Family-of-Origin Therapy
and Diversity

Family-of-Origin Therapy and Diversity

H. Russell Searight, Ph.D.

Department of Family Medicine
Deaconess Hospital
and
Department of Psychology
Saint Louis University
and
Department of Community and Family Medicine
Saint Louis University School of Medicine
St. Louis, Missouri

Taylor & Francis
Publishers since 1798

USA	Publishing Office:	Taylor & Francis 1101 Vermont Avenue, NW, Suite 200 Washington, DC 20005-3521 Tel: (202) 289-2174 Fax: (202) 289-3665
	Distribution Center:	Taylor & Francis 1900 Frost Road, Suite 101 Bristol, PA 19007-1598 Tel: (215) 785-5800 Fax: (215) 785-5515
UK		Taylor & Francis Ltd. 1 Gunpowder Square London EC4A 3DE Tel: 171 583 0490 Fax: 171 583 0581

FAMILY OF ORIGIN THERAPY AND DIVERSITY

1 2 3 4 5 6 7 8 9 0 BRBR 9 8 7

This book was set in Times Roman. The editors were Catherine Simon and Kathleen Sheedy. Cover design by Ed Atkeson, Ber Design.

A CIP catalog record for this book is available from the British Library.
♾ The paper in this publication meets the requirements of the ANSI Standard Z39.48-1984 (Permanence of Paper)

Library of Congress Cataloging-in-Publication Data
Searight, H. Russell.
    Family of origin therapy and diversity/H. Russell Searight.
        p. cm.

    Includes bibliographical references.

    1. Psychotherapy patients—Family relationships. 2. Psychotherapy. 3. Family psychotherapy. 4. Intergenerational relations. 5. Family–Psychological aspects. 6. Parent and adult child. 7. Cultural psychiatry. I. Title.

RC489.F33S43   1997   96–47173
616.89.156–dc21   CIP

ISBN 1-56032-463-5 (case)
ISBN 1-56032-464-3 (paper)

*For
my parents
and
Barbara and Alicia*

Contents

Preface

Family-of-origin therapy was originally developed by Murray Bowen to account for the role of family history in shaping both individual development and current relationship patterns. The historical perspective developed by Bowen and other family therapists such as James Framo provides a unique vantage point with its emphasis on implicit legacies transmitted across multiple generations. These legacies are experienced as templates for current relationship patterns. Family-of-origin therapy is a useful framework for family and marital treatment and has considerable value for working with individuals as well.

However, despite family-of-origin therapy's emphasis on historical contexts, little attention has been paid to the surrounding social contexts shaping many of these basic family worldviews. Gender, ethnic diversity, and religion all play significant roles in shaping perceptions of marriage, family, and individual identity. The family of origin is the setting through which these norms are transmitted.

This book was written for practicing therapists as well as for students in training programs in family and marital therapy, psychology, counseling, and social work. The book has several goals. First, family-of-origin therapy has often been difficult to grasp because of the complexity of the concepts involved. In Part 1 of this book, the goal of the first three chapters is to provide a user-friendly description of family-of-origin therapy. After a discussion of family-of-origin assessment tools and research in chapter 4, Part 2 of the book focuses on integration of family-of-origin therapy with diversity.

Chapter 1 provides an overview of the background and basic concepts of family-of-origin therapy. Bowen's constructs of the emotional system and differentiation are described. Related concepts such as Framo's object relations approach to family therapy are also included.

Chapter 2 focuses on the practical issue of clinical assessment in family-of-origin therapy. The importance of eliciting family rules is a key part of the assessment process. In addition, the clinician will benefit from determining levels of differentiation and accompanying reactivity within families.

Chapter 3 moves into the treatment phase. The efficacy of the extended history as a treatment technique is emphasized. In addition, the coaching approach for family work in the context of individually focused therapy is given considerable attention.

Concepts such as differentiation, reactivity, and intergenerational legacies often appear to be too abstract to be systematically assessed or empirically investigated. However, for the clinician and the researcher, there are several psychometrically sound instruments. These tools, discussed in chapter 4, include the Family-of-Origin Scale, Personal Authority of the Family System Questionnaire, and the Differentiation of Self in the Family Scale. Chapter 4 goes on to discuss related research in attachment, identity, and adolescent development that supports the basic tenets of family-of-origin theory.

Beginning with chapter 5, the book moves into an exploration of diversity from the family-of-origin perspective. Some of the most fundamental assumptions about ourselves and others stem from gender. Chapter 5 discusses identity differences in men and women as well as gender-related relationship patterns. The role of the family of origin in shaping basic assumptions about what it means to be male and female is explored. Family therapy, including family-of-origin treatment, has often perpetuated harmful gender-role stereotypes. In addition, family-of-origin therapy has often been accused of neglecting the larger social assumptions surrounding gender. Chapter 5 highlights these issues and presents a revised family-of-origin therapy that promotes gender-role flexibility.

Gay and lesbian relationships are the focus of chapter 6. Gay and lesbian issues are only recently beginning to be discussed in family therapy. Family-of-origin therapy has considerable value as a treatment approach with gays and lesbians. The process of coming out to family members is heavily influenced by the historical relationship between the gay and lesbian adult and his or her family. The chapter also includes attention to characteristics of gay and lesbian relationships, including recent research on children growing up in gay and lesbian households.

Chapter 7 focuses on ethnic and cultural diversity. African Americans, Asian Americans, and Native Americans are discussed in some detail. Hispanic and ethnic groups of European background are also described. This chapter focuses on how basic dimensions of family life, such as boundaries, communication styles, management of emotion, gender roles, and parenting, reflect cultural assumptions. These cultural worldviews are transmitted to individuals through the unspoken rules of the family. This chapter emphasizes the diversity of cultural and ethnic backgrounds found among families in the United States.

Religion and spirituality, an important dimension of family life, has received little attention in family therapy. Although the field of mental health and religion both examine similar issues—how one should live, the nature of commitment to others, the meaning of life—these two perspectives have not been well integrated. The family is one of the primary means of transmitting religious and spiritual values. Chapter 8 explores a number of religious belief systems, including Judaism, Christianity, and Islam as well as Native American and Asian belief systems. The role of religion as an implicit organizing force within families is discussed.

In real life, families and individuals do not fall into the neat compartments determined by the chapters in a book. Gender, ethnicity, sexual orientation, and spirituality all combine into a complex variegated pattern within family life. The therapist will have to include attention to each of these influences and how they interact in clinical practice. The final chapter of this book addresses this integration. In addition, therapists also grow up in families and bring their own history of diversity to the clinical encounter. It is hoped that this book will make therapists more aware of their own assumptions about families and diversity and how these dimensions influence their daily clinical practice.

Acknowledgments

Although this book required about a year to actually write, the background for *Family-of-Origin Therapy and Diversity* extends over a 10-year period. My original interest in this area arose through teaching a course and providing clinical training in family therapy in Saint Louis University's Psychology Department. I am very grateful to the members of Family Vertical Team, the clinical supervision group at Saint Louis University that I have led for the past 10 years. The students' openness, honesty, and courage in presenting and exploring their families of origin has been the primary Inspiration for this book. I only hope that my students have learned half as much from me as I have from them.

This book would never have been written without the continuous and generous support of Dr. David Campbell, Director of Family Medicine at Deaconess Health Sciences Center and Associate Chair of the Department of Community and Family Medicine at Saint Louis University School of Medicine. Dave has successfully created a climate that encourages faculty self-development and he actively encourages faculty to set and achieve meaningful professional goals. Dave's consistent encouragement of personal development allowed me to pursue this book along with my other activities. As always, I am very grateful for Dave's support for my research and writing within the Department.

I also want to acknowledge the Deaconess Family Medicine residents. Many of the case examples in the book were drawn from observations in the residency clinic. In addition, discussions and informal corridor consultations prompted a number of the ideas incorporated in the diversity section. I particularly wish to thank Dr. Haifaa Younis for her insights into Arabic and Islamic families. Ms. Susan Hubbard, LCSW, provided helpful comments on the gender chapter.

Although the clinical psychology faculty at Saint Louis University have consistently been supportive of family training, there have been two faculty members who have been influential in my own professional development. More than 15 years ago, Dr. Joan Oliver had both the patience and the skill to teach me how to write for professional publication. In addition to helping me to acquire the ability to compose coherent sentences and to recognize when a paragraph should start and stop, Joan encouraged me to seek an academic career. I hope that this book embodies one important lesson that Joan taught me—wordiness is not necessarily related to meaningfulness.

I owe a long-standing debt of gratitude to Dr. Paul Handal. Paul has encouraged my writing and academic pursuits for many years. His support for family training as well as for me personally as I developed professionally was immeasurably important. I doubt that I would have experienced the confidence to take on this project without his years of encouragement. Paul's willingness to talk with me and provide guidance at different choice points in my career has been deeply appreciated.

I wish to thank Ms. Elaine Pirrone at Taylor & Francis for her persistent encouragement for writing this book. Through her support and numerous helpful suggestions, Elaine made this initially anxiety-provoking process far less threatening—even enjoyable. Ms. Bernadette Capelle at Taylor & Francis saw this work into its final form and made a number of important contributions to the completed manuscript. Her enthusiastic feedback about the final draft was gratefully received.

I can never fully thank my wife, Barbara, for her ever-present caring, emotional support, and continuous encouragement while I wrote this book. Barbara's unselfish belief and confidence in my ability has been a sustaining gift through our marriage. My daughter, Alicia, has understood, without complaint, my long internment in my study while this project was being completed. Alicia was like having a personal cheerleader; she often asked me when she would actually get to see this book.

Last, I wish to thank my parents. They encouraged independence, self-discipline, and the importance of having a life that includes meaningful goals. These values allowed me to begin and complete this book.

PART ONE
INTRODUCTION AND DESCRIPTION

Chapter 1

Family-of-Origin Therapy: An Overview

Nearly everyone was raised and influenced by a family of one type or other. Family experience is carried over multiple generations and becomes a Weltanschaungen or worldview—a set of unspoken, largely unlabeled assumptions about the nature of relationships. Because these patterns were communicated from birth, they were present before language developed. Unlabeled experience is typically uncritically internalized. Dimensions of daily life such as the acceptability of emotional expression, closeness versus distance with friends or acquaintances, and style of handling crises are all shaped by multigenerational family history.

These patterns typically exist outside of awareness until a rule is broken. An analogy is riding an elevator. No one is ever formally taught the rules or etiquette for riding an elevator, one simply gets on, pushes the button for the correct floor, and thinks little about it. However, there are implicit rules for elevator riders. To see the rules, do the following: Rather than quietly standing side by side with fellow elevator riders, turn around and face them. The reaction will be one of extreme discomfort.

Family rules have the same power to shape conformity. Many people begin to be aware that their family's way may not be the only way during adolescence, when they start having more contact with peers and their families. Assumptions about the way the world is are likely to be challenged when it is learned that many families yell, scream, and carry on acrimoniously with one another but still seem very happy together or that a messy home does not mean that a friend is lazy. These implicit rules are more sharply challenged when significant relationships are developed in adulthood. Fundamental views about emotion, conflict, work, or gender may undergo upheaval as one becomes increasingly close to someone who operates from a different assumptive world. McGoldrick (1995) pointed out that rapid social change has moved many people out of insulated homogeneous family enclaves and into new social arenas that may readily challenge prevailing family rules. Changing gender roles, increased mobility, and the reduced influence of centuries-old religious traditions, as well as a rise in new family forms,

3

make many individuals acutely aware of the clash between their assumptions about social life and the relationships that they actually experience. Another dimension that has contributed to this sense of upheaval is the acceleration of social change. Current events, music, politics, and the arts change at a dizzying pace. Former Vice President Quayle's quest for family values seems to reflect a reaction to the challenges of social and relationship changes and a wish to return to a supposedly traditional, more homogeneous lifestyle.

Family-of-origin therapy focuses on the patterns that are carried from early family experience and translated into adult experiences such as marriage or raising children. The goal of family-of-origin therapy is to help clients understand the rules, relationship patterns, and behaviors that arose in their own family development. Equipped with this knowledge, clients may alter the unproductive, emotionally trying, and repetitive sequences that occur in their current relationships.

OVERVIEW OF BASIC THEORETICAL CONCEPTS

Murray Bowen, a psychiatrist, is usually seen as the founder of family-of-origin therapy. A major theme that runs through Bowen's theory is that of counterbalancing forces. Bowen, in contrast to strategic therapists such as Haley (1976) or structural therapists such as Minuchin (1974), emphasized the individual against a backdrop of family processes. Changes occur within the individual. As a result of those intrapsychic and corresponding behavioral alterations, systemic change follows. Bowen (1978) described two sets of forces, which fluctuate in their importance throughout development. One pair of forces centers around individuality versus togetherness, and the other set of forces involves intellectual versus emotional functioning. The individuality–togetherness dimension centers around a striving for independence, autonomy, and one's own identity on the one hand versus a strong need to be socially connected with others on the other hand. The intellectual versus emotional dimension centers around operating cognitively and choicefully versus being emotionally determined and immediately reactive. Bowen argued that the psychologically healthy person can maintain these two types of functioning as distinct but may also choose to operate on an intellectual, objective basis or an emotional, subjective basis. When these two systems are not separate, the element of choicefulness is lost, and behavior automatically becomes emotionally determined. When behavior becomes emotionally determined, it frequently centers around a reaction to others. People become overresponsive to others' behavior.

For example, consider a therapist working in a community agency who experiences a conflict with a supervisor or colleague at work. The conflict may be so emotionally disruptive that it becomes impossible for the therapist to give full attention to clients the rest of the day. When the therapist goes home that evening, he or she spends an hour or two rehearsing the event with a significant other and then has difficulty falling asleep because of ruminating about the conflict. In situations like this, the reaction to the colleague or supervisor has disrupted the therapist's sense of choicefulness, and his or her behavior becomes emotionally determined. In a very real sense, the supervisor or colleague comes home with the therapist and disrupts his or her emotional as well as social life.

Emotional–Intellectual Polarity

Bowen's (1978) emotional system is a shared phylogenetic structure with nonhuman organisms. Subcortical structures such as the limbic system are shared with nonhuman animals and are involved with basic instinctive reactions (e.g., fleeing, fighting, feeding, and mating; Carlson, 1981). Emotional forces are automatic reactions—the immediate panic when a parent sees her 2-year-old in the middle of a busy street or the angry helplessness of watching a large truck back into one's parked car. As posited in classical Freudian theory, anxiety becomes aroused under conditions of perceived threat. At these times, the emotional system takes over and supersedes intellectual functioning.

In contrast, the intellectual system operates in a planful, goal-directed manner. Persons who have ready access to their intellectual system are focused, experience themselves as being choiceful in their daily activities, and do not become readily frazzled by external crises or distractions. An adult's ability to return to writing a report after answering the phone and hearing that the water pipes in his or her basement have just burst is an example of the relative influence of the intellectual system. Bowen has been misunderstood at times as viewing the emotional system as innately inferior to the intellectual system. Feminist family therapists, in particular, have been critical of this perspective (Luepnitz, 1988). It is more accurate to say that Bowen (1978) viewed the intellectual system as one that enables individuals to choose to be emotionally focused or to be cognitively focused and goal directed. The intellectual system is similar to meta-cognitive processes such as self-monitoring. Thus, there are times in which persons may choicefully be emotionally governed, such as during a romantic moment, listening to a symphony, or gazing out on a snowfall.

A third component, to which Bowen (1978) gave significantly less attention, is the feeling system. The feeling system centers around affective states that are conscious and usually labeled (Knudson-Martin, 1994). Bowen did not develop the role of the feeling system in his theory. Critics have argued that the feeling system may actually be a more appropriate pole against which to juxtapose the intellectual system (Knudson-Martin, 1994) than the more visceral, unlabeled emotional system.

Individuality–Togetherness Polarity

The other key duality in Bowen's (1978) theory is the force for togetherness and the complementary drive toward autonomy. The togetherness force is also, to some extent, biologically based. Papero (1990) noted that primates such as chimpanzees tend to live in groups. At the same time, there is a counterbalancing force toward personal independence and self-sufficiency. Developmentally, these forces are particularly evident in early adolescence. The young teenager will, within the span of minutes, shift from childlike dependency on parents to a strong need for personal privacy and space.

Differentiation

The emotional–intellectual and togetherness–separateness forces become integrated through the concept of differentiation. Differentiation refers to one's ability to maintain cognitive and emotional independence in the face of strong togetherness forces.

People whose functioning tends to be dominated by emotion are described as having a low level of basic differentiation between the emotional and intellectual systems. Those who can maintain this distinction—particularly in emotionally intense situations—have a high degree of basic differentiation. The greater the degree of fusion, or absence of this differentiation, the greater the influence of the togetherness force on the individual's functioning. When the togetherness force is particularly strong, there are several common results: poorly defined boundaries between the self and other, emotional reactivity to what others say and do, and an experience of being pressured to think and act in ways specified by others (Bowen, 1978).

This upsurge in reactivity is, in effect, an anxiety-management strategy. In work situations, this interplay can be observed when a coworker is suddenly fired. The tension will be managed through intense, repetitive, and anxiety-driven interactions among employees. For several days, the amount of social activity and processing of the event will prevent much work from being accomplished. Groups of employees will be huddled about as they anxiously share and reshare the information and rumors they have heard.

In families, this lack of differentiation emerges through reactivity to one another. Family members emotionally and automatically respond to one another's behavior. Everyday language suggests support for Bowen's (1978) view that human beings often experience themselves as controlled by significant others ("She drove him to drink," "My kids drive me crazy," "My husband's depression is bringing the whole family down"). Another aspect of undifferentiation is the tendency to predict or anticipate what others want from us and to shape our behavior accordingly.

As he did with the emotional system, Bowen (1978) linked the concept of differentiation to humans' phylogenetic heritage. One body of research cited by Papero (1990) is Calhoun's (1962) "behavioral sink." Calhoun found that increased density of rats in a colony resulted in deteriorated social functioning. Rats who were less physiologically stable exhibited more fighting and were less reproductively successful. At the higher end of population density, the more physiologically stable rats began to exhibit behavioral difficulties. Calhoun's work demonstrates how emotional reactions are related to external social forces. The rats, in a sense, became increasingly reactive. Even those rats with less physiological loading for social reactivity exhibited behavioral changes when the population density increased. Thus, differentiation is, in part, based in the biologically based emotional system and its relative influence on behavior under external stress.

In human systems, well-differentiated persons are able to maintain the intellectual and emotional systems as distinct even under relatively intense social demands. These individuals are able to engage in close intimate relationships while maintaining a clear sense of personal identity and goals. Behavior is not determined by the other party. Bowen (1978) assumed that a person's basic level of differentiation is similar to the concept of early childhood temperament and is constitutionally determined early in life. However, although persons may vary in their innate reactivity, this predisposition may be altered through planful effort and overt behavioral change.

Triangulation

Bowen's (1978) theory, up until this point, was largely intrapsychic. However, with the concept of triangles, Bowen linked intrapsychic concepts such as differentiation to interpersonal interactions. At the dyadic level, he proposed, persons tend to seek out and develop relationships with persons exhibiting similar levels of differentiation. As a result, the dyad may be characterized by surges in anxiety and tension associated with reactivity when individual-level boundaries are poorly defined or maintained. When anxiety exceeds a critical point in one dyad member, a third party may be brought into the relationship. This temporarily reduces tension in a two-person relationship, such as a marriage. For example, Whitaker and Bumberry (1987) argued that a common unlabeled conflict in many marriages is the wife's desire for emotional intimacy and the husband's inability to provide it—a pattern they described as "hopeful women and hopeless men." Because of the unstable nature of this process, which stems from unmet emotional needs, a child may be brought into the relationship. The child's presence often has an initial calming effect on the marital dyad. The husband, who is aware of the tension with his wife but often unaware of its meaning, is typically initially relieved by her involvement with the child. The mother may experience emotional connectedness with the child, thus reducing her need and therefore her efforts to engage her husband. This pattern may persist until the child moves toward independence—either in a small way such as beginning school or in a big way such as leaving home in early adulthood. The mother's differentiation level will be an important determining factor in whether larger or smaller moves toward independence evoke anxiety. Thus, the child's beginning elementary school may make the triangle unstable and either provoke a return to the former pattern of the wife as pursuer after her husband or stimulate a renewed effort on the wife's part to re-engage the child. In this process, the wife may develop somatic or psychological symptoms, which functionally serve to elicit caretaking by the child or husband (or both). Although the above pattern is probably one of the most common ways of managing dyadic tension, Bowen (1978) also described several other resolutions.

Other Forms of Dyadic Tension

In response to dissatisfaction around unmet individual needs, couples may also exhibit increased marital conflict. This is a situation encountered by many marital therapists. Conflict may oscillate with intense togetherness ("The best part of breaking up is making up"). One clue that underlying historical issues are being enacted is that the couple seems to be fighting intensely over relatively superficial issues. Conflicts over such things as who takes out the garbage or who feeds the cat that appear to have incredible emotional energy surrounding them are likely to represent underlying conflicts around individuality and separateness. In these situations, the couple is likely to view negotiation as a major threat to their individuality. So rather than having a fight about who takes out the garbage, the couple is in essence really having a fight about whether or not one party controls the relationship and the accompanying struggle for independence. The strong reactivity that the spouses exhibit toward one another is indicative of poor levels of individual differentiation. The endless bickering and sarcasm also reflects the strong emotional pull for closeness while simultaneously indicating the accompanying anxiety associated with intimacy. Bowen (1978) argued that the more effectively this tension can be managed within the marital dyad, the less likely it is to adversely affect any children in the home. Parents who are anxious about the impact of this conflict on their children often overcompensate through overinvolvement or have difficulty being objective as a parent. For example, a father who worries excessively about how marital conflict may be influencing his adolescent daughter may go easy on her and not set behavioral limits. Although the father's intent is to compensate for the adverse effects of his marital conflict, the result will likely engender greater anxiety for the teenager because of the absence of limits and structure.

Another common pattern is one in which one partner absorbs the distress; the relationship may become patterned around an overfunctioning and an underfunctioning partner. One partner may readily take on the patient role. In addition to psychiatric disorders such as major depression, panic disorder, or substance abuse, this patient role may also include physical problems in which there is a psychological component, such as migraine headaches or lower back pain. Haley (1976) noted that physical distress can be seen as a metaphor for the relationship. "I have a headache" is often a way of communicating that "This is a painful relationship." Although symptomatology may remain solely in one spouse, one variation on this pattern occurs when there is fluctuation between spouses around who is sick and who is well. Another variation is one of symmetrical escalation—each partner competes with the other for the title of sickest. A diabetic woman may require hospitalization when her blood sugars are out of control. In response, the husband's low back pain may flare up, requiring sedation and bed rest. Each spouse is managing anxiety about their dependency needs not being met by upping the sickness ante and becoming more symptomatic. These processes are usually not conscious and are somatic representations of the emotional system.

A third mechanism for managing anxiety is emotional distancing. In U.S. society, men are particularly prone to relying on this mechanism. Emotional disengagement and social distancing often emanate from intense fears of dependency and interpersonal engulfment. Although the apparent source of distancing is the other person, the actual causes are intrapsychic. The intense reactivity and accompanying anxiety are the actual motivating factors. Common mechanisms for distancing include long work hours, travel, and many social engagements. More subtle internal processes may include detachment:

> Chronic irritability, involvement in a book or activity to the exclusion of all else, a stony or troubled countenance, and the ability to tune out the efforts of the other to communicate all may manifest an internal shutting down of emotional response. At the same time that one is closing off contact, thoughts of the other may fill thinking time. (Papero, 1990, p. 52)

Multigeneration Projection

Bowen (1978) included an interaction between triangulation and projection to account for how undifferentiation is transmitted from one generation to the next. An example of this interaction: A mother may feel insecure about her social skills and general abilities in interpersonal relationships. Because this is an ongoing area of sensitivity for her, she will be highly attuned to any minor social inadequacies in her child. If the child shows one or two small weaknesses in social skills, the mother unconsciously decides that the child is just like her and begins behaving toward the child in a way that is compatible with these expectations. Concerned about her child's self-esteem, the mother may shield him or her from social opportunities (e.g., birthday parties, summer camp, scouts, sports), with the result that the child has little opportunity to develop and practice social skills. In a sense the child's poor social skills become a self-fulfilling prophecy. Many clinicians are familiar with projection processes of this type. It is not uncommon for a child to be brought to a therapist and a parent to state, "You know he becomes explosive. He is just like I was at his age," or "He is just like his father was at this age." Although this may seem to be a uniquely human process, Papero (1990) described an intriguing example among primates, which demonstrates how reactivity can be socially transmitted. In Jane Goodall's (1979) studies of chimpanzees, she focused on a mother and son dyad (Flo and Flint). Goodall noted that Flo was generally successful in raising competent independent children. However, with one of her younger offspring, Flint, Flo was unable to complete the weaning process, and Flint continued to cling to her and did not join with age peers. This reactivity was particularly pronounced when Flo died. Flint died less than a month later. In humans, this process is likely to be a circular one in which the parent appears to generate specific behavioral patterns in the child. However, the child soon automatically learns how to trigger parental solicitousness.

According to Bowen (1978), this process occurs over multiple generations. Bowen argued that this transmission process follows a set of guidelines. First, if parents are individually not well differentiated from their own families of origin and they have only one child, that child will become highly impaired because one or both parents will intensely fuse with him or her. Again, it is important to recall that adults tend to develop close relationships with those of comparable levels of differentiation. Over succeeding generations, this lack of differentiation influences subsequent children. The ultimate pathological process that may emerge is the family with few individual boundaries in which members are highly reactive to one another. Bowen referred to this as an undifferentiated ego mass. Spouses and children are immediately reactive to one another. "Borderline" families with chronic conflict and frequent crises typify the undifferentiated ego mass.

Role of Birth Order

Bowen (1978) also argued that the child's birth order may play a role in this process. Bowen drew from the work of Toman (1976), who developed personality descriptions of children based on sibling position. Toman argued that there are certain social expectations of oldest, youngest, and middle children that are deeply rooted in cultural values and have very little to do with what parents or children consciously desire. For example, the oldest child tends to be oriented toward responsibility and decision making. The youngest child may be more dependent. Bowen incorporated Toman's ideas and added the concept of the family projection process. The projection process may result in characteristics associated with the oldest child being projected onto the youngest or vice versa. Although the role of oldest, youngest, and middle child is relatively fixed, the children that actually take these roles are influenced by family members' expectations or transgenerational emotional legacies. If, for example, the oldest child is caught in an intense triangle with the parents, he or she may grow up with exaggerated characteristics of the youngest. In this family, the younger child may exhibit characteristics that are functionally associated with being the oldest. Sibling position may also become an issue in marriages. For example, if two youngest siblings marry, there is likely to be a symmetrical escalation of conflict centering around dependency and being cared for. By contrast, two oldest siblings may compete for dominance and responsibility. Complementarity in sibling roles (e g , an oldest child marrying a youngest child) may be associated with greater marital stability. However, as is the case with children, these roles can be modified by projections, which are in turn influenced by individual reactivities.

The Cut-Off

Adults who have little or no contact with their families of origin may appear to be well-differentiated but in reality are not. The emotional cut-off is a strategy used to manage intense reactivity. We often encounter adults who say "I am completely independent of my family because I rarely see or talk with them." In reality, these individuals are extremely dependent on their families. Rather than being able to maintain some level of contact with family members, these persons are so highly controlled by family dynamics that they cannot tolerate any sustained interaction. The inability to resolve these issues and to maintain a separate identity while interacting with important family members is a key deficit that will emerge in other interpersonal relationships. Close relationships such as marriage are likely to be the next arena for enacting the dynamics underlying the cut-off. Intense closeness may alternate with explosions of angry distancing. Similar to the well-known dictum about history, those who have not resolved issues in their families of origin are destined to repeat them in their next relationship. A commonly observed pattern among adults in therapy is to move from one relationship to another. Usually, ending of the relationship is provoked by increased feelings of closeness, which are closely followed by anxiety about engulfment.

Societal Implications

As Freud (1961) did with his late-life application of psychoanalysis to society, Bowen (1978) also examined how anxiety and reactivity operate on a societal level. Bowen noted the impact of increased population density on human anxiety. As suggested by Calhoun's (1962) "behavioral sink" research with rats, the growth of populated geographic space increases anxiety and, in turn, heightens togetherness. Bowen neglected another force, which has become very prominent in the past decade—the constant and rapid transmission of information. A reactive news media that responds in an intense crisis-oriented mode to even trivial details creates anxiety and emotional reactivity among citizens. This, in turn, generates further efforts to obtain more news and prevents people from formulating and following well-conceived personal goals. Indeed, the constant bombardment and push to become part of a "global community" heightens reactivity and distracts citizens from personally held values, such as maintaining close relationships with others.

OBJECT RELATIONS THEORY

James Framo (1982) added to Bowen's model by including object relationships in family-of-origin therapy. As with Bowen's concept of differentiation, inclusion of the role of internalized representations of early relationships provides a bridge between the individual and family. Object relations theorists such as Fairbairn (1952) developed their ideas within the psychoanalytic tradition but later broke from Freudian thought around certain key concepts such as the nature of instincts. Whereas Freud argued that the key motivating force for human behavior was instinct gratification, Fairbairn asserted that humans' primary drive is to develop satisfying object relationships. These objects are significant others. Thus, Freud's sexual and aggressive drives were replaced with the drive to seek out and emotionally attach to others. Finkelstein (1987) noted that object relations theories were derived from two types of observational contexts. One source has been psychoanalytic treatment of adults, and the second has been observations of parent–child interaction among infants and toddlers. Although there are a number of object relations theorists, including Kohut (1977) and Kernberg (1976), the writings of Fairbairn (1952) have been the most commonly incorporated into marital and family therapy.

Fairbairn (1952) viewed early childhood as a period in which internalized representations of relationships with adults are generated. These objects are, in a sense, like unconscious schemas and serve as reference points for other relationships throughout childhood and adulthood. The objects are templates for what relationships are like. These templates, derived from experience with one's parents, are likely to be activated when other intimate relationships are being formed.

The above statement is a more contemporary, cognitive interpretation of Fairbairn's (1952) theory. Fairbairn devoted considerable attention to the role of internalized objects in psychopathology. Parents who temporarily abandon, physically reject, emotionally reject, or abuse the child precipitate an intrapsychic dilemma. Because of the reality-based helplessness that goes along with being a young child, there is little control over the immediate environment. The child cannot give up the external object or change reality. As a result, the child may handle the frustration and disappointment by internalizing the unpredictable, loved-and-hated parent to control the object in the only domain where control is possible— intrapsychically. These internalized objects exist at an unconscious level where they color all significant relationships. When the relationship with the primary caretaker has been an intensely ambivalent one, splitting occurs. In the case of splitting, there are two introjects for the parent—a good one and a bad one. The "good" representation reflects the nurturing and giving behavior of the parent. In extreme situations it may also include the engulfing, smothering style as well. The "bad" representation reflects the rejecting and critical aspects of the parent. According to object relations theory, the earlier in life that a process such as splitting occurs, the greater the reliance the child has on the internalized object to deal with significant adult relationships. The earlier in life that this process occurs and the greater the degree of associated trauma, the more likely the person will be to rely on the object to transact with the external world. The developing child and the adult will be less able to perceive and respond to objective characteristics of important others.

Individuation and Attachment

A key interpersonal process that occurs simultaneously with the early development of these internalized objects is the movement toward independence. Mahler, Pine, and Bergman (1975) highlighted the importance of the delicate interplay between dependence and autonomy that becomes pronounced during the second year of life. Cognitively, this is a period in which the child is developing object constancy through internalized representations of people and things that they can intrapsychically summon when the external object is not present. However, for consistent and stable representations to be formed, the child should experience a supportive and predictable relationship with at least one primary caretaker. When the relationship is unpredictable, harsh, or alternates between engulfment and abandonment, the child will, because of cognitive limitations, be unable to integrate these contradictory experiences into the same representation. As a result, the child will have two distinct schemas of intimate relationships—closeness (perhaps overly intense) and rejection or exploitation.

A particularly critical interpersonal dynamic that occurs during the second and third years is movement toward greater independence while maintaining attachment. Parents who encourage age-appropriate autonomy while providing a secure base of attachment will foster an identity comparable to the well-differentiated adult described by Bowen (1978). A common game played by 2-year-olds is to briefly run out of the area where their parent is seated, pick up an object, and bring it to the parent. Most parents will readily recognize that an appropriate response is to positively acknowledge the child's gift. This response conveys acceptance of the child's drive toward independence while assuring him or her of the parent's availability.

A pathological variation was presented by an adolescent mother of a 17-month-old girl. The dyad was receiving therapy as part of a group of high-risk mother–infant pairs (Searight, Graham, Rae, & Parker, 1989). When her young daughter walked away to explore the room, the mother would respond in one of two ways. When the toddler began to walk away from her, she would grab the child from behind and hold her firmly on her lap while smiling and saying, "Get your butt over here, you're not going to get away from me." This engulfing response would alternate with a pattern in which the mother would respond to the child's exploration by turning away from her and remarking, "Go on ahead, I don't want you either." When the child later tried to reengage her, the mother would not respond.

Projection and Internalized Objects

The rejecting and engulfing pattern may become a template or set of unconscious expectations for relationships. Importantly for family theory, there are often unconscious attempts to project these representations onto significant others in one's adult life—such as spouses and children (Framo, 1982). In a sense, these representations, when projected onto others, are attempts to force one's spouse or children into fitting these internalized role models. This may occur even when the spouse's or children's objective behavior or personality characteristics contradict these prototypes. This pattern is often very apparent in families with multiple children. In these families, different children may take on the good or bad part of the parent. The "good parent" child is likely to become parentified themselves. Such a child will often have the role of taking care of the mother—a dynamic that is frequent in families with a disengaged or absent father. The "bad child" is often characterized as harsh and rejecting of the mother. Framo argued that when parents have lost their own parents at a very young age, their relationship with their children may center around recapturing the lost love relationship. In these families, children may seem to be symbiotically tied to their families and discouraged from extrafamilial relationships; this pattern may be punctuated with intense conflict as both parties become fearful of dependency. From the parent's perspective, a conflict often represents a defensive attempt to deny the need for the object because this relationship could suffer the same fate, and the child could leave him or her. In these dyads, normative moves toward independence by the child or adolescent are extremely threatening to the parents and trigger anxiety stemming from feared abandonment.

Object Relations and Marriage

Object relations theory in a family or marital context represents a synthesis of attachment and psychoanalytic perspectives. The key dynamic of movement toward autonomy while maintaining intimacy becomes a repetitive theme throughout development in a relationship context. One's early representations of caregivers become the unconscious guides that predispose individuals to enter into similar relationships in adulthood. Framo (1982) pointed out that active attempts are made to force others to fit these internalized role models.

Marriage or a similar dyadic relationship becomes the primary arena in which dynamics or attachment and introjected objects become enacted in adulthood. In a sense, these issues may have been dormant until the challenge of intimacy arises in the late teens and early 20s. Marital theorists argue that the parent–child relationship is the model for intimacy in later life (Dicks, 1967). A common pattern seen in therapy with men in their 30s is ambivalence around commitment to a heterosexual relationship, as seen in the following example:

> A 33-year-old man came for treatment so that he could make a decision about marriage. James had been involved with a 30-year-old woman, Susan, for the previous 5 years in an exclusive relationship. Susan would often spend the night at his apartment. However, after two to three consecutive overnight stays in a row, James would become increasingly agitated and tell her to stop "moving in." After about a week of cooling off, the relationship would re-intensify. This cycle had become more prominent in the previous year. Neither party was dating anyone else. Finally, Susan had given James an ultimatum—he needed to propose marriage within 6 months or Susan would end the relationship.
>
> At the beginning of therapy, James was very agitated—he did not want to end the relationship but was very frightened about the notion of commitment. James expressed love for Susan and could not find any specific flaws that would prevent him from marrying her. He repeatedly, however, expressed intense yet vague fears

that he would be "tied down" or "on a leash" if he were to marry Susan. When the therapist probed further, James alluded to his own mother who had stayed at home with James and his brother and at times "stifled" them with her care. When asked to be specific about what he would actually lose if he committed to Susan, James spoke angrily about having to give up deer hunting or playing cards with his male friends. These were the only specific examples of "being on a leash" that he could describe. The therapist encouraged James to talk directly with Susan about the importance of these activities to him and how these could be preserved in a marriage. James agreed to do this. The therapist noted that James was somewhat angrily defiant, as if he were preparing for a major confrontation with Susan.

When he returned the following week, James appeared both relaxed and perplexed. He described how he confronted Susan with his "need for freedom." When she had asked what he meant, James then overbearingly told Susan the importance of hunting and card playing. He was mystified by her response: "She said, 'Is that all? What's the big deal? Sure, I don't care if you play poker and shoot deer. Why would I stop you?' " The nonargumentative response thoroughly confused James, who was geared up for a major battle. Subsequent therapy focused on James's relationship with his mother and how he was projecting her controlling, intrusive behavior onto Susan.

CONTEXTUAL THERAPY

Contextual therapy, although less commonly practiced, also includes family-of-origin theory. Developed by the psychiatrist Ivan Boszormenyi-Nagy (Boszormenyi-Nagy & Spark, 1973), the contextual approach contributes the useful concept of invisible loyalties. Intergenerational legacies refer to a group of expectations, debts, and missions that are rooted in the acts of previous generations but that frame important life choices and interpersonal interactions in the present. This legacy is accompanied by a ledger featuring statements of entitlement or indebtedness for each family member. Contextual therapy argues that one does have certain ethical responsibilities to family members. Indeed, individual symptoms arise from breakdowns in caring and accountability between family members (Boszormenyi-Nagy & Spark, 1973). Marital issues, as well, are likely to arise because one or both family members cannot balance competing loyalties to spouse and children and to the intergenerational debts incurred from the family of origin.

Besides the accumulation of intergenerational debt, the ledger also includes entitlements and merits. A child is entitled to basic caregiving and nurturance from a parent. The parent, by providing this support, has earned merit. If the child is given up and placed in foster care at a young age, the parent has little or no merit, but the child maintains the entitlement to the biological mother's support and concern. For those working in the child welfare system, this pattern is very familiar. The child, while having little to no contact with a biological parent for many years, persists in the view that the parent will come and rescue him or her. The foster parents—particularly if they are relatives of the biological parent— experience a sense of merit. At the same time, they may be fulfilling a previous generation's mission. For example, one of the foster parents may have been raised for a period of time by an extended family member. The current caretaking arrangement takes care of an old debt. The child, however, may not be able to balance the competing loyalties to the biological mother and the foster parents and may begin acting out aggressively.

ADULTS AND THEIR FAMILIES

Neither Bowen (1978) nor Framo (1982) focused exclusively on historical family patterns, but they did include attention to current relationships between adults and their parents and siblings. The emphasis was on developing a better understanding of family history as a basis for more satisfying relationships with family members.

Framo (1976) described four basic patterns of relationships between adults and their families of origin. The most common type he termed superficial. This pattern involves nonpersonal relating and minimal contact. These adults make the customary duty visits home and send cards for the necessary holidays. Often, however, family members get together only for major events like weddings or funerals. Interactions are polite but not terribly meaningful. The second type, overinvolved, is characterized by adults who live with their parents or nearby. Even if they live at a distance, there are almost daily contacts. Often, all vacations are taken together, and parents have significant input into all life decisions. These adults may talk on the phone with their parents several times a day. In one example, a man in his late 50s was the family patriarch. He was seen by me for a rehabilitation consultation for low back pain in a hospital setting. The referring physician believed that the patient was overexerting himself and that this was contributing to the low back pain. In interviewing the patient, I noted that he lived in a compound with all his adult children. He had a large amount of land out in the country, and when each of his adult children got married, he bought them a mobile home, deposited the mobile home onto his compound, and expected the child and his or her spouse to move in. The man's flare-up of back pain was believed to be partially related to the growing responsibilities of supporting this clan.

A third pattern is the emotional cut-off. Both Framo (1976) and Bowen (1978) described this pattern. One way that many adults respond to family turmoil is to physically or psychologically cut themselves off from their family of origin. The more intense the emotional fusion during early development, the greater the likelihood of a cut-off. The cut-off is an attempt at obtaining some differentiation from the family's reactivity. The cut-off is paradoxical; it does not really solve the problem. As Bowen noted, the cut-off reflects, solves, and creates a problem. At the solution level, the effects are relatively brief; some anxiety is reduced. However, there are several ways that this is traumatic. First, both parties, the person and his or her family of origin could benefit from contact if they could meaningfully interact with each other. Second, when a cut-off occurs, people are highly vulnerable to fusion in other relationships. It has been argued that they simply recapitulate the family-of-origin pathology in their next intimate relationship. Thus, people who say that they have little or no contact with their family because their family drives them crazy are likely to repeat those disturbed family dynamics in their marriage or in raising their children.

In the healthy family, the adult is able to develop a solid sense of identity before separating from the family of origin. Such adults do not have a strong need to stay with or get away from their parents. They relate to their parents more as adults. While recognizing that they are still their parents' children, their relationship is more one of equals. Affection and a desire to help family members are still present but not at the expense of personal integrity.

A major contribution to family theory by Bowen (1978) and Framo (1976) is an examination of how adults relate to their families of origin. These concepts are useful both in conducting therapy with adults as well as for therapists attempting to understand their own family dynamics. As is discussed further in chapter 2, Bowen emphasized the value of family therapists' developing a thorough understanding of their own families of origin.

CONCLUSION

Family-of-origin theory emphasizes the role of early experience with parents as a determinant of adult relationships. Bowen (1978) as well as Framo (1976) accounted for how these patterns are transmitted across multiple generations. Whereas Bowen emphasized the role of the emotional system and accompanying interpersonal reactivity, Framo highlighted internalized representations of early relationships as determinants of intimate adult interactions. Another useful conceptual scheme to account for the distancing–closeness dynamic observed in adults is Mahler et al.'s (1975) observation of young children. When synthesized, these models provide a unique historical vantage point on clinical marital and family difficulties.

Chapter 2

Clinical Assessment

Family-of-origin therapists are unique among family clinicians in several ways. First, there is a disproportionate emphasis on theory versus clinical techniques. Whereas much of family therapy is devoted to intervention techniques, such as symptom prescription (Haley, 1976), paradoxical injunctions (Selvini-Palazoli, Boscolo, Checchin, & Prata, 1978), boundary establishments (Minuchin & Fishman, 1981), or generating new cognitive frames and solutions (deShazer, 1985), family-of-origin treatment sees understanding of historical patterns as the key to therapeutic change. The *genogram*, a schematic family history discussed in greater detail later in this chapter, is a tool used to depict these patterns. Armed with these historical insights, the client will then be less emotionally reactive to relationship triggers, and a calmer, more choiceful behavioral pattern will follow. Therapies can be placed on a continuum with respect to the relative emphasis on affect, cognition, or behavior as the fulcrum of change. Family-of-origin therapy is heavily weighted toward the cognitive end of this spectrum. However, the cognitive aspect of this treatment is not directed toward present-centered thought patterns as in Beck's (1976) therapy for depression but instead focuses on history and its meaning. The client and therapist become engaged in a process similar to that of an anthropological historian—the goal is to elucidate family themes and how they are behaviorally symbolized.

Second, family-of-origin work, while attending to systems, is largely individual in focus. Change occurs within individuals through analysis and labeling of introjected objects. Once the power of these representations is understood by the client, the projection process is appreciated and then can be interrupted. Although couples may be seen conjointly, an observer would see that each partner is working with the therapist individually while his or her spouse looks on.

Family systems therapy, in general, is to be understood as a perspective for viewing and interviewing in emotional distress and is not defined by the number of people in the treatment room. Empirical support for this position comes from the work of Szapocznik and colleagues (1986) with adolescent substance abusers. Szapocznik et al. found that family therapy conducted primarily with the identified patient alone was as successful as conjoint treatment.

CLINICAL PRESENTATIONS SUGGESTING FAMILY-OF-ORIGIN THERAPY

In clinical practice, family-of-origin therapy is of particular value in several situations. First, this approach is helpful in families presenting with a child-focused problem in which there is capacity for insight on the part of the parent and there is some evidence of solid marital connectedness. Many strategic or behavioral family therapists are well aware of the clinical phenomenon in which the therapist helps the parent set rules and limits and the child's problem rapidly disappears in about six to eight sessions. However, at this point, more pervasive marital issues come to the surface. At this juncture, marital or family therapy with an historical emphasis is often very helpful.

Although genograms and extensive family histories are the defining feature of family-of-origin therapy, this assessment process is often useful prior to strategic, structural, experiential, or behavioral marital or family therapy. By spending the first two to three sessions gathering a thorough history, the therapist can impart a sense of cohesiveness and optimism to the family by focusing on their shared history. It is striking to see an angry, argumentative couple become suddenly warmer and supportive of one another when the therapist asks about their dating period and choice to be married. Another useful by-product of the extended family history is that husbands and wives develop an appreciation of the sources of many of their current differences. By examining each spouse's family of origin, current conflicts around dimensions such as childrearing and finances may be more sympathetically understood as outgrowths of family history rather than as deliberate antagonism.

This perspective often allows couples to step back from the intensity of current arguments and appreciate the differences as products of history. The result is often a rapid reduction in defensiveness and anger. The history also presents an opportunity for the strategic or other action-oriented therapist to buy time to observe family dynamics before prescribing a directive. Many family therapists are familiar with the phenomenon of selling a directive before its time and the therapeutic setbacks that are inevitably produced. With a genogram and accompanying picture of family dynamics, the therapist is better able to package a strategic or structural intervention in a manner compatible with the family's worldview. As a result, the directive will be more readily followed (Searight & Openlander, 1987).

A second clinical situation in which family-of-origin interventions are useful are those in which long-term, insight-oriented marital therapy is the treatment of choice. Prior to marriage or similar commitment, adults are likely to have relatively open one-to-one relationships. Over time, the emotional and physical closeness, together with a desire to be free of tension, results in a more guarded communication pattern. Although many people defensively state that they do not bring up important yet threatening topics to protect their partner from undue emotional distress, the primary reason for this guardedness is self-protection from anxiety. Bowen (1978) argued that gradually and usually imperceptibly, the relationship becomes closed, and important, sensitive subjects are forced underground. Access to the intellectual system with its clearer sense of values and goals can prevent this defensiveness from occurring. However, over time, the conditioned, unthinking avoidance of certain topics becomes status quo. Without outside assistance, it becomes difficult for the individual or couple to surmount this almost visceral inhibition.

In terms of marital expectations, object relations theorists argue that husbands and wives come together through a mix of healthy and largely pathological reasons. These issues may take several forms. If a person's parenting lacked something, he or she often tries to find a partner who provides what mother or father did not. On the other hand, if a person was subjected to some sort of tyranny from his or her parents and felt helpless, he or she might be drawn to someone who has these same characteristics, with the goal of obtaining control over that individual in adulthood. For example, someone who has been subjected to abuse by an alcoholic father may be drawn to a man with a drinking problem, with the unconscious agenda of being able to change a behavior pattern that was not changeable during childhood. In addition, someone a person is close to as an adult can become the target of projected issues. In pathological couples, these projections often conflict. For example, someone who as a child had to be extremely responsible may look to a new marriage as a way of being cared for and casting off the mantle of responsibility. Thus, a newly married man may want his spouse to take over the checkbook, pay the bills, and make important decisions about buying a car or house. However, according to Bowen's theory, it is very likely that the new partner has similar needs. The object relations theorists assume that people's basic need is for connectedness and that people's experience with their parents—particularly their mothers—programs them for the next intimate relationship that involves dependency.

Long-term psychiatric illness in one family member is usually part of a deal that has been unconsciously struck (Framo, 1982). The wife of an alcoholic may incur huge credit card debts. The husband of a depressed woman may have frequent extramarital affairs. The "bargain" prevents a direct challenging of the illness. ("Why shouldn't I spend my evenings shopping at the mall; it's the only way I can stand living with him. Besides, with all his drinking, he *owes* it to me"). Another variation is when the family member's symptoms have become a permanent piece of the fabric of family life. Somatoform patients often have organized their marriage and families around illness. Social outings center on doctors and clinic visits. The days are spent setting appointments and completing health insurance forms.

Framo (1982, p. 47) poignantly described the family organized around a psychiatrically ill member:

> One can witness the melancholy ritual every Sunday in all the state hospitals across the country: Family members visiting the hospitalized one year after year, bringing food, asking the same questions of the patient and staff, and not really expecting any change. Some of these families, feeling the illness of the patient as the cross they have to bear, do get some surplus advantages from the arrangement; for some, the only social life they have is involved with hospital visits and activities, and such situations can become so calcified that attempts to get the patient out of the hospital will be sabotaged by the family.

Another useful perspective added to object relations therapy is Carol Gilligan's (1982) view of female identity development. Gilligan's writing on gender is discussed in more detail in a later section. Gilligan noted that relatedness for women plays a major role in self-definition, whereas masculinity is defined through separation. Thus, male identity is threatened by intimacy, and female identity is threatened by separateness (Finkelstein, 1987). The theory also implies that men are not innately skilled at being in a relationship. In addition, both parties define themselves in ways that are not instinctively understood by the other:

> Frank was a 45-year-old businessman who owned a small chain of successful restaurants. He was brought to marital therapy by his wife, who opened the first session by exclaiming, "I can't take it anymore! This man is married to his computer and the telephone. We don't have a relationship; the children hardly know him."
>
> Frank had grown up as an only child. Frank's father owned and operated a small grocery store. During Frank's adolescence, the business had folded under competition from a large grocery chain. Frank remembered his father as being devastated and haunted by failure until he died when Frank was in college. With questioning from the therapist, Frank said he felt he had met his father's goals. The restaurants were stable and secure. Frank also was satisfied that he had met his personal goals: "I'm worth nearly a million; most of it is in safe stocks and bonds."
>
> The therapist then asked Frank about his goals as a husband and father. There was a long silence. Frank seemed bewildered and confused. He stammered that he didn't understand the therapist's question. His only definition of a spouse and father

was that of a good provider. Frank was genuinely surprised by his wife's distress; he felt he had done well for his family. The importance of his presence and emotional availability to his wife and children was totally new to him.

Family-of-origin work is also useful when working with individuals. Family-of-origin issues are likely to take several forms. First, an adult may continue to be overly involved with his or her family. This may not be experienced as a conflict until demands of adult life, such as marriage or work, conflict with the relationship with one or both parents—for example, a newly married husband who spends 2 to 3 hours every night with his mother; a newly married woman who discusses all her marital conflicts with her parents; or situations in which parents of either spouse become intrusively involved with daily life decisions.

An additional way that this family influence may occur is when family-of-origin issues become enacted in current relationships with one's spouse or children. For example, in one family presenting with an adolescent daughter who was exhibiting some minor defiance of rules and frequent arguments with parents, the mother and father seemed particularly concerned about the daughter's making a suicide attempt. When asked if the daughter had made a suicide attempt in the past or had spoken of suicide, the parents both indicated that this had never happened. However, the mother had had the experience of finding her own mother after she had hung herself.

GATHERING A FAMILY HISTORY

Current distress is seen as the culmination of a multigenerational process. This belief guides the clinical assessment. In the first stage, an extremely thorough history, including three to five generations of information, is developed. This is often organized with the aid of a genogram—a schematic family tree. The basic genogram format has been well described (Guerin & Pendagast, 1976; McGoldrick & Gerson, 1985). An example is shown in Figure 1. There are a number of variations on the genogram construction. However, the basic format is straightforward: A square signifies a male, and a circle indicates a female. A horizontal line denotes marriage. For example, Figure 1 shows that Jeff and Cheryl were married in 1976, and Julie and Justin were married in 1985. A dotted horizontal line indicates a significant nonmarital relationship such as cohabitation. Jeff and Cheryl's daughter, Jana, is living with Chuck. A set of parallel lines at an angle indicates a divorce. Robert and Ellen were divorced in 1940. They had one child, Jack, who was in the custody of his mother, Ellen, after the divorce. They also had a stillborn child in 1934. A pregnancy is denoted by a triangle; Julie is

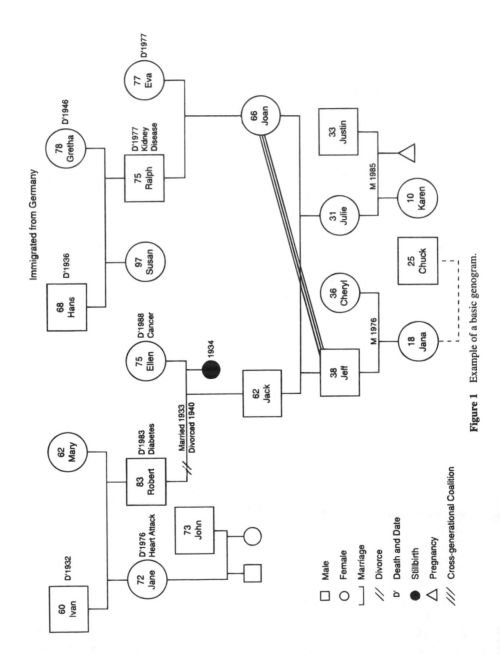

Figure 1 Example of a basic genogram.

24

pregnant with her second child. A D' indicates a death; the date of death, if known, is often noted. For example, Ralph died in 1977 at the age of 75. A set of lines across generations is often used for cross-generational coalitions; Jeff has a particularly close relationship with his mother, Joan.

A genogram is helpful to clients in that they can see the connections between events and also can see broader scale family patterns and how they may be handed down. It also helps the therapist in highlighting themes that are likely to be contributing to current family problems. The genogram is a useful place to start because it is factual—names, dates, and so on are obtained—and it is a relatively nonthreatening way to begin family-of-origin exploration.

Nuclear Family

Information about the nuclear family should include educational and occupational backgrounds of adults. Age at courtship and marriage should also be obtained. Information about previous marriage and past pregnancies is elicited. If there are ex-spouses, the interviewer should attempt to understand the current status of the relationship between former spouses (Kerr & Bowen, 1988).

The courtship process should be inquired about. How long did the couple see each other before getting married? Did they live together prior to marriage? In the case of nonmarital relationships such as with gays, lesbians, or heterosexual cohabitants, what factors led them to define their relationship as a significant one? What made each partner decide that this was to be an enduring relationship? Each partner's family-of-origin reaction to the relationship should also be elicited.

The decision to have children should be a focus of discussion. Each child likely altered the family or marital relationship in some way—the impact of each child should be the subject of inquiry. A picture should be obtained of the development of each child as well as the child's school and social adjustment (Kerr & Bowen, 1988). The childrens' and parents' response to beginning school is a useful indicator of the ease of separation within the family.

Each spouse's occupational and educational history should also be obtained. Significant family stressors—moves, serious illness, unemployment—are also important for the therapist to understand.

Extended Family

Similar factual information should be obtained for each partner's family of origin. Parents' and siblings' ages, occupations, and significant physical and mental health history should be noted. Divorces, separations, desertion, and remarriages are important to establish. Often clients may not have important information about family members. A very useful stance for the therapist is to encourage the client to obtain more information from their relatives about extended family functioning. A good stance for the client is to say something simple to family members, such as, "I'm in the process of learning more about myself and to do that I'd like to learn more about our family." This nonaggressive, nondefensive request will be difficult for family members to turn down. It places the family member being asked in a position of being helpful and does not raise defensiveness.

In gathering this information the client may find that there are holes or inconsistencies. For example, a client may say, "No one ever talked about my grandmother's death. I never knew what she died from; it just seemed sudden. My parents never talked about it." Another puzzle that often emerges in the information-gathering process is that there are major cut-offs in families. The client often does not understand the origin of these cut-offs and in fact may not even have reflected on them until gathering a history. A client may say, "We hardly ever saw my mother's side of the family; my dad never spoke to his older brother and his name was never mentioned in our home." A blanket of silence around a seemingly significant event or around particular family members suggests a loaded issue (E. Carter & McGoldrick-Orfanidis, 1976). The client may report that the major players—often their own parents—in these dramas aren't talking and that they refuse to when the subject is brought up. They simply change the subject and criticize the client for dredging up the past.

The genogram-oriented historical assessment may also allow an open discussion of family stressors that have been chronically affecting the family as an emotional undercurrent. Illnesses, divorces, geographic moves, job changes, and deaths may all be producing emotional shockwaves that the family has heretofore been too anxious to address (Kerr & Bowen, 1988).

Another source of anxiety in the information-gathering phase is that a client may become fearful of opening the door to contact with dysfunctional extended family members. There is often concern that the impaired member will become dependent on the client or a generalized fear that the relative's depression, anxiety, or other emotional distress will be transmitted like a contagious illness.

Family Secrets

Areas to encourage clients to reflect on while developing the genogram include communication rules in the family, how stressful events were managed, sexuality, and finances (McGoldrick & Gerson, 1985). Communication rules are rarely explicitly stated but more commonly take the form of implicit, unspoken norms around what is left *un*said. These norms are often far more powerful than any stated injunctions. Anne Tyler's *Dinner at the Homesick Restaurant* includes this powerful account of how the absence of communication about the father's sudden departure created a pervasive family rule:

> One weekend their father didn't come home, and he didn't come the next weekend either, or the next. Or rather, one morning Cody woke up and saw that it had been a while since their father was around. He couldn't say that he had noticed from the start. His mother offered no excuses. Cody, watchful as a spy, studied her furrowed, distracted expression and the way that her hands plucked at each other. It troubled him to realize that he couldn't picture his father's most recent time with them. Trying to find some scene that would explain Beck's leaving, he could only come up with general scenes, blended from a dozen repetitions: meals shattered by quarrels, other meals disrupted when Ezra spilled his milk, drives in the country where his father lost the way and his mother snapped out pained and exasperated directions. He thought of once when the Nash's radiator had erupted in steam and his father, looking helpless, had flung his suit coat over it. "Oh, honestly," his mother said. But that was way back; it was years ago, wasn't it? Cody journeyed through the various cubbies and crannies of the house, hunting up the trappings of his father's "phases" (as his mother called them). There were the badminton rackets, the butterfly net, the archery set, the camera with its unwieldy flashgun, and the shoe box full of foreign stamps still in their glassine envelopes. But it meant nothing that these objects remained behind. What was alarming was his father's half of the bureau: an empty sock drawer, an empty underwear drawer. In the shirt drawer, one unused sports shirt, purchased by the three children for Beck's last birthday, his forty-fourth. And a full assortment of pajamas; but then, he always slept in his underwear. In the wardrobe, just a hanger strung with ties—his oldest, dullest, most frayed and spotted ties—and a pair of shoes so ancient that the toes curled up. (Tyler, 1982, pp. 39–40)

Family secrets are particularly relevant dimensions because they often implicitly define a family's boundaries (Boyd-Franklin, 1989). Secrets often are the source of unspoken mythology or domains of silence. Key family members may go to great lengths to avoid recognition of a child's out-of-wedlock birth, a suicide, or a parent's previous jail term. These secrets may lead to alliances among those who have been let in on the information. Secrets may also generate patterns of familial blackmail. A mother who seems to go much easier on one of her daughters and seems reluctant to discipline the child may be doing so out of an implicit threat that the daughter will expose her maternal grandfather's attempt to sexually molest her. Secrets may lead to relationship patterns that are not understood by those involved (McGoldrick, 1995). A father may seem more detached from his middle daughter than his two other daughters. This distance is evident, and the extended family frequently comments on how the middle daughter and her father just don't seem to "click." However, only the mother and father know that the daughter is the result of the mother's extramarital affair.

Families in which there is sexual, physical, or severe emotional abuse or in which drug or alcohol addiction is an ongoing problem are often aware of the issue within the home but have strong sanctions around disclosure to outsiders. In addition to guilt and shame, family members are often afraid of exposure as well as the intrusion of social service and legal agencies.

The presence of family secrets is often suggested by one of several indicators. First, there is a generalized avoidance of talking about the past. Often there is anxiety that discussing one issue could lead to another and so forth until the secret would spill out. Second, there is a sense of tension, often with rapid subject changing, whenever a particular person, time period, or issue is discussed. Another clue is the presence of greater emotion than would be expected around a particular event or person (McGoldrick, 1995).

Family Themes

Important family themes are also made apparent through over- and underachievement patterns (e.g., mother overfunctions while father underfunctions at home; Ault-Riche, 1988), the family's reaction to stressful events (cohesiveness vs. disengagement; coping with the event head-on vs. multiyear shock waves), and how losses were managed (stoically?, emotionally?, denied?; McGoldrick & Gerson, 1985). Other issues to consider include whether gender roles and childrearing norms of the particular time period were followed or whether there were radical departures from historical expectations. For example, a family in the 1920s in which the father was the primary caretaker of the children while the mother was employed 70 hours per week is a significant departure from the norm. Sibling position patterns are also important to examine. Toman's (1976) notion of socially prescribed roles based on birth order is a useful guide.

As noted in chapter 1, the sibling position of the parents in relation to one another and to their children should be considered. For example, loading of a sibling role— for example, an adult who is the oldest son in a family in which his father was also the oldest son—can result in a highly exaggerated version of the oldest child role. In addition, birth order interacts with differentiation and the degrees of influence exerted by the emotional system. A well-differentiated oldest sibling is aware of the social legacy associated with the role of oldest child. Thus, she may choicefully behave as a responsible leader but also knows when to back off and let others take charge. The less-differentiated oldest child is likely to be rigid and authoritarian in relation to others and, in particular, his or her younger siblings (Kerr & Bowen, 1988).

Views of marriage are also important organizing principles. Marriage may reflect an almost legalistic contract in which each spouse is expected to perform specific duties. If these roles are not fulfilled, divorce is an acceptable response. In other couples, the marriage is of two large clans—the extended family is part of each spouse's daily life. Is the marriage based on shared responsibility, or is this highly skewed, such as when the man leaves the home and periodically returns for brief periods? These questions are examples—many more themes will arise in later chapters.

Emotional Shockwaves

In addition to structural patterns, the genogram should also include temporal sequences. Emotional shockwaves (Bowen, 1976) often occur in the months or years following a significant family event. These upheavals are not the overt mourning that family members go through but are the subterranean patterns of emotional reverberations occurring following serious illness or loss. Bowen noted that many people minimize or deny the significance of a deceased relative, and the interpersonal crises occurring in the aftermath may be presented as unrelated to distress or life change. The therapist who attempts to make these connections may find the interpretation strongly rejected. Bowen first described emotional shock-waves in the 1950s and observed that deaths were often followed by increased respiratory illness, diabetes, allergies, surgeries, and psychiatric disorders ranging from depression to full-blown psychoses. Research in family systems medicine in the past decade has found considerable support for Bowen's clinical observations (Rolland, 1994). The following case illustrates the domino effect of a death:

> Father John was a 48-year-old Catholic priest. He was the oldest of three children. Father John's brother, James, had been married for 20 years and had three children. His sister, Claire, was a nun and worked as a teacher in a school run by her religious order. Their father had died 5 years earlier after a long painful bout of cancer. All three of the adult children were very supportive of their mother. They were devastated when she died suddenly of a heart attack. Within 18 months of their mother's funeral, Father John and his siblings had embarked on major life transitions. Father John had left the priesthood and was working on a novel as a writer. James divorced his wife and was living with a much younger woman. Sister Claire had left her religious order and was managing a politically progressive bookstore. Of the three adults, only John exhibited some insight into the changes, saying, "I loved Mom very much. I knew she would be devastated if I left the priesthood. When Mom died, it was as if a weight had been lifted from my shoulders; I wouldn't disappoint Mom by leaving; I could finally be free."

Ongoing or recent individual therapy should be elicited. Individual therapists are often foci of triangulation. Woody Allen's movie *Annie Hall* presents a humorous example of each partner talking with their respective therapist about the relationship and then sharing the therapist's wisdom with the other partner. Family therapists should be particularly judicious when accepting a client or family for treatment when another therapist is currently involved. Therapists may refer clients for family treatment out of their own reactivity when individual work seems to be at an impasse. The family therapist should consider the individual therapist to be part of the system (Kerr & Bowen, 1988). Unfortunately, the individual psychotherapist or even the psychiatrist providing medication management may be an unintentional stabilizing force that hinders meaningful change (Selvini-Palazolli et al., 1978.)

Issues in Obtaining the History

It is important to make a distinction between a client's personally held theories about how the family should be and how the family actually functions. Global questions often elicit equally global and vague descriptions. (Question: "How is your relationship with your brother?" Answer: "Good, we get along very well.") In contrast, questions about specific relationship parameters often are far more revealing. (Question: "How often do you see, write, or call your brother? What do you talk about? Do you see him alone or with other family members?"; Nichols & Schwartz, 1995.)

It is important that the therapist's process of asking questions not become a Socratic inquiry in which family members are pushed in a particular direction. Rather, the information gathering should be factual and neutral. This style of inquiry, by itself, has considerable interventive power.

As the history is gathered, the therapist should begin looking for patterns. Some of these may be fairly obvious, such as an intergenerational alcoholism or early deaths by adult males. However, other dynamics may be more subtle, including the overfunctioning mother and underfunctioning father, a history of geographic cut-offs, or of more involvement with the paternal extended family with little contact on the maternal side. Patterns of alliances and themes will become apparent as information is gathered.

The Therapist's Case Conceptualization

The clinician should also keep in mind that the family's level of adaptive flexibility will be a function of its emotional reactivity. The family lifestyle is a series of developmental stress points, including marriage, birth of first child, children entering school, adolescence, children leaving home, retirement of spouses, and so forth (B. Carter & McGoldrick, 1989). An adaptive family in which parents (and even children to some extent) flexibly trade off roles such as nurturer, keeper of family finances, manager of the household, and disciplinarian will respond in a healthier way to these external changes than a reactive family with more rigid role prescriptions.

Certain conditions may reduce the effectiveness of conjoint marital sessions. Spouses who are too intensely joined may have difficulty getting beyond the *we* position to an *I* posture. Change occurs at the individual level. Conjoint sessions may obscure this focus because each spouse may perceive his or her change to be contingent on the other. In addition, with a high level of reactivity, it may be difficult for each partner to think clearly within sessions and obtain the necessary focus on personally held goals and responsibilities.

In either case, the clinician should include attention to conditions around a marriage. Extended or very brief courtships suggest poorer levels of differentiation. Similarly, couples who managed to live together with little distress but who become highly conflictual soon after marriage were probably able to manage reactivity through distance (Kerr & Bowen, 1988) and now find it manageable only through the emotional wall associated with conflict. Similarly, having children out of wedlock or becoming pregnant very soon after marriage may, in certain cultural groups, suggest poor differentiation.

For adolescents and adults who are pushed into therapy by parents or spouses, it is important to recognize and openly discuss the coercive element surrounding their presentation. Ignorance of this issue or refusal to address it by the therapist only continues a pathological family projection process (Kerr & Bowen, 1988).

During the history gathering, the therapist should try to formulate some initial hypotheses. These will be based on themes that arise in the intergenerational legacy of the client's family. The family's interaction in relation to the client's key conflicts should be examined. Although making judgments about the symptom's function has been criticized by family therapists (Bogdan, 1986), it is often helpful to consider what the symptom prevents the individual, couple, or family from doing. The answer to this question should provide the therapist with clues as to "disasters" that are feared (Bentovim & Kinston, 1991; Nichols & Schwartz, 1995). For example, a husband may have anxiety attacks if his wife is more than 10 minutes late coming home from work. The intensity of his reaction might suggest abandonment as central fear or conflict. In gathering the husband's family history, the therapist notes that his father died when he was 5 and that his mother died 3 years later. This information provides further support for abandonment as a core issue. The potential current function of the anxiety attacks is that they elicit caretaking from wife and children and over time are likely to result in a restriction of the wife's activities. Equipped with the history, the therapist will actively and repeatedly point out the husband's predisposition for perceiving abandonment as rooted in his family-of-origin traumas. He, in effect, is projecting abandonment onto his wife. As the process continues and she feels increasingly trapped in his projections, she may tire of the growing constraint to be present at all times and leave the relationship. Thus, the projection process results in the feared catastrophe.

By the end of the assessment, the therapist should be able to describe the following:

> 1) the nature of the patterns of emotional functioning in a nuclear family; 2) the level of anxiety a family has experienced in the past and the level it is currently experiencing; and 3) the amount of stress a family has experienced and is experiencing. (Kerr & Bowen, 1988, p. 295)

The family's anxiety is the built-in reactivity transmitted across generations. This reactivity interacts with external stressful life events.

It is important for the therapist to recognize that the client's degree of differentiation with his or her family of origin is likely to be recapitulated in nonfamily relationships. Thus, an emotionally driven client who obtains greater objectivity may, him- or herself, gradually pull away from old friends. Although in the past the client was very reactive to a friend's frequent crises, he or she is now less responsive and more detached. The friend may complain that the client is not "there for me anymore." The client is likely to be there for the friend but with a level of involvement that is less intense and more thoughtful. Similarly, increased differentiation may carry over to the work place. Emergencies at work may be experienced as less emergent. In addition, triangulation in the form of anxious gossip or excessive involvement with coworkers outside of the employment setting may be reduced as a result of therapy. Coworkers may complain that the client has become "too good for us" or that she "just doesn't care anymore."

The therapist may also become reactive and inadvertently climb inside the family. This is a particular risk when the family presents with a crisis that appears to warrant immediate resolution. The therapist who is able to control his or her own reactivity will be better able to remain engaged with the family while simultaneously maintaining enough distance to be objective.

CONCLUSION

The assessment process in family-of-origin therapy is difficult to distinguish from the active ingredients of treatment. The collaborative process of obtaining a detailed family history often contributes to new insights and new perspectives on individual functioning. In addition, the client who engages in one-to-one interaction with key family members to obtain factual information is likely to be altering a long-standing pattern of disengagement or superficial exchanges. The therapist's ability to integrate historical information in a sensitive yet objective manner will help provide clients with useful feedback about unspoken legacies and themes that are affecting their current relationships.

Chapter 3

Concepts and Intervention Techniques

For both Bowen (1978) and Framo (1982), family-of-origin therapy was a long-term, multiyear process. Those who have adapted family-of-origin work to other contexts or include family-of-origin assessment as a precursor to other types of family therapy often have departed from the long-term nature of the therapy process.

The traditional approach to family-of-origin therapy begins with an extensive multigenerational family history—often developed with the aid of a genogram. The history-taking is one of the core curative factors in family-of-origin therapy. This is usually followed by a focus on spouses' intrapsychic issues and how they are being enacted in the family or marriage. Interpretations that link each person's history to his or her current relationship issues are made. Transference and projection are seen as key processes leading to these conflicts and are pointed out. Framo (1982) and Bowen (1978) both developed several variations on this general approach. One of these methods, coaching, involves changing family relationships by working with one person alone.

INTEGRATING THE HISTORY INTO THE PRESENT

Although gathering family information and discussing it with a neutral observer may appear to be a minimal intervention, it is the heart of family-of-origin work. Therapists who were trained in strategic or behaviorally oriented approaches may have difficulty with what superficially appears to be a very passive style of therapy. However, being seriously and actively listened to can be a profound and novel experience for family members. Rather than being preoccupied with generating directives, the therapist empathically attempts to enter into the family narrative that is unfolding while mentally labeling patterns and themes. For family members to begin to confront their distortions, there needs to be a noncritical and supportive holding environment, which can be created by the therapist's empathy

33

(Nichols & Schwartz, 1995). Without this safe arena in which to examine the split, contradictory object representations that are projected onto significant others, the process becomes overwhelmingly threatening, and family members shut down. The holding environment is the psychological anesthetic that makes the anxiety of therapeutic work tolerable.

Although *transference*—the projection of unresolved historical issues onto the therapist—occurs in family therapy, it is usually weaker than in individual treatment. Family-of-origin therapy argues that *all* significant relationships are colored by transference. Psychodynamically oriented family therapists have long recognized that a person's behavior and emotional reactions are a function of his or her historical analogues. Thus, if a person was raised by authoritarian, punitive parents, being summoned to an immediate supervisor's office may fill him or her with anxious dread. Similarly, if a person was raised by a parent who did everything for him or her, that person's search for a mate is likely to include a quest to be dependent and cared for. Therapists should periodically ask themselves "What does this pattern (e.g., alliance, style of handling loss, married late in life, having large numbers of children) *mean* for the couple or family in treatment?" This should be considered both in terms of the expectations and representations of family life brought to marriage and in terms of how these themes become enacted with a spouse and children. The same historical pattern may have very different meaning at the individual level:

> Karen and Eric were both the oldest of six children in Midwestern farm families. While growing up, each had considerable responsibility for younger siblings as well as for duties on the family farm. In late adolescence, Eric rebelled and went on strike, refusing to perform farm chores or take care of the younger children. Shortly afterward he went away to college and saw his family only once or twice each year. Karen, on the other hand, enjoyed her caretaking role. Her mother was frequently ill, and Karen took great pride in being able to run the household while still helping out on the farm. Even after she began college, Karen returned home frequently and maintained involvement with her siblings. Karen and Eric met after college when they were coworkers in the same business. Within a year they were married. Although Karen was somewhat confused by Eric's rare contact with his family, and Eric periodically felt claustrophobic with Karen's "overinvolvement" with her family, these tensions were manageable. However, during their third year of marriage, Karen became insistent about becoming pregnant, and Eric became increasingly angry in his refusals to discuss having children.
>
> In therapy, the different meaning attached to very similar family-of-origin conditions became apparent. Karen wanted a large family much like the one she was raised in. She found that her family role was very satisfying for her. Eric, on the other hand, viewed the caretaking, parenting role as oppressive and confining.

Although Karen and Eric initially felt that they were a natural match because of their families of origin, differences in how these conditions were experienced led to the eventual conflict regarding child bearing. Both Karen's and Eric's views of children were shaped by their family-of-origin experiences. Each person's anticipation was that children would recapitulate the desired or undesired climate of their own early family life.

In developing case conceptualization to guide therapy, the clinician should not assume that spouses will interpret objectively similar family histories in the same way.

INTEGRATING FAMILY HISTORY INTO THERAPY

Bowen (1978) and Framo (1982) both worked with individuals, conjoint families, marital couples, and family groups. To the external observer, conjoint sessions often look more like individual therapy with a set of related persons. If a child is presented as a problem, there is an immediate assumption that marital conflict must be addressed. Family members may deny this, but the history that is being gathered is used to provide low-level interpretations (Framo, 1982). These interpretations relate individual and marital histories to the child's presenting problem.

In the next phase of treatment, transference to the therapist and other family members is interpreted. As in Yalom's (1985) model of group therapy, family therapy includes multiple transferences and reactivities. Although there is often transference to a therapist, there is also substantative transference taking place among marital partners or among parents of children. In the context of therapy, particular attention is paid to the historical issues or introjects that color these interactions. The therapist will point out how these assumptions initially arose in the parent's own family of origin and how they have come to influence relating with children and spouse.

It is also useful to interpret family members' behavior directly. For example, the therapist might say to a woman that "you say you want your husband to share with you more, but every time he does talk here you interrupt him" (Bowen, 1978). In addition, there is often more forcefulness and openness than in traditional dynamics therapy. This is particularly true when family myths are exposed. For example, Bowen gave the description of a case in which a wife, rather than wearing her husband's wedding ring, had been wearing the engagement ring of a fiance who had been dead for 30 years. This was an unquestioned behavior that undoubtedly had considerable symbolic significance. The therapist directly labeled this symbolic yet unspoken conflict.

The early phase of therapy is typically directed toward alleviating significant distress. Kerr and Bowen (1988) noted that most families entering therapy undergo symptom and anxiety reduction. Differentiation—requiring more extended work and the ability to tolerate greater levels of emotional discomfort—will be achieved by only a small number of the family members in treatment.

As noted in the preceding chapter, the presence of cut-offs has harmful effects on current relationship patterns. However, in therapy, individuals and families believe that they can improve without addressing these cut-offs. This view is likely to be particularly pronounced when both spouses have cut themselves off from their families of origin. When only one spouse has cut off the family of origin, there is likely to be some recognition of the pattern, particularly by the spouse who is more appropriately engaged with his or her family. Kerr and Bowen (1988) argued that unless cut-offs are dealt with, the improvement that does occur will be less substantial and less enduring.

Bowen and Framo also argued that it is often useful to work with subsystems, particularly when there is an impasse. Framo (1982) described a case in which a husband's mother was involved in the family's life. She called him every day, and there were several sessions with the mother and son dyad. In these sessions, the mother's guilt-inducing statements were confronted directly ("Don't worry about me, I'm going to an old ladies' home. Go back to that wife of yours"). Eventually new patterns of relating begin to develop. Often, some regression is seen immediately prior to termination, and this is similar to what is seen in individual psychodynamic therapy.

Framo (1982) and Bowen (1978) differed around how the therapist should deal with the family of origin. For Bowen (1978), once intergenerational processes are understood, the focus should be on reducing reactivity and becoming a more objective observer of family processes and one's role in them. Members of the family of origin are not directly included in therapy sessions. In Framo's (1982) approach, therapy typically goes through an initial child-focused stage and then through a stage in which marital issues and relationship to family of origin are the focus. At this point, the format shifts and the couple may meet with other couples in a couples group. The major focus of these groups is to have each spouse bring in his or her own family of origin for sessions with the therapist. These sessions are usually not conducted in a couples-group format. There is typically considerable anxiety and resistance about these "in vivo" family-of-origin sessions.

In these extended family sessions, the mate is not present. This prevents inappropriate intrusions into the couple's relationship and reduces the tendency for triangulation, which could serve as an unproductive diversion. The goal of these sessions is to collaboratively examine the family life cycle, with particular attention to traumas, alliances, and roles. This allows for in vivo corrective emotional experiences. As with many brief family therapies, seemingly small interventions can have wide-ranging effects. Opening up a previously closed path of communication or being able to recognize how history has permeated a spouse's view of a husband or wife can have pronounced and enduring effects. At the same time, however, family-of-origin therapists are suspicious of early rapid therapeutic change because it represents symptom removal alone and does not include the necessary intrapsychic work to prevent the symptoms from being reshuffled.

COACHING: DIFFERENTIATION FROM THE FAMILY OF ORIGIN

A major contribution made by both Framo (1982) and Bowen (1978) centers around adults' current relationships with their families of origin. Bowen, in particular, emphasized that by harnessing the intellectual system and relying upon a well-developed history of one's own family, adults could develop more satisfying relationships with parents and siblings. The key to this outcome was to be able to maintain a strong sense of individual identity without reactivity while relating to family members.

Working with the therapist on the genogram may be an initial first step in this process. Generating the genogram, as described in chapter 2, is often a successful strategy for opening up closed systems and beginning to develop one-to-one relationships. However, discussing family history may be anxiety provoking, and triangulation may also occur. For example, a client may try to elicit historical information from his mother but be interrupted by his father. Another way that triangles arise is when a client attempts to engage a parent in a one-to-one manner, but the parent consistently talks not about him- or herself or about personal experiences but about one of the client's siblings, friends, or other relatives.

In terms of intervening further, the client who is desiring a more fulfilling relationship with his or her own family of origin should be aware that change in these patterns is likely to be a three-step process. First, the client's own behavior will change. Second, the family will react to the change. Third, the client will, of necessity, need to respond to the family's reaction. Often, the client returns to habitual ways of interacting in response to the family's reaction. There are several useful strategies for this process. Humor is often very useful in detoxifying repetitively painful family processes. Thus, for the client with an intrusive mother, it is sometimes useful to humorously point out that the mother is overflowing in her love. Another useful strategy is the reversal. In the reversal, the client changes a habitual pattern by exhibiting the opposite behavior. For example, if the client

finds that he always withdraws from his mother's affection, he should be encouraged to initiate it (E. Carter & McGoldrick-Orfanidis, 1976). If the client calls on
the phone and always talks to her mother, she should call and ask deliberately to
speak to her father. Triangling is a useful strategy for those who frequently get
caught up in conflicts, particularly with their parents. A common pattern is one in
which a mother will complain to an adult child about the father. At these times, it
is useful for the client to approach the father and say something like, "Your wife
seems really upset. I hope you can help her. I don't know why she came to me"
(E. Carter & McGoldrick-Orfanidis, 1976). Often in the history process, particularly with respect to loaded issues, relevant adults may refuse to talk. For example, if a father won't talk about his first marriage and that seems to be important,
the client should be encouraged to go to the father's brother. It is likely that the
uncle's conversation will get back to the father, who will want to give the client
the "real" facts.

If the client is attempting to change a repetitively painful pattern of interaction with key family members, it is extremely important that Bowen's concept
of differentiation be underscored. The client should take an "I" position.
Because the client is part of this family system, doing therapy with the family is
unlikely to be successful. The goal is for the client to have an improved relationship with individual family members, not to produce change at the family
systems level or to get relatives into psychotherapy to cure pathology. In addition, the client should have a clear plan and should know what he or she is going
to do in relation to family members before doing it. Role playing in the context
of therapy is often helpful in this regard. If the client seems angry, hurt, or can
only see the family in terms of victims and villains, then it is likely that he or she
has succumbed to the emotional power of the family. At these points, it is helpful for the therapist to assist the client in getting more emotional distance, examining his or her feelings from a detached perspective, and going back to the
historical pattern of family dynamics (E. Carter & McGoldrick-Orfanidis,
1976). Regaining a perspective on triangles, sibling position, and cut-offs is very
useful in regaining the intellectual perspective and simultaneously gaining some
emotional distance. As a general rule of thumb, when the family is described in
terms of good guys and bad guys, the client has lost the ability to objectively see
larger patterns of family interaction.

Often a family member may seem to block efforts to connect with another. For
example, every time James tries to have a one-to-one conversation with his brother
John, his sister-in-law, Julie, is always either on the phone or in the room. This is
often a very frustrating process. In American society, there appears to be a pervasive myth that, once one is married, the relationship with one's in-laws is somehow as close as that with ones' own parents, siblings, and children. If an in-law or

relative is a source of frustration, he or she should be dealt with directly. One strategy would be for James to call Julie at a time when he knows she will be home alone as a means of getting to know her better rather than continuing to deal with her as an obstacle.

Kramer (1985) noted useful parallels between the concept of second-order change (Watzlawick, Weakland, & Fisch, 1974) and differentiation in family-of-origin work. First-order change is the typical pattern of response to another's behavior based on a logical, rationale premise. Thus, a common reaction to an adult sibling who does not attend family gatherings and does not respond to letters is to more vigorously pursue them. If, for example, this is the first such concerted effort by a client to engage his or her sister, more vigorous pursuit is probably a reasonable response. However, if the distancer–pursuer dynamic is long-standing, it is time to consider alternatives. Typically, the pursuer is contributing as much to the distance as the distancer; a recurring cycle has emerged. Often it is difficult to see around the frame one is locked into—a very limited set of possibilities is apparent. Second-order change reflects a shift to a higher order perspective and the ability to appreciate the presence of multiple ways of constructing the behavior sequence. The new perspective may lead to changes in behavior (e.g., waiting for the distancer to initiate contact rather than continuing to chase him or her), or the change in perception alone may be enough (e.g., "I want to continue to initiate contact with my sister because it is important to *me*, but I am not so dependent on *her* responses").

Developing a more differentiated identity in relation to one's family requires sustained effort. Often, motivation for change is short-lived or reduced considerably after an initial flurry of activity, particularly in the face of roadblocks or strong emotional reactions (Nichols & Schwartz, 1995). Bowen (1978) noted that disclosures of important information, including age-old family secrets, are often more likely during family crises such as acute illness or death. However, the person seeking change needs to continue his or her efforts after family functioning has returned to the status quo.

One important insight that can emerge from understanding family patterns is that *all* family members, including one's parents, are part of an extended multigenerational emotional matrix. Each individual has the responsibility to be as mature, reflective, and goal directed as possible (Kerr & Bowen, 1988). A thoughtful history will ideally unhook adults from blaming their parents for not giving them what they needed and also guide them to reflect on wherever they are expending considerable frustrated energy in attempting to extract some compensation from coworkers, friends, and spouses for what was not given to them by their family. By being able to examine their own motives and relationship agendas, clients will be less caught up in how family members should be and more accepting of how they are. This acceptance will, with time, extend laterally to their spouse or significant other, coworkers, or boss and extend downward to their relationships with their children.

INTEGRATIVE MODELS

Recently, there has been movement toward integration of different family therapy models. In particular, intrapsychic approaches have been integrated with those that focus more on family organization patterns. One useful complementary integration has been of family-of-origin treatment with structural family therapy (Minuchin, 1974). Structural therapy focuses on roles and boundaries. Each role—parent, child, spouse, sibling, grandparent—has accompanying rights and responsibilities. Pathology occurs when these roles become diffuse or unclear. For example, children may function in the role of parent, or a grandparent may override parental authority when dealing with grandchildren. Minuchin also emphasized that families are not democratic institutions but are hierarchically organized for effective functioning. Parents are the authorities in the family and should, as a unit, make all important decisions for children and for the family as a whole. Parents should have a marital relationship separate from their parental role, which is not intruded on by their own parents or their children. Melitio (1988) noted a parallel between Bowen's concept of differentiation and the hierarchical, boundary-determined interdependence of the structurally healthy family.

Although structural therapy accounts for how families become distressed at a molar organizational level, there is little attention devoted to the molecular, intrapsychic factors that account for the breakdown of family roles and boundaries. Although the therapist may clearly discern the presence of a cross-generational coalition between a grandparent and grandchild, structural models do not address the question of why this pattern might have emerged. The addition of Framo's (1982) concept of unconscious role assignment provides the missing link in this account. Thus, the grandparent who has formed a coalition across generational boundaries with a grandchild is likely to be perceiving the child as a means of meeting his or her own needs for nurturance and may co-opt the child into becoming dependent on him or her (Melitio, 1988). The outcome of these distortions is an absence of differentiation; identities are merged. Whereas family-of-origin therapists interpret and clarify the historically based introjects that fuel the projections, the structural therapist achieves separateness through the establishment of interpersonal boundaries. An example of a structural boundary-setting analogue that promotes differentiation is found in Minuchin and Fishman's (1981) account of therapy with an anorectic young woman:

Minuchin: Let's jump out of the groove. (Touches Miriam's hands.) Miriam, are these your hands?

Miriam: Um-hum.

Minuchin: They are not your father's hands?

Miriam: They are not.

Minuchin (touching her biceps): Is this your muscle?

Miriam: Yeah.

Minuchin: Are you certain?

Miriam: Yes.

Minuchin (touching her nose): Is this your nose?

Miriam: Um-hum.

Minuchin: Not your father's nose?

Miriam: Yeah.

Minuchin: Are you certain? Absolutely certain?

Miriam: Yes.

Minuchin: Is that your mouth?

Miriam: Um-hum.

Minuchin: Who eats when you eat?

Miriam: Me.

Minuchin: Where does the food go?

Miriam: In me.

Minuchin (gently pinching some skin on Miriam's arm): Is this fat your fat?

Miriam: Yeah.

Minuchin: Yeah. So why do they tell you what to eat? Is it right that your father tells you what to put in your mouth?

Miriam: I guess it is right.

Minuchin: No. It's wrong. It's wrong. It's your mouth.

Miriam: Yeah.

Minuchin: Can you open your mouth? Open it. (Miriam slowly opens, closes, then opens her mouth.) Close it. Open it. Can you bite your lips? (Miriam does this.) It's your mouth. When you eat, will you eat by yourself the food that you want? And then when you come here, you will go with the therapist to weigh yourself. (Picks up father's hand.) Whose hand is this one?

Miriam: My dad's.

Minuchin: You are certain it's your dad's? (Lifts Miriam's hand.) And whose hand is this?

Miriam: Mine.

Minuchin: You are certain? Okay, so it's your body, you will feed it. How old are you?

Miriam: Twenty.
Minuchin: Does your father need to tell you what to eat?
Miriam: No.
Minuchin: Does your mom?
Miriam: No.

These structural interventions occurring in session are termed *enactments* and are the heart of this therapeutic approach. Enactments may be akin to the working-through phase of historically oriented therapy, when the client applies therapeutic insights to current interactions with family members. Melitio (1988) noted that in later structural theorizing, Minuchin and Fishman (1981) devoted increased attention to intrapsychic dimensions. These included cognitive schemas held by family members. The beliefs about relationships were supported and justified by family organization and vice versa. These cognitive schemas and familial behavior patterns are recursively validating. The entry point into change may occur at the intrapsychic or interpersonal level; structural and family-of-origin theorists differ in terms of which dimension is emphasized. The structuralists emphasize interpersonal behavioral change as the key to altering beliefs, whereas historically oriented therapists emphasize the opposite sequence (Melitio, 1988).

OUTCOME RESEARCH

Although family-of-origin therapy has not been the subject of significant outcome research, there are several studies suggestive of its effectiveness. In an early study, Winer (1971) used a coding system that measured the ratio of differentiated verbalizations to undifferentiated verbalizations ("we," "our," "us"). It was assumed that as the individual began to change in treatment and became more differentiated, the number of "I" statements would increase, with a corresponding decline in collective pronoun use. Examples of "I" statements include "It's a question of finding out who I am and how I got that way" and "I am convinced there are two problems—hers and mine" (Winer, 1971, pp. 245–246). The study was based on a small sample involved in multiple-family group psychotherapy. Results indicated that for six of the eight individuals studied, the ratio of "I" to "we" statements shifted in the more differentiated direction over the course of therapy. It was also noted that early in treatment, husbands and wives showed very similar differentiation ratios. However, by later sessions, couples exhibited greater variability between spouses.

More recent studies have not been as directly grounded in Bowen's theory. However, they are more sophisticated methodologically. Szapocznik, Kurtines,

Foote, Perez-Vidal, and Hervis (1983, 1986) developed an approach called one-person family therapy to address substance abuse among young adolescents. One-person family therapy involves only the identified patient attending the treatment sessions. One-person treatment assumes that the identified patient is involved in a series of complementary repetitive behavioral processes such that each family member's behavior influenced and is affected by that of other members. Szapocnik et al. (1983) described this approach as an integration of Bowenian coaching with structural and strategic therapy. To enact key family sequences, the therapist and client use role playing, with the client depicting several family members. The therapist also may use the Gestalt empty-chair technique, diagramming of family dynamics on a chalkboard, and therapist–client role playing to develop alternative styles of relating to family members. It is assumed that when the client depicts another family member's behavior, he or she must be acting in a complementary role to maintain the other's behavior. As an intervention, the therapist focuses on establishing structural boundaries around introjected representations of family interactions. These introjects are addressed through procedures such as role reversal and Gestalt fantasy techniques. Homework assignments are then given to the client to alter stereotyped styles of relating. The client and therapist then address the family members' responses to these new behaviors. Szapocznik et al. (1983) indicated that through complementarity, these changes often produce a crisis response in family members. The therapists may have one or two conjoint sessions at this point.

In evaluating this approach, it was found that when compared with conjoint treatment, one-person family therapy was equally effective in bringing about individual-level symptom reduction in the identified patient as well as improved family functioning. Family measures were based on observations as well as reports from all family members on the Family Environment Scale. This pattern of findings was replicated in a subsequent study, which found that single-person treatment was associated with somewhat better family functioning at followup (Szapocznik et al., 1986). One qualification of these findings is that these families were of Hispanic background. It has been suggested that Hispanic families are particularly cohesive, so that change in one member is very likely to arouse complementary behaviors in other family members, leading to change. This approach may have markedly less effect in more disengaged families.

THE THERAPIST'S OWN FAMILY

Both Bowen (1978) and Framo (1982) emphasized the value of family therapists' developing a thorough understanding of their own family of origin. This is in contrast to many of the strategic and structural therapists, who regard working on their own family as irrelevant and as a pointless distraction from getting down to business.

Bowen's (1978) approach came from his observations that trainees had more clinical success when they had been coached to address issues in their own families. He also used this coaching when only one member of a couple or family was motivated to participate in treatment. Bowen's work in this area has influenced a number of training programs such that family-of-origin training has become a common component (Wells, Scott, Schmeller, Hilmann, & Searight, 1990).

In being a coach for trainees, it is important to recognize that families operate as tightly interwoven systems with characteristic, repetitive interpersonal sequences. Although family interactions can often be considered linear and causal ("She nags, causing him to leave the house"), these sequences are arbitrarily defined. A common heuristic for making sense of one's own family is to see members in the roles of victims and villains. These arbitrary dualistic percepts prevent one from recognizing higher order patterns that usually involve more players than the victim and the villain. The strength and constancy of these patterns will be evident when one of the participants changes their habitual behaviors. If one person in the family is able to overcome the pull of the emotional system and accompanying interpersonal reactivity, the recurring behavioral sequences will be disrupted, with resulting systems change.

Bowen (1978) discussed his work with his own family at a family therapy conference with a number of well-known family theorists present. Bowen noted that, while developing his family theories, he often would make visits to his own parents. Bowen said that he was able to understand intellectually how his family operated. He could analyze his family brilliantly. However, he seemed to have difficulty maintaining his conceptualization and how he wanted to relate to his family during his visits home. He often described how he lost his sense of differentiation and became absorbed into the emotional system of his family. Bowen argued that what he ended up doing was maintaining a superficial, detached relationship with the family. In his early work with his family, Bowen, similar to many therapists in training, made the cardinal mistake of attempting to "do therapy" with family members. A common goal of trainees in their initial family-of-origin work is to help their family in some way. Goals such as getting an older brother into a drug treatment program or helping another family member with depression are inappropriate. The trainee is part of the family system and will likely be unsuccessful in his or her efforts. The goal of single-person family-of-origin work is not to change family members but to help the trainee develop more satisfying one-to-one relationships with family members as well as reduce reactivity.

Personal family-of-origin work is helpful for conducting therapy because it is likely to reduce countertransference and improve the therapist's ability to work with certain types of families. For the therapist, family therapy, as opposed to individual therapy, is likely to evoke stronger countertransference. Particularly in families that evoke unresolved issues of the therapist's own family of origin, the treatment process may be contaminated. For example, if a therapist works with a mother who is critical and controlling of her child and this was a big issue for the therapist as a child, the therapist is likely to perceive this mother similarly to his or her own and to relate to her in the same way. This process is much stronger in family therapy because the therapist is viewing clients in the context of family roles (mother, father, older sister, older brother), whereas in the case of individual therapy a client may be seen as, say, a 38-year-old White woman with dysthymic disorder. Therapists need to be alert to this process so they don't fuse, cut off, or relate to clients out of their own set of internalized introjects. It is important for therapists to maintain that Bowenian balance between intellectual and emotional functioning.

The family therapist is also more likely to experience a "pull" to form an alliance with one member of the family against another. Therapists can unwittingly become the focal point of a triangle designed to reduce dyadic tension. The therapist who has successfully differentiated from his or her own family is less likely to be emotionally reactive to client families. Kramer (1985) noted that therapists, unless they are aware of their own family-of-origin issues, may reconstruct, through the projection process, their own family of origin in the treatment room. Strong emotional reactions, confusion, feeling overwhelmed, distancing, or shutting down should be cues for the therapists to consider whether their own family issues are being activated.

For the past 10 years, I have supervised a family-therapy training group that includes family-of-origin work by therapists in training. This application of coaching raises a number of ethical issues. Family-of-origin work in small groups has become a common training experience, but it raises concerns about confidentiality, the distinction between supervision and therapy, and informed consent (Wells et al., 1990). In a training context, evaluation anxiety is likely to be fairly high. Trainees should be assured that the content of their presentations is confidential and will not be used as part of their evaluation. In my use of coaching, the supervisor always presents his or her own family first, which enhances trust as well as provides an example of how to present this material. Trainees are not mandated to present their family, nor are they pressured into divulging information that they prefer to keep private. An issue that has been raised is whether a trainee's family should be informed that material about them will be disclosed. The majority of trainees tell their family about the upcoming presentation and typically request their help in obtaining historical information.

The distinction between personal therapy and supervision in family-of-origin work may appear hazy. Kramer (1985) pointed out that family therapy always involves at least three families in the consulting room—the family in treatment, the "therapeutic family" (therapist and family), and the therapist's own family. In training, family-of-origin work is seen as an educational endeavor that may have indirect therapeutic benefit:

> Family therapy, because of its immediacy and aliveness, much more than indi-
> vidual therapy, elicits therapist responses which relate to the therapist's own
> family-of-origin or family of procreation. We do not view this as "unanalyzed
> counter-transference phenomena." Rather we see this as an inevitable and natural
> process and one which the therapist will be encountering throughout his profes-
> sional lifetime. The supervisor's task is not to help the therapist "solve" his fam-
> ily problems, but to teach him to be aware of, and to cope with, the secret
> presence of his own family in the treatment room. (Mendelsohn & Ferber, 1972,
> pp. 441)

Thus, family-of-origin therapy helps clinicians be more aware of the "third family" in the treatment room as well as assisting the development of more satisfying relationships with their own extended families.

CONCLUSION

Family-of-origin therapy is a fairly intellectually oriented approach with considerable emphasis on understanding factual and symbolic aspects of family history. The therapist actively interprets the client's historically based projections as they emerge in current marital and parent–child relationships. Coaching is an application of family-of-origin work designed to help adults develop more satisfying relationships with parents and siblings. The other goal of coaching is to work with adults to reduce their reactivity to family members and themes. Bowen's work has had considerable impact on family-therapy training through the inclusion of family-of-origin work for trainees.

Chapter 4

Clinical Assessment Tools and Relevant Research

Family-of-origin therapy, though theoretically and clinically sophisticated, has been criticized for its poor empirical foundation. Concepts such as triangulation, reactivity, and differentiation have been difficult to investigate with conventional quantitative methods. Indeed, a recent meta-analysis of family therapy (Shadish et al., 1993) noted that despite their widespread acceptance among clinicians, psychodynamically oriented family approaches were characterized by a paucity of research support.

However, during the past 10 years, several clinical assessment instruments have been developed that are based on family-of-origin theory. These instruments, although still undergoing further validation, have demonstrated acceptable psychometric properties. The tools that are reviewed in this section—the Family-of-Origin Scale, the Personal Authority in the Family System Questionnaire, and the Differentiation of Self in the Family Scale—all exhibit acceptable test–retest and internal consistency reliabilities. In addition, these instruments are able to quantitatively discriminate between clinical and nonclinical groups in the directions predicted by family-of-origin theory. These scales generally correlate with other instruments measuring marital satisfaction, family well-being, and individual distress.

While providing empirical support for the role of intergenerational processes in current individual and relationship adjustment, these scales are also relatively brief, easy to complete, and efficiently scored. They can be readily used by clinicians as an assessment tool at the outset of individual, marital, or family treatment. All of these scales are multidimensional; thus, they may direct the therapist to specific target areas of intergenerational influence.

A second focus of this chapter is to highlight research that supports, both directly and indirectly, the core assumptions of family-of-origin theory. Although generally not addressed in the classic writings of Framo and Bowen,

47

research in adolescent–parent relationships and the newly developing field of adult attachment is yielding findings that converge with family-of-origin theory. The balance between connectedness and a secure, independent identity is a consistent dynamic found in the psychologically healthy adolescent and young adult. The research on family–adolescent relationships provides an intriguing vantage point on individual and parental dynamics associated with the development of qualities important for differentiation. As this review suggests, a secure sense of identity, ego strength, and freedom from emotional distress have all been found to be strongly related to the parent–child relationship. Similarly, parental attachment patterns characterizing infancy and early childhood appear to be predictive of intimate relationships in adulthood. The latter part of this chapter examines this research.

FAMILY-OF-ORIGIN ASSESSMENT MEASURES

Differentiation of Self in the Family Scale

Anderson and Sabatelli (1992) developed the Differentiation of Self in the Family Scale (DIFS) as a self-report measure to assess Bowen's construct of differentiation. Anderson and Sabatelli described differentiation as a "family level variable involving interactions that enable individuals to maintain both a sense of ongoing emotional connectedness (support, involvement, personal relationships) and a sense of separateness (autonomy, uniqueness, freedom of personal expression)" (p. 77). The DIFS focuses on the respondent's view of dyadic exchanges. Anderson and Sabatelli argued that although multigenerational family patterns are important, they are founded on a series of reciprocal dyads. "Whole-family" assessment measures such as the Family Environment Scale (Moos & Moos, 1986) or the Family-of-Origin Scale (Hovestadt, Anderson, Piercy, Cochran, & Fine, 1985) are likely to reflect measurement error as well as provide a cloudy picture of true family interactions. Items dealing with family-level conflict and support will not be helpful in determining dyadic conflicts, alliances, or cross-generational coalition. Anderson and Sabatelli also noted that the observational studies of Cooper, Grotevant, and Condon (1983) and Hauser et al. (1984) are not capturable by whole-family assessment tools. The DIFS, focusing on multiple dyadic relationships, was developed to provide a usable family assessment tool to assess similar dimensions. The 11 Likert-scale items are rated for each dyadic relationship. In addition to rating other family members in relation to the respondent, the DIFS also allows the rater to assess differentiation between other family dyads (e.g., mother–father; sibling–father). Example items are

My (father, mother, sister, etc.) or I:
... responds to my _____'s feelings as if they have no value.
... demonstrates respect for my _____'s privacy.
... tells my _____ what she/he should be thinking.

These positions are rated 1 (*never*), 2 (*almost*), 3 (*sometimes*), 4 (*almost always*), or 5 (*always*). Higher scores are associated with greater levels of differentiation. Internal consistency for the DIFS is reported to be in the .84 to .94 range (Anderson & Sabatelli, 1992). Validity for the instrument comes from studies in which the DIFS scores were found to be related to family conflict and identity status (Bartle & Sabatelli, 1989). The DIFS has also been found to correlate positively with degree of family support and negatively with reported depression and anxiety (Anderson & Sabatelli, 1992; Sabatelli & Anderson, 1991). The DIFS was able to discriminate between clinical and nonclinical groups.

The individual DIFS items are designed to reflect actions conveying respect for personal identity as well as the degree of healthy intimacy existing between family members. Research with adolescents provides indirect support for Bowen's (1978) view of differentiation as an intrapsychic traitlike construct (Anderson & Sabatelli, 1992). As would be expected from Bowen's family theory, adolescents perceived considerable consistency in how individual members interacted across multiple family relationships. Fathers were perceived as showing similar patterns of respect for individuality while simultaneously supporting intimacy with both spouses and children. Adolescents generally perceived themselves as equally differentiated with their mothers and fathers. Ratings on selected dyads (e.g., husband–wife) are determined by multiplying individual dyadic scores. Anderson and Sabatelli noted that if one spouse rates the relationship as a 20 and the other rates it as a 40, this would provide the same spousal score as the situation in which each spouse rated the relationship as a 30. To capture these discrepancies in differentiation, they recommended that the scores be multiplied ($20 \times 40 = 800$; $30 \times 30 = 900$). Thus, the system in which one partner is less differentiated will achieve a lower score. Research with the DIFS has also supported the adverse effects of an adolescent's involvement in a cross-generational parental coalition as described by Minuchin (1974), a variant of the pattern of triangulation described by Bowen. Adolescents involved in these parental coalitions perceived less family support and reported greater anxiety as well as depression (Anderson & Sabatelli, 1992).

The DIFS is well grounded in Bowenian theory, yet focuses on current patterns of interaction. Most of the existing research support for the instrument involves use of the scale with adolescents. The salience of the balance between connectedness and independence may be greater for families with adolescents than for those with younger children or for childless couples. The scale's simplicity and ease of scoring and the ability to present feedback data to family members suggests that it could be of value in clinical practice.

Family-of-Origin Scale

The Family-of-Origin Scale (FOS; Hovestadt et al., 1985) is a 40-item, 10-subscale measure centering around the polarity between autonomy and intimacy. The scale's development was influenced by Bowen's (1978) views of the importance of differentiation from the family of origin as a determinant of healthy adult intimacy, as well as by Framo's (1976) balance between closeness and separation in relationships. The specific subscales of the FOS were based on Lewis, Beavers, Gossett, and Phillips' (1976) study of healthy families. Hovestadt et al. generated five dimensions of family functioning seen as important for individual adjustment: power structure, family individuation, acceptance of separation and loss, and perception of reality and affect. All items were worded in the past tense to obtain a retrospective view of the family in which the respondent was raised. The items are all in Likert-scale (1–5) format. Example items include

> My parents encouraged me to express my views openly.
> If a family friend moved away, we never discussed our feelings of sadness.
> In my family, people took responsibility for what they did.

The FOS has demonstrated reliability and criterion validity with adults. Evidence of criterion validity comes from correlational studies in which the scale has been found to be related to measures of individual adjustment, such as the Multiple Affect Adjective Checklist (MAACL; O'Leary, Searight, Rogers, & Russo, 1992) and the State–Trait Anxiety Scale (Spielberger, Gorsuch, & Lusken, 1970), and to measures of family and marital adjustment, such as the Healthy Family Functioning Scale (HFFS; Sennott, 1981).

Of interest to clinicians, the FOS has been consistent in its ability to discriminate between male prison inmates and college students (Mangrum, 1989), adult children of alcoholics and a nonclinical sample (Capps, Searight, Russo, Temple, & Rogers, 1993), and psychotherapy patients and a nonclinical group (Lee, Gordon, & O'Dell, 1989).

However, there has been considerable controversy surrounding the adult FOS. As a result of factor analytic studies, several investigators have concluded that the adult FOS does not, in reality, measure multiple dimensions of perceived family functioning but instead reflects a global appraisal of the family ("all good" or "all bad"). However, it has still been argued that the adult FOS has value as a tool for clinical descriptive use even though it may have construct validity limitations when used for research (Mazer, Mangrum, Hovestadt, & Brashear, 1990). Several recent clinically relevant investigations provide support for this perspective.

In a study of female college students, Reeves and Johnson (1992) found that the FOS was significantly associated with self-reported eating-disorder attitudes and behaviors, as measured by the Eating Disorder Inventory (EDI; Garner & Olmsted, 1984). The pattern of relationship indicated that women who were less aware of feelings and internal experiences saw themselves as less competent and had difficulty trusting their own judgment as well as trusting others (Reeves & Johnson, 1992). These data provide some empirical support for the application of family therapy to young adults with eating disorders. Minuchin and Fishman (1981) emphasized that effective treatment involves a balance of parental limit setting, boundary establishment, and support. Psychodynamically, eating disorders have been interpreted as reflecting conflict between parental introjects regarding personal independence and parental loyalty (Bruch, 1977).

The FOS has also been found to be sensitive to family trauma. Young adults who reported significant family trauma, such as sudden death of a family member, rape, serious illness, or sexual or physical abuse, rated their family as less healthy on 9 of the 10 FOS subscales (Brett, Brett, & Shaw, 1993).

Of particular interest to clinicians practicing family-of-origin therapy are several studies relating perceptions of the family of origin to current views of marital and family relationships. Fine and Hovestadt (1984) found that positive perceptions of marriage and greater levels of rationality were associated with healthier ratings of the family of origin. Similarly, current family functioning ratings were positively related to perceived family-of-origin climate (Canfield, Hovestadt, & Fenell, 1992). Thus, research with the retrospective FOS suggests that current perceptions of family or marital well-being are a function of intergenerational factors that are transmitted through individual psychological make-up (Canfield et al., 1992).

I have used an alternative version of the FOS for adolescents in a series of studies. The adolescent FOS assesses current rather than retrospective perceptions of one's family by changing all items from the past to the present tense. The adolescent FOS has demonstrated temporal and internal consistency reliabilities similar to the adult version (Manley, Searight, Skitka, Russo, & Schudy, 1991). Validity support has come from the scale's ability to discriminate between nonclinical adolescents and those in inpatient drug treatment (Searight et al., 1991) and psychiatric facilities (Niedermeier, Searight, Handal, Manley, & Brown, 1995). Neidermeier et al. (1995) also found that the adolescent FOS correlated moderately with the Brief Symptom Inventory (BSI; Derogatis & Spencer, 1983) and other family inventories such as the Family Environment Scale (FES; Moos & Moos, 1986) and the Family Adaptability and Cohesion Evaluation Scales (FACES; Olson, Portner, & Lavee, 1985). Factor analytic studies with the adolescent FOS suggest that this version is a multidimensional instrument, in contrast to the adult version (Manley, Wood, Searight, Skitka, & Russo, 1994). Our research suggests that the adolescent FOS does measure two distinct overarching constructs roughly corresponding to the concepts of autonomy and intimacy, as intended by the scale's developers (Hovestadt et al., 1985).

Personal Authority in the Family System Questionnaire

Similar to the FOS, the Personal Authority in the Family System Questionnaire (PAFS–Q) was developed to empirically assess intergenerational influences on current adjustment as well as differentiation in current relationships (Bray, Williamson, & Malone, 1984). In addition to being the name of the measure, personal authority in the family system is also viewed as a set of "relational skills, interactional behavior patterns, and as a way-of-being in the world" (Bray et al., 1984, p. 169). Unlike the FOS, which measures a set of personality constructs, the PAFS–Q is a constellation of interpersonal behaviors. Specifically, these reflect the ability to

> direct one's own thoughts and opinions; to choose to express or not to express one's thoughts and opinions regardless of social pressures; to make and respect one's personal judgments, to the point of regarding these judgments as justification for action; to take responsibility for the totality of one's experience in life; to initiate or to receive (or to decline to receive) intimacy *voluntarily*, in conjunction with the ability to establish clear boundaries to the self-at will; to experience and relate to all other persons *without exception*, including "former parents," as peers in the experience of being human. (Williamson, 1982b, p. 311, cited in Bray et al., 1984, p. 168)

It is assumed that personal authority in the family system requires an understanding and freedom from intergenerational mandates that emerge in current work, marital, and family relationships. Bray et al. (1984) argued that this behavioral pattern will emerge in adults during their 30s and 40s. The absence of personal authority in the family system, including differentiation, is evident through continual overinvolvement of an adult in his or her parents' marriage. In addition, the adult lacking in personal authority in the family system is continuing to behave out of legacies to preceding generations.

There are three versions of the PAFS–Q, with differing numbers of items: Version A is for adults with children; Version B is for adults without children; and Version C is for college students without children. The instrument consists of between 84 and 132 items in a Likert-scale (1–5) format. The items are grouped into seven subscales, as follows:

1. *Spousal Fusion/Individuation*—extent to which the respondent is able to differentiate self in relation to spouse or significant other ("I have difficulty attending most social events without my mate").
2. *Intergenerational Fusion/Individuation*—extent to which respondent is able to function in an individuated way in relation to parents ("I am usually able to disagree with my parents without losing my temper").
3. *Spousal Intimacy*—the ability to maintain closeness while simultaneously maintaining a distinct self in relation to a spouse or significant other ("My mate and I frequently talk about the significant events in our lives").
4. *Intergenerational Intimacy*—satisfaction with the quality of the relationship with parents as well as the degree of intimacy in the parent–adult child relationship ("I share my true feelings with my parents about the significant events in my life").
5. *Nuclear Family Triangulation*—this scale is only relevant to adults with children; it assesses the extent to which children are triangulated into marital issues ("How often do you intervene against your mate in a disagreement between your mate and your son or daughter?").
6. *Intergenerational Triangulation*—the extent to which adult children become involved in their parents' marital issues ("When your parents are having a significant problem in their marriage, to what extent do you feel personally responsible to provide a solution to their problem?").
7. *Intergenerational Intimidation*—extent to which adults feel controlled by their parents ("How necessary is it to you to meet your parents' expectations concerning your work?").

All of the scales—with the possible exception of Intergenerational Fusion/Individuation—have exhibited acceptable test–retest and internal consistency reliabilities (Bray et al., 1984; Grotevant & Carlson, 1989).

Validity support comes primarily from studies in which relevant PAFS–Q subscales have been moderately correlated with the Dyadic Adjustment Scale (Spanier, 1976) and with life stress and health distress among college students (Bray & Harvey, 1992). Construct validity support comes from factor analytic studies in which seven factors emerged, with an eighth factor (Nuclear Family Triangulation) being present for respondents with children (Bray et al., 1984; Grotevant & Carlson, 1989).

The PAFS–Q may be useful for clinicians as a quantitative guide to describing the individual adult from a three-generational family perspective (Bray et al.,

1984). The pattern of subscale scores can be examined to provide the clinician as well as the client with a focus for therapy. Thus, collaborative discussion of a PAFS–Q profile may direct early treatment efforts to a pattern of triangulation in the marriage of the adult client's parents. Addressing this issue is likely to have positive benefit for the client's own marriage. Bray et al. also noted that completing the PAFS–Q often prompts profitable reflection on extended family patterns by the client.

Grotevant and Cooper (1986) as well as Hauser et al. (1984) have used direct observation with coding schemes to assess differentiation of family members with adolescents. Coding focuses on dyadic interactions as the unit, with key processes centering around individuality and connectedness. There are four central dimensions in Grotevant and Cooper's scheme: (a) *self-assertion*—demonstrating an awareness of one's own distinct viewpoint and being able to clearly communicate it; (b) *separateness*—taking responsibility for feelings and thoughts and being able to distinguish them from others' viewpoints; (c) *mutuality*—exhibiting a sensitivity to others' beliefs and feelings; and (d) *permeability*—being responsive or open to input from others.

RESEARCH ON THE BALANCE OF SEPARATION AND CONNECTEDNESS IN DEVELOPMENT

Adolescence and Young Adulthood

Separation and adjustment. Although Bowen's (1978) systems theory and Framo's (1982) object relations theory may seem difficult to empirically investigate, adolescent research provides support for many of the core concepts. The tension between maintaining a separate identity while still being emotionally connected to parents is a central struggle of middle to late adolescence. This process has been the focus of considerable research, and although these studies were not guided by family-of-origin theory, the conclusions drawn from them have been that adolescent self-esteem, identity, and other personality constructs are strongly influenced by parent–child interaction patterns. This body of research provides indirect convergent support for concepts such as differentiation and the influence of introjected objects.

Autonomy, support, and healthy development. Research on adolescents and young adults suggests that young people who experience the greatest levels of autonomy are more likely to maintain close relationships with parents and rely on them for guidance (Grotevant & Cooper, 1986). The adolescent with a secure, solid identity is able to become aware of others' perspectives while being able to maintain his or her own views as distinct from others. There is also evidence for intergenerational transmission of these patterns. In analyses of dyadic communication data, support was found for the view that parents who exhibited an individuated relationship with one another were more likely to have more differentiation in relationship to parents and peers (Grotevant & Cooper, 1986). Further support for this transmission process comes from Kleiman's (1981) study of the relationship of adolescent boys' self-image to parental marital adjustment. Boys with healthier self-images came from families in which parents were able to maintain a separate marital relationship. Parents indicating that they were able to exclude the adolescent from parental decisions, argue constructively between themselves, and prevent marital conflict from leaving the bounds of the marriage had better adjusted adolescents. These couples indicated greater marital satisfaction and reported engaging in couples' activities apart from their teenager (Kleiman, 1981). Although these findings support family-of-origin theory's view of family health as being transmitted through individuals, the data is also compatible with the importance of family boundaries and rules, as emphasized by structural therapists (Minuchin, 1974).

Adolescence and identity integration. Hauser et al. (1984), as well as Powers, Hauser, Schwartz, Noam, & Jacobson (1983), examined parent–adolescent interactions and their impact on adolescent ego development. Their research represents a blend of family systems theory with psychoanalytic and cognitive psychology. Adolescents with higher levels of ego development came from families in which the family's verbal communication included a balance between stimulation and support. Although focusing, explaining, asking for clarification, and recognizing differences were all important communication processes, they were not sufficient in promoting ego development. It was essential that communicative clarity and effective problem solving were combined with supportive interactions, including acceptance, affect recognition, and validation (Adams, Dyk, & Bennion, 1987; Hauser et al., 1984; Powers et al., 1983).

Block and Block (1980), in their investigations of adolescent development within the family, relied on the concept of ego resiliency and ego control. These constructs, which have been operationally defined, have parallels to Bowen's (1978) intellectual–emotional polarity and the concept of reactivity. Individuals with high ego resiliency are able to adaptively respond to internal need states and external environmental demands. They can withstand greater stress without impaired performance and are able to manage conflicting demands. Persons with lower levels of ego resiliency are more rigid and less adaptable. Ego control exists on a continuum as an independent dimension, with overcontrolled persons being emotionally constricted, overly conventional, and inhibited. Persons with ego undercontrol are impulsive, often undirected, and prone to immediate and intense emotional expression (Block & Block, 1980). Similar to Bowen's theoretical constructs, ego resiliency and ego control have exhibited considerable empirical stability from adolescence to adulthood.

Grotevant and Cooper's (1986) research led them to conclude that adolescence is not simply a process of severing ties with parents but instead is a time of renegotiating relationships. As in Bowen's theory, the teenager and his or her parents are posited to be struggling to establish a balance of individuality and connectedness. Individuality is exhibited by adolescent–parent exchanges that communicate the adolescent's distinct unique perspective, including viewpoints not shared with parents. Connectedness is shown through respect for others' perspectives and values as well as openness to considering others' viewpoints. Teenagers in families that connote and support individuality while maintaining a moderate degree of connectedness have better self-images as well as higher levels of identity integration. The key element in Grotevant and Cooper's perspective is that rather than a reduced relationship with parents, adolescence involves a qualitatively different pattern of involvement. Positive parental behavior emphasizing support and acceptance has been found to be associated with greater levels of self-esteem as well as higher levels of identity formation and integration (Grotevant & Cooper, 1986).

Identity formation is often assessed through the categorical scheme of Marcia (1976, 1980). The interview developed by Marcia is designed to evaluate the Eriksonian identity categories of achievement, moratorium, foreclosure, and diffusion (Erikson, 1968). Marcia's *identity achievement status* is comparable to Bowen's conception of the mature, differentiated individual who maintains relationships but is guided by a clear set of personally held internal standards. Identity in the Erikson–Marcia scheme focuses more on the internal processes of the individual than on social relationships. The *moratorium* describes someone who is currently and actively searching for a perspective for his or her own life but who has yet to find it. A person using the *foreclosure* style adopts the values of goals and others—usually parents—and uncritically incorporates them as his or her own. The foreclosure pattern is likely to emerge out of the symbolic, overly close parent–child relationship. This identity type is often a reaction to the anxiety generated by the possibility of independence and the struggle for one's own value system and goals. To reduce this seemingly intolerable anxiety level, foreclosure occurs. Finally, the *diffusion* pattern is exhibited through a chronic inability to commit to a value set or goals. In contrast to the moratorium style, the diffusion style describes a person who is not actively struggling with a life direction but instead is drifting aimlessly.

Research has found that the moratorium and identity achievement patterns are more likely to be found among adolescents who experience their parents as emotionally supportive. Parents who are rejecting or overly controlling are likely to have teenagers experiencing identity diffusion or foreclosure (Adams, 1985; Adams & Jones, 1983). Other investigators have found gender differences in this pattern (O'Connor, 1995), which can be meaningfully integrated with family-of-origin theory. Among girls, foreclosure has been associated with greater parental emotional support. Marcia's (1980) research suggests that foreclosed adolescents and young adults may be engaging in a "love affair" with their families (O'Connor, 1995). This age-inappropriate overinvolvement appears to be more problematic for girls than for boys. Autonomy for girls within families may be more challenging for both parents and young adults because girls may be socialized toward greater social responsibility for family members. Boys, on the other hand, are likely to be socialized toward independence and separateness, and family support is therefore a healthy complementary force (O'Connor, 1995; Steinberg, 1987). As discussed in chapter 5, there appear to be important gender differences in both the content and process of differentiation.

Redefining the parent–adolescent relationship. Apter (1990), through interviews and observation of mother–daughter dyads, found that adolescence involves an ongoing struggle to redefine this relationship. Like the toddler, the adolescent looks to the mother or father for approval of his or her independence, a process called *mirroring.* Mirroring allows the teenager to see the meaning of what he or she is doing. The parental response may be approval, anxiety, humorous condescension, pleasure, or indifference—these responses reflect the parents' views of the teenager's moves toward greater autonomy. Strong expressions of differing views are an important part of this process. Outward disagreements between mother and daughter trigger self-exploration. Apter argued that these arguments push internal reflection—helping the adolescent to highlight his or her own thoughts and feelings. In particular for adolescent girls, observing significant verbal conflicts between parents also appears to be associated with a more secure sense of identity, if these conflicts are successfully resolved. Direct observation of a woman holding her own and being able to articulate differences in relation to her husband or significant other is powerful role modeling.

Apter (1990) noted that for adolescent girls the primary context for individuation and identity development is the relationship with their mother. The maternal relationship is often internalized and serves as a source of values, which are incorporated, rebelled against, or modified. In her interviews, Apter often elicited internal dialogues that adolescent girls engaged in to grapple with their mother's voice:

"Sometimes I'm walking, or sitting on a bus, and I feel her voice inside me. It's like my own nerves are twanging, but making the sound of her voice. And I get so angry—I know it's funny—she isn't even there—but I say to her, in my thoughts, 'Leave me alone!'. She says, 'Think for yourself!'. And then somehow she gets inside me, like this," admitted 16-year-old Lindsay who smiled away the conflict with her distinctive calm English manner. (Apter, 1990, p. 95)

Mothers attempted to respond to their daughters' disclosures and confidences but at the same time felt frustrated by the sense of "missing something." The missing dimension often centered around mothers' perceived failure to validate their daughters' separateness. Apter observed that a frequent cue was the girls' saying"'mo-o-ther' with the elongated vowel exhaled in a sigh" (p. 16). These were identity reminders and served to communicate to the mother the daughter's strong opinion or ability to do something on her own. Mothers would often attempt to reassert control by laughing or smiling or with angry statements like, "I've had enough of that."

Adolescent girls similarly erect verbal boundaries to preserve their identity and prevent overly close, symbiotic relationships with their mothers. Mothers' attempts to establish connectedness with their daughters often take the form of urging agreement with "tag" questions such as "Isn't that right?", "Don't you think so too?", or "That's really nice isn't it?" (Apter, 1990, p. 97). Apter observed that even at age 11, girls often rejected these verbal overtures with a flat out "No" or "I don't care." As they became older, girls would respond with a ping-pong effect such that "anything a tagging mother would say would be thrust back to her with a tidy spin such as 'It's nice for you, but not for me, so you can do it and leave me out if you want nice all around'" (Apter, 1990, p. 97).

As discussed further in the next section, after the rapprochement period of early childhood, adolescence represents the second major developmental period in which separation and connectedness become a major dynamic. This body of research, from a different background than family-of-origin therapy, provides considerable support for certain key assumptions, such as the individual as the receptacle for transmission of family interaction patterns and the process of internalization of marital and parent–child dynamics. This research also provides considerable empirical support for Bowen's (1978) view of healthy relationships as characterized by a choiceful fluctuation in self-direction versus respect, sensitivity, and support for others.

Childhood and Adult Attachment: Research and Implications for Assessment and Therapy

Assessment may also include attention to attachment processes in the family of origin (Pistole, 1994). Attachment can be defined as seeking physical and emotional closeness with another person. Attachment dynamics are seen as biologically based and rooted in the evolutionary advantage conferred by protection (Bowlby, 1980). In childhood, the attachment figure serves as a source of security from which exploration of the environment can occur. Even when the relationship with a parent is harshly abusive, attachment still occurs.

Early childhood basis of attachment. Developmental psychologists believe that attachment evolved as an adaptive mechanism to maintain proximity between caretakers and infants under conditions of danger (Bartholomew & Horowitz, 1991; Bowlby, 1977). Bowlby's observations were derived from infants who underwent involuntary separations from caregivers. Bowlby argued that when forcibly separated from their primary caregiver, infants exhibited a three-stage process characterized by protest, despair, and detachment. The infant would eventually realize that the parent would not be returning. Bowlby believed that this disruption impaired subsequent relationships in childhood and adulthood. Ainsworth developed an assessment approach—the Strange Situation—to determine the extent which an infant relies on the caretaker for security (Ainsworth, Blehar, Waters, & Wall, 1978; Bartholomew, 1990). The Strange Situation typically involves an observation of a sequence in which the parent interacts with the child, leaves the room and the child, and then reenters the room and attempts to interact with the child. On the basis of this sequence, Ainsworth et al. described three basic patterns of attachment—secure, anxious–resistant, and avoidant. The securely attached child responds positively to the parent's return and, if the separation was distressing, will readily respond to the parent's comforting. The anxious–resistant child exhibits more ambivalence during reunification with the parent and is less readily comforted. The avoidant child appears emotionally and behaviorally detached from or rejecting of the parent when reunited.

Attachment patterns have been found to be fairly stable over time through early childhood (Bartholomew, 1990). Of particular interest to family-of-origin therapists is recent research relating the quality of current mother–child interactions to the mother's account of her own attachment during early development (Bartholomew, 1990; Main, Kaplan, & Cassidy, 1985). Bartholomew (1990) and Pistole (1994) included the more developmentally sophisticated capacity of adults for self-evaluation and integrated this with childhood attachment patterns.

Adult attachment patterns. The template for attachment is a cognitive–affective schema established during early childhood. Although the attachment schema may be modified by subsequent experience, this model for intimate relationships is likely to remain consistent through adulthood. Although the attachment schema is conceptually similar to that of introjected objects, attachment theory and research adds the therapeutically useful dimension of distance regulation in intimate relationships. Pistole (1994) categorized adults as exhibiting one of five attachment patterns—preoccupied, avoidant, fearful avoidant, dismissing avoidant, and secure.

Secure, attached adults are well differentiated, view themselves as worthy of care (Feeney & Noller, 1990), and view their partner realistically and positively. They are able to tolerate some emotional and physical distance from their partner without becoming significantly anxious. Adults who are preoccupied with attachment exhibit a possessive, clinging style. They are likely to have poor self-esteem while seeing their partner in an elevated light (Pistole, 1994). Their partner is "much better" than they are. Preoccupied adults are likely to be vigilant and devote considerable energy to monitoring the partner's whereabouts.

The adult with avoidant attachment does not exhibit concern with intimate relationships. Little affect is experienced—these individuals are likely to be intellectualized, with energies directed toward inanimate things and activities rather than people (Cassidy, 1988).

The fearfully avoidant adult is characterized by poor self-esteem and an expectation of rejection by others. The combination of a fear of intimacy as well as a hypersensitivity to rejection cues may play a role in bringing about rejection as a self-fulfilling prophecy (Bartholomew & Horowitz, 1991). Last, the adult who dismisses avoidance is characterized by inflated self-worth. Similar to the narcissistic personality style, idealization occurs as a defense. Significant others may be viewed in a somewhat deprecatory manner and as unavailable or unresponsive (Bowlby, 1980; Pistole, 1994).

In contrast to young children, adults are better able to maintain attachment security through language and other symbolic means. However, a key issue in the development of adult intimacy is distance regulation. The couple must come to some agreement—usually implicit—about the degree of closeness necessary to avoid separation anxiety. A common marital pattern is one in which spouses spend considerable time together during the first few years of marriage. Trips to the grocery store, bank, and carwash are all conjoint endeavors. During this early marriage period, a spouse who takes a several-day trip for work or to visit a friend may elicit considerable separation anxiety in his or her partner. The partner who is planning to leave may have some characteristics of dismissive or avoidant attachment and may not be distressed by the separation. However, for the spouse with preoccupied attachment, the anticipation of the separation, by itself, is likely to produce protest and possibly anger. After 3 or 4 years together—particularly if there have been multiple brief separations with no adverse consequences—the attachment system may become calmer, with the breaks no longer eliciting anxiety (Pistole, 1994).

Mahler's rapprochement phase (Mahler, Pine, & Bergman, 1975), usually seen as an important developmental process during the second year of life, reemerges as an important interaction in early adulthood (Quintana & Kerr, 1993). The adolescent initially focuses on separation from parents, with the establishment of independent competence. Once independence is achieved, the older teenager then attempts to reconnect with parents. The key issue in this reestablishment of ties is to obtain parental validation and support for the teenager's newly acquired values and ideas. Similar to family-of-origin theorists, Josselson (1980) proposed that young adults' patterns of attachment to peers mirror the parent–child relationship. There is empirical evidence that the quality of these attachments is related to psychological distress among college students. Relationships that allowed for maintenance of individual identity while providing emotional support and mirroring were associated with less depression and anxiety (Quintana & Kerr, 1993). By contrast, students who denied dependency (such as in an emotional cut-off) experienced distress about separation or rejection and were more likely to be depressed. For women, relationships that gratified dependency needs were particularly important for mental health, whereas men experienced more depression when they were engaged in a major, prolonged struggle for independence.

THERAPEUTIC IMPLICATIONS OF IDENTITY AND ATTACHMENT RESEARCH

Adult and adolescent identity attachment research has a number of practical implications for therapists. The adolescent or young adult who is being treated is likely to be struggling with achieving the optimal balance of distance and closeness with parents. The therapist treating a college student who seems overly involved with family may be inappropriately working toward a lessening of ties (Quintana & Kerr, 1993). A common therapy issue is the college-aged adult who seems overly concerned with parental approval. Rather than pushing for greater independence, the therapist should consider helping the young adult to maintain contact with family members while establishing his or her own identity. Similarly, therapists who view emotional emancipation from the family as a treatment goal should seriously reflect on the consequences of cut-offs. Cutting off as a means of denying dependency or to manage anxiety around symbiosis is likely to be associated with greater distress (Quintana & Kerr, 1993). Importantly, the adult and adolescent attachment research literature provides considerable empirical support for the impact of family-of-origin interaction patterns on identity development and the formation of satisfying, healthy, intimate relationships with peers. This case from a college counseling center (Openlander & Searight, 1983) illustrates how the relationship between parents and a young adult may be redefined to maintain connectedness while supporting age-appropriate independence:

> A first-year resident student came to the counseling center for feedback on a standardized test she had taken. She hinted at a family crisis that would affect her remaining at the university. The matter was pursued with the counselor, and it was found that the young woman had a younger sister at home who had become pregnant.
>
> The student believed that she needed to go home to help her sister deal with her parents. There was a history of friction between the parents and the younger daughter. Using Bowen's (1978) approach to coaching, the counselor posed a series of questions. The student was asked how her parents and her sister would ever learn to interact successfully if she intervened. She was also encouraged to examine her past style of relating to the conflict between her parents and her sister.
>
> Through questions and basic explanation of family systems, the young woman was helped to become a skillful observer of her family's relationships. Essentially, she was encouraged to avoid the repetitious cycle of being drawn into the conflict and providing a type of escape valve for the family's tensions. During four meetings she became so impressed with the new perspective gained and the correspondingly greater freedom that she decided to avoid the possibility of interfering with the interaction adjustments of her parents and sister. She chose to attend summer school at a university that was about 100 miles from her parents' residence rather than to spend the summer at home. Her plans to return to school the following year were not altered.

This young woman was on the verge of withdrawing from school. By helping her to take a more individual stance in this family crisis, instead of accepting her usual role of mediator, the counselor helped the young woman accomplish two goals. First, she distanced herself and acted more responsibly and independently. Second, she gave her family the opportunity to reorganize in a way that permitted more diversity, complexity, and appropriate independence for its members (Openlander & Searight, 1983).

These attachment patterns interact with levels of differentiation. For adults who are less differentiated and whose functioning is dominated by the emotional system (Bowen, 1978), there is likely to be considerable reactivity to separation. The four less securely attached behavioral patterns described above may be amplified by the emotional system (Kerr, 1985; Pistole, 1994). In the context of therapy, attachment issues may be interpreted similarly to internalized object representations. The attachment schemas currently operative were generated in early childhood experience with parents but are now being misapplied to an adult relationship. These attachment schemas, however, are resilient, and their influence is unlikely to be remedied through interpretation alone. When working with couples, therefore, therapists should help partners to become aware of each other's attachment pattern and the accompanying interpersonal interpretations and affect. For example, understanding the childhood origins and cognitive–affective interplay associated with a spouse's preoccupied attachment style may help the partner to show greater tolerance and be less likely to experience the partner as intrusive or controlling. Because attachment patterns are seen as being transmitted across generations, the genogram history should include attachment to these dimensions.

Attachment is largely a visceral experience and at times may appear highly irrational. One common example of this is the angry, strong overengagement that ex-spouses often experience for one another (Berman, 1988). This hostile, clinging attachment may be based in a fundamental survival instinct (Pistole, 1994). The intense anger and jealousy that occurs when an ex-spouse begins dating or remarries reflects the threat to the availability of an attachment object.

Berman's (1988) research supports the well-known clinical observation that even when an unhappy marriage ends, divorce is still associated with strong emotional reactions. Even when an adult recognizes intellectually that the relationship was not healthy or satisfying, there continues to be a longing for the familiarity of and connectedness with the ex-spouse. This phenomenon appears to be a variation on attachment in infancy. Of note, Berman found that postdivorce attachment reactions were distinct from emotional distress but contributed to and were amplified by divorce-related emotional turmoil. Continued emotional and cognitive engagement with an ex-spouse is a common experience and should be considered by the therapist. This is particularly likely to be an issue in situations with subsequent remarriage soon after a divorce. Lingering attachment to the ex-spouse may impair connectedness with the current spouse.

CONCLUSION

Although the concepts of family-of-origin therapy are often seen as abstract and too complex to be reduced to quantitative investigation, developmental research provides considerable support for several key elements of family-of-origin theory. Attachment research suggests that early childhood experiences with the primary caretaker exert influence in adult relationships with child, spouse, and significant others. Data from diverging perspectives indicate that internalized representations of the parent–child relationship are formed during development and continue to exist, albeit in somewhat altered form, in adulthood. These representations or schemas, conceptually similar to Framo's (1982) internalized objects, do seem to serve as guides for adult interpersonal relationships. The research on relationships between adolescents and their families provides considerable support for Bowen's (1978) concept of the importance of a balance between separateness and connectedness with one's family as critical for mental health. Similarly, the increased ego strength and identity maturity found among adolescents who achieve this balance support Bowen's view of differentiation. For clinicians, several assessment tools can be used to efficiently evaluate clients' perceptions of their family of origin as well as their relationships with family members.

PART TWO
INTEGRATION OF FAMILY-OF-ORIGIN THERAPY WITH DIVERSITY

Chapter 5

Gender and the Family

The family of origin transmits powerful messages about gender—largely through the daily exchanges that mothers and fathers have with their sons and daughters. The impact of gender is most apparent by its gross neglect in family-of-origin therapy. Fathers appear to rapidly disappear:

> The mother's first child was conceived when her life was unsettled and anxious. . . . The child, a girl, was tense and fretful and required more than average mothering attention. A second child was born 18 months later. (Bowen, 1978, p. 426)

As noted by Luepnitz (1988, p. 40), "The father in this family is alluded to only through the fact of impregnation."

As in this example, fathers in family-of-origin therapy are noteworthy by their absence. They are often characterized as weak or unavailable figures who are unsuccessful in their efforts to keep their engulfing wives at bay or from harming their children (Framo, 1977; Luepnitz, 1988). Men's intellectualized, emotionally disengaged relationships with their wives are often found in Framo's cases (Framo, 1977, 1982). On the other hand, adult men raised in enmeshed environments as children are described as either overinvolved with their own mothers—one married man "kissed his mother . . . full on the lips and [his mother and sister] sat on his lap often and he patted their rear ends" (Framo, 1982, p. 226)—or cut off from their families of origin. These unprotective, identityless men provide no models for men as partners to women or as husbands and fathers. For children and men, women—as mothers—can be depended on, but at the expense of one's independence. Personal goals are sacrificed for the maintenance of the mother–adult child relationship.

A theme that emerges in family-of-origin theory is *mother as heroine, father as devil*. Mothers become internalized as giving and supportive, whereas fathers are seen as undependable, befuddled figures standing out on the distant outskirts of family life. Men's relationships with women are often sexualized but with little true intimacy.

67

Family therapy's emphasis on interactional patterns has in many respects ignored gender differences. The systems model that family-of-origin therapists have incorporated to varying degrees tends to treat men and women as "gender-less cybernetic units" (Merkel & Searight, 1992). Many of the classic cases presented by family-of-origin therapists feature variations on the overinvolved mother–underinvolved father theme (Walsh & Scheinkman, 1989). However, these case analyses, although featuring traditional gender interactions, do not include attention to the distinct intrapsychic and social worlds of men and women.

At the individual level, there is growing evidence that key concepts in family-of-origin theory—autonomy, intimacy, identity, differentiation, individuation, and the self—differ in content, process, and development for men and women. Autonomy, intimacy, identity, differentiation, and the self appear to be distinct entities for men and women. Feminist critics of Bowen have begun to translate and extend his theory to account for the unique experience and relationship patterns of women (Knudson-Martin, 1994). The newly developing field of men's psychology will also result in a redefinition of family-of-origin theory. Serious clinical theorizing and research about men's development as fathers and relationship partners is in an embryonic stage but is likely to lead to a more complex understanding of autonomy, intimacy, and relationship development for men.

Although gender differences in identity and relationship are important microlevel processes in family-of-origin theory, macrosystems issues are also relevant. The broader societal context of the family, though mentioned by Bowen (1978), has not been addressed in discussions of gender. With their emphasis on personality dynamics, family-of-origin theorists have paid little attention to the family's embeddedness in a social–political matrix. This larger social system is itself altered by the forces of historical change. Gender roles, in particular, are shaped by a complex interplay of social, historical, and economic factors. This chapter examines gender in the family from extrafamilial as well as intrapsychic perspectives. Family-of-origin therapy is then critiqued, and directions for reconceptualization of concepts such as identity and relatedness are discussed.

GENDER AND SOCIETY

The past 200 years have witnessed significant changes in the organization of economic, educational, and childcare responsibilities (Goldner, 1985; Mintz & Kellogg, 1988). Before extensive industrialization, most important life functions took place in the home. Production through farming and small scale domestic industries often meant that there was no separation between the family and work worlds. Similarly, medical care and education also took place within the home.

During this period, the bifurcation of gender and public versus private life was less pronounced. As society became more industrialized in the mid to late 1800s, the centrality of the home declined. Work occurred in factory and office settings away from home (Goldner, 1985). Childbirth occurred in hospitals, and education became the province of an organized school system. Previously private, domestic activities became part of the public sphere. The home became a retreat from public life. The writings of Rosseau and others who emphasized the importance of back-to-nature, Eden-like experiences influenced domestic life. In the United States, Victorian homes often had a lush garden, which was seen as a place for men to retire after a day in the competitive, stressful work world (Mintz & Kellogg, 1988).

Women became the keepers of this private domestic sphere. Detailed instructional manuals emerged for women, describing household management. The field of domestic science blossomed in the United States in the early 1900s. This field, in effect, established a "scientific" basis for household maintenance and elevated domestic chores to a businesslike enterprise (Welter, 1983). The family became women's domain.

There have been brief periods in U.S. history when this pattern was altered. During World War II, women in industrial jobs were characterized as hard working, dedicated, and as productive as men (Douglas, 1995). Factory jobs were popularized as a glamorous way for women to contribute to the war effort. At war's end, however, there was considerable concern that there would not be enough available jobs for returning servicemen. Television, movies, radio, and magazines all began to reglorify the role of housewife and mother: "The war was over, and they were supposed to sashay back to the kitchen and learn to make green beans baked with Campbell's cream of mushroom soup" (Douglas, 1995, p. 47). Day care was negatively construed as a Communist approach to childrearing. Popular television shows of the 1950s, such as *Father Knows Best* and the *Donna Reed Show*, emphasized women's roles as wives and mothers "with their self-effacing pearl-clad moms who loved to vacuum in high heels" (Douglas, 1995, p. 36). Sociologist Talcott Parsons (Parsons & Bales, 1955) developed an early gender-role theory that influenced several decades of psychological understanding of men and women. Parsons characterized men as fulfilling instrumental, rational, and task-oriented functions and described women as emotional, nurturant, and relationship oriented. These personality dimensions are very comparable to those described by Bowen.

Even with women increasingly in the work place, the theme of family as the women's responsibility and domain still persists. Women who work outside of the home still have a disproportionate amount of domestic responsibility (Nichols & Schwartz, 1995). In Russia, where large numbers of women have been in the work force much longer than in the United States, cooking, cleaning, and child care still are disproportionately women's responsibilities. In the United States, studies have found that working wives still do substantially more domestic work than their husbands. However, as women's earnings approach that of their husbands', husbands do greater amounts of house work. It is possible to buy one's way into an equal partnership (Goldner, 1985).

GENDER AND THE POLITICS OF FAMILY THERAPY

A casual perusal of the child and family therapy literature supports the conclusion that mothers are more likely than fathers to be held accountable for the behavior of their children. In a review by Caplan and Hall-McCorquodale (1985) of 125 clinical articles in nine mental health journals, there was considerable evidence for "mother blaming." Therapists held mothers responsible for 72 different psychological disorders. They attributed children's pathology to mothers 82% of the time and to fathers 43% of the time. Judgmental labels were applied to mothers in 74% of the articles and to fathers in 41%. There is a pervasive stereotype that mothers exert a powerful primary and negative impact on family interaction (Caplan & Hall-McCorquodale, 1985).

Family-of-origin therapists, in particular, have been prone to placing women at the center of the triangulation process. Women are seen as engulfing their own children as they were purportedly engulfed by their own mothers. Mothers are seen as incurably dependent figures whose overwhelming needs for emotional closeness result in irreparable harm to their infantilized children. Adults continue to fend off the encroachment of mothers into their lives. In Framo's (1982) cases, marriages are continually threatened by grasping elderly mothers who sabotage their sons- or daughters-in-law while desperately clinging to their own grown sons or daughters. These struggles take place while husbands and fathers are shuffling about in the background.

Goldner (1985), examining the social–historical role of family therapy, noted that therapists are the last in a lineage of professionals that women have turned to for legitimation of their power. In the mid to late 1800s, when women did not have the right to vote, they often turned to Protestant clergy for social power. Dorothea Dix, Jane Adams, and Harriet Beecher Stowe all relied on church support for their efforts to create humane social changes. In a complementary manner, these women increased the power of their sponsor churches. As women became increasingly involved in the work force, they functioned in roles that men continued to dominate. Female teachers were legitimated by male principals, and nurses' power was supported by male physicians and hospital administrators. Similarly, women may turn to marital and family therapists to legitimate their disempowered role at home. In a complementary manner, therapists need wives and mothers to give them access to the private arena of family life. Whereas women usually are engaged in treatment from the outset, husbands and fathers often are uncomfortable with therapy and let the therapist know that he or she had better tread lightly or they won't be back (Goldner, 1985).

It has been argued that those who conduct family therapy operate from a premise that men and women are equal partners in families, that they function at the same level and have equivalent power. Goldner (1985) and others (Bernard, 1972) have argued that this equality is far more illusory than real and have provided demographic and economic data to support their position. First, women often earn only about 75% of what their male counterparts earn (Schmittroth, 1995). Second, women have more to lose economically if a marriage comes apart. In a divorce, women's standard of living drops dramatically. Women's income declines by 33%, whereas that of their ex-husbands actually increases (U.S. Bureau of the Census, 1991). Third, responsibility for children continues to be disproportionately allocated to the mother. Only about half of female-headed families receive the total amount of child support actually awarded. Nearly one quarter of these households receive none of the legally mandated financial support (Holden & Smolk, 1991). From a demographic perspective, men are more likely to remarry and to do so more quickly after a divorce. From a statistical point of view, men have more "staying power" as they get older in terms of remarriage. As women get older, their remarriage rate declines. For example, only about 10% to 15% of women divorced in their 50s remarry. The longer a women stays with a bad marriage, the lower her chances of having a second satisfactory relationship (Goldner, 1985).

Social roles stemming from gender are not neutral. Family therapy has often ignored these roles or viewed them as noncontributory to individual and family dysfunction. There are several dangers in uncritically accepting traditional gender roles or viewing them as irrelevant to therapy. Both tacit acceptance and denial of the broader social context of treatment have characterized family-of-origin therapy. Although it is not a historically oriented approach, Alexander and Parsons's (1982) functional family therapy includes three constructs that are similar to Bowen's model. First, there are behaviors that promote interpersonal closeness and intimacy—*merging* functions. Second, there are actions that promote distance and separateness—*distancing* functions. Third, there are interactions that maintain a balance between closeness and distance—*midpointing* functions. Alexander and Parsons argued that these functions are neutral and are not evaluative. More important, they argued that these functions are biologically based and should not be challenged during the course of therapy (Alexander & Parsons, 1982; Avis, 1985). "No matter how noble our motivation we cannot afford to prescribe therapist behaviors which alienate one or more family members who then drop out of treatment" (Alexander, Warburton, Waldron, & Mas, 1985).

Although Alexander et al. presented these merging and separateness functions as value neutral, they are in effect gender based. Men nearly always exhibit separateness, with women demonstrating merging. This allocation of function is similar to family-of-origin case accounts, which typically include men who are intellectual and disengaged from family lives and women who are emotional and overinvolved. Alexander's model accepts and positively connotes existing localization of functions by gender as the basis for subsequent strategic and behavioral intervention (Avis, 1985).

For example, a husband who is quiet and reluctant to share his feelings is reframed as being considerate and not wanting to burden others with his problems. Similarly, authoritarian and rigid fathers are construed as active leaders. Women are seen as sources of emotional support and nurturance, and this too is positively connoted. This view of family therapy and family life was harshly critiqued by Avis (1985). Women in the family

> are sexual and emotional service stations for men and children. Their exploitation involves systematic socialization which prepares them for unpaid domestic labor, exclusion from the mainstream of economic and political life, and surrender of self-development and self-interest in favor of serving others. This socialization process actively promotes merging functions in women. (Avis, 1985, p. 130)

This relabeling or reframing approach to family therapy can be used to continue harmful patterns in which women are held almost exclusively responsible for closeness and nurturance. One example that Avis presented is a couple in which the wife wanted her husband to share more of his feelings, but the husband did not want to talk about his feelings. During the communication training module of functional family therapy, the husband was able to communicate that he was not good at and did not like to share his feelings. He never actually shared any affect. The therapist, however, interpreted this as a "very high level of self-disclosure . . . the most intense closeness of which he was capable" (Barton & Alexander, 1981, p. 428).

The woman was encouraged to take responsibility for determining her husband's mood and initiating exchanges with him when she desired contact. This approach clearly establishes who is being held responsible for intimacy and nurturance in the relationship. The case examples presented at the beginning of this chapter highlight how family-of-origin therapy includes implicit responsibility of women for their children, with few domestic expectations for men.

The denial of the impact of gender roles on psychological health occurs despite considerable research evidence that these traditional functions are harmful to women. Married women, particularly those with young children at home, have a higher incidence of depression. This pattern is most pronounced for women who are not employed outside of the home (Baruch, Biener, & Barnett, 1987). Domestic violence is associated with power imbalances in the marriage (Strauss, Gelles, & Steinmetz, 1980). A major contributor to the greater psychological distress found among married women is that their roles involve substantial, ongoing interpersonal demands with little corresponding control:

> A major component of the roles of wife, mother, and homemaker is the obligation to see to it that another person—spouse, child—is well and happy, a success in school or at work. Yet, in reality, one has relatively little control over the welfare and happiness of another person and such responsibility thus exposes one to many frustrations and failures. (Baruch et al., 1987, p. 131)

These socially prescribed roles do appear to affect marital and family therapy outcomes. Taffel and Masters (1989) analyzed data from families in therapy and found that treatment outcomes directly related to the woman's employment and to the number of young children at home. In families with "economically viable" women, therapeutic success was much more likely In addition, the presence of preschool-age children and the total number of children in the family were inversely related to positive treatment outcomes. Therapy often cannot be effective unless the underlying patterns of gender role responsibilities are addressed. Families cannot be treated in isolation from the larger society, which has defined the roles of caretaker for women and breadwinner for men.

INTRAPSYCHIC GENDER DIFFERENCES

Family-of-origin therapy emphasizes concepts such as differentiation, cognitively driven decision making, and individuation as hallmarks of psychological health and successful relationships. There is a growing body of literature—frequently derived from psychotherapy—indicating that these processes have different pathways and meaning for men and women. This section examines the self-in-relation models of female identity development and the newer relationship-oriented masculine identity theory in the context of family-of-origin theory.

Moral Reasoning and Gender

Gilligan's (1982) research highlighted differences in moral reasoning between men and women. Beginning in early childhood, boys make moral judgments on the basis of absolutes—usually in the form of abstract principles such as laws that reduce dilemmas to right or wrong. Thus, for boys, stealing is a crime and is wrong. Alternatively, they might conclude that laws are wrong and should be violated if there is a higher principle to help others. Girls, on the other hand, make judgments on the basis of the specific relationship involved. These social commitments are unique to each situation, and blanket "laws" cannot be invoked. As they grow older, girls engage in a cognitive process of taking the perspectives of multiple others, including themselves, in arriving at a moral judgment. Boys often reduce responsibility to others to a mathematical equation and then apply the principle to the social situation. Girls examine social situations from others' perspectives, then examine their own role in the situation, and finally come to a judgment reflecting the interplay of their own and others' needs.

Gilligan's (1982) Heinz dilemma involves a man named Heinz who decides whether to steal a drug that he cannot afford but which will save his wife's life. In answering the dilemma, respondents are guided through a series of questions to determine how their decisions are made. Boys responded with clear-cut references to the values of property versus life. They recognized that to save a life it was necessary to steal from the druggist. Girls, on the other hand, tried to find reconciliation between the competing demands:

> If he stole the drug, he might save his wife then, but if he did, he might have to go to jail and then his wife might get sicker again, and he couldn't get more of the drug, and it might not be good. So, they should really just talk it out and find some other way to make the money. (Gilligan, 1982, p. 28)

Girls viewed the dilemma as involving a network of relationships extending in time.

Women perceive moral dilemmas in terms of conflicting responsibilities to others versus conflicting rights or laws. Candib (1995) noted that despite Gilligan's (1982) work, discussions of development and moral reasoning in pediatric textbooks continue to reflect the male model as the prototype.

As young women develop, an interplay of the self as connected yet distinct comes to dominate their experience:

> I'm trying to tell you two things. I'm trying to be myself alone, apart from others, apart from their definitions of me, and yet at the same time I'm doing just the opposite, trying to be with or relate to—whatever the terminology is—I don't think they are mutually exclusive. (Gilligan, 1982, p. 53)

Activity is present as a component of women's identity, but these are actions of care rather than impersonal achievement or solitary self-enhancement. Aggression and even anger are seen as fragmenting forces that break connection (Gilligan, 1982).

Family-of-origin dilemmas, particularly those implying separation, are not rule-governed decisions for women. These issues are not perceived as either–or dichotomies. Marriage is seen as the addition of a relationship to the one with the family of origin. The struggle for women in early marriage is often how to maintain connection with siblings (particularly sisters) and parents (particularly mothers) while committing to a spouse. Wives are often puzzled and even frightened by their husband's rule-governed approach to these issues—"I'm married, my wife comes first and foremost." Women's contextual decision making and ethic of care views these dilemmas not as choices but as a struggle to connect with all concerned.

Identity Development: The Role of Relationships

Bowen viewed his basic polar concepts as resting on a biological or instinctual foundation. Gender differences in the ability to connect socially may also be, in part, innate. At birth, boys appear to have less well-developed neurobehavioral systems (Pollack, 1995; Silverman, 1987). As a result, boys' ability to socially respond to their mothers through reciprocal gazing may be compromised relative to girls (Pollack, 1995). The result may be fewer sustained and successful interactions between mothers and infant boys.

As they develop, relationships with the primary caretaker have a different dynamic for boys and girls. Boys are socialized to be different and to move away from their primary caretaker (Chodorow, 1978). Empathic relating is discouraged because boys need to develop an autonomous, distinct self (Pollack, 1995).

Girls have a different experience. Because the primary caretaker during the early years is almost always female, girls experience themselves as being the same as their mother (Chodorow, 1978). Attachment and identity formation become part of the same process. Connection is the basis on which female identity is founded. With the basic connection always intact, girls then compare other experiences with this relationship as well as develop greater complexity within the mother–daughter bond itself. Underlying this boundary-determined self is a sense of oneness or merging with the mother that continually challenges this separateness (Pollack, 1995). In contrast, men, as they develop, live with a chronic undercurrent of threatened merger with another—particularly with the mother. When this neglected experience "breaks through" periodically, usually in relation with women, there is an accompanying burst of fear and anxiety.

Among boys, there is the added dimension of the unavailability of an adult male model to learn about masculinity. Fathers, if present, are often disengaged through activity, work, hobbies, and sports. In addition, about half of U.S. marriages end in divorce (Peck & Manocherian, 1989). After divorce, fathers become even more scarce.

Miller's (1976) psychology of women replaces the moving away of separation as normal development with connection as both a beginning and end of development. This is not a stagnant dependence but, instead, is a building of relationships into a complex network. At a dyadic level, affiliation becomes more sophisticated and multifaceted with time. This web of connection is an integral part of female identity, and the rupturing of a relationship bond may be experienced as a loss of one's own being.

Surrey (1991) argued that women develop a more encompassing sense of self, in contrast to the boundary-determined self of men. An early stage of this self in girls is the circular or oscillating development of empathic understanding between the young girl and her mother. Empathy is a key component in self-in-relation therapy. Empathy has received somewhat of a bad rap in object relations theory. It has been seen as a less mature level of functioning, occurring through a temporary suspension of boundaries (Jordan, Surrey, & Kaplan, 1991). Current theorizing about women's identity includes a more sophisticated conceptualization of empathy as a complex interplay between emotion and cognition (Jordan et al., 1991). The maintenance of boundaries while entering into the affective world of another is probably differentially developed in men and women. If personal boundaries are overly rigid, it will be difficult to grasp the others' affective experience. The result will be "a distanced intellectual effort to reconstruct what is going on or a projection of one's own state into another" (Jordan et al., 1991, p. 29). Poor boundaries lead to a merger, in which the other or the other's feelings are seen only as an extension of one's own experience. Accurate empathy is a quality of the well-differentiated person. Men probably overemphasize the personal cognitive boundary of empathy, whereas the struggle for women is to maintain a separate self while being open to others' experience.

These gender differences in empathy form one basis for conflicts arising in communication between men and women. Women describe their needs, desires, and conflicts with the hope of better self-understanding through dialogue. The other person is more than a sounding board; they are being asked to temporarily enter the woman's experiential world and help her sort it out. Men, because of their boundary-determined self, often respond with direct advice or challenge. The result is that the woman feels confused, disorganized, and often alone (Surrey, 1991).

For boys, the experience of premature separation from their mother without an affiliative experience with their father is likely to leave the adult male with strong needs for connection that are simultaneously defended against. The disruption in their interaction with their primary caretaker leaves men needy for emotional connectedness but also extremely fearful of it (Pollack, 1995). When these early, largely unconscious templates are reactivated in adolescence and early adulthood, these dynamics are enacted through the approach–avoidance cycle that men often exhibit in relationships with women. An additional strategy may center around attempting to control and capture women in adulthood as a means of preventing the profoundly painful loss from reoccurring.

The angry frustration and flight into activity shown by many men in response to intimacy obscures their underlying needs. Men themselves often focus on the perceived injustice that superficially triggers their anger rather than on the underlying fears of abandonment and deep needs for nurturance (Bergman, 1995). For many men, all negative emotion—fear, threat, sadness, loss—has the final common affective pathway of anger. In daily life, men devote considerable energy to defending against closeness. Men who have multiple relationships, or even sustained involvements including children, often do not see these others as important parts of their identity (Candib, 1995). This void may take the outward form of seeming indifference toward others or a sense of control, as if the partner were a material commodity. Even when men are able to recognize—albeit dimly—their own emotional needs, they are likely to devote their energies to maintaining some distance from them.

For men, a significant relationship is often a way of compartmentalizing emotional needs or of having empathy conveyed vicariously through their spouse (Brooks & Gilbert, 1995; Pleck, 1980). Wives convey sympathy to ill colleagues, phone with social invitations or regrets, send gifts for a friend's new baby, and write the requisite thank you notes for gifts. These gender roles are again often handed down uncritically from the boy's observation of his parent's relationship. There is some indirect support for this pattern as an intergenerational process. Brooks and Gilbert (1995) found that men who were positively oriented toward sharing household roles also viewed their fathers as shouldering significant household responsibility. However, this splitting-off of functions by gender suggests that traditional sex roles support opposite ends of Bowen's (1978) social–emotional polarity for men and women, respectively.

Men may project their less dominant function onto their female mates. Adult men have an extensive social network but few close friends (Gilligan, 1982). Men's stories of relationship belie a fear of intimacy; it is seen as a threat. Close relationships may result in betrayal, humiliation, or entrapment. Women often express a complementary fear of autonomous goal directedness as leading to isolation and abandonment by others. Disturbingly, violence is often the solution to resolving these anxiety-provoking relationships for men (Gilligan, 1982).

Although men usually have one primary (and often the only) source of intimacy—their spouse or significant other—women often have a broader network of meaningful connections. These include friends, sisters, and an ongoing relationship between the adult woman and her mother. The quality of the connection between sisters, and between mothers and daughters, is often transformed to include strong elements of mutual friendship (Candib, 1995).

Recent writing on the psychology of men (Brooks & Gilbert, 1995; Pollack, 1995) suggests that the concept of men as internally directed individuals who are not susceptible to others' influence is not accurate. The ability to remain connected and empathically perceive the world through others' eyes is an important, yet neglected, aspect of men's development. Pollack (1995) reviewed findings from the Boston University Parenthood and Pregnancy Project, a longitudinal study of mothers' and fathers' interaction with young children, beginning during pregnancy. Bowen's view of healthy functioning was supported; parents who maintained relationships with significant others while simultaneously exhibiting the ability to focus on personal goals reported greater marital satisfaction and healthier family functioning, and their children exhibited higher levels of positive mood (Pollack, 1995). However, men experienced connectedness with their children differently from women. Fathers interacted with young children through physical play, teaching, and attention, whereas mothers exhibited affiliation with their child through holding and hugging (Pollack & Grossman, 1985). Research has suggested that being a father and success in carrying out parental tasks plays a significant role in men's well-being (Barnett, Marshall, & Pleck, 1992; Pollack, 1995). This relational dimension warrants attention and indicates that men's identity is more complexly determined than just through work achievement or marriage.

IDENTITY DEVELOPMENT THROUGH THE LIFE SPAN: ACHIEVEMENT VERSUS CONNECTION

Identity development through the life span has historically been presented as a process of separating oneself from others to find one's inner being. Achievement has been one of the primary yardsticks for assessing identity in existing stage theories. This theme emerged consistently in the writings of developmental theorists such as Valliant (1977), Levinson (Levinson, Darrow, Klein, Levinson, & McKee, 1978), and even Erikson (1968).

Longitudinal studies of "great" men such as those conducted by Erikson reveal a profound detachment from those around them. Luther and Gandhi seemed to distance themselves from others: "Thus Luther in his devotion to faith like Gandhi in his devotion to truth, ignore the people most closely around them while working towards the glory of God" (Gilligan, 1982, p. 155).

Men finding themselves through solitary exploration is a central theme in Western film and fiction. Somerset Maugham's (1944) classic *The Razor's Edge* (made in two different film versions) features a protagonist, Larry Daryl, who experiences a spiritual crisis when a fellow soldier is killed during a World War I battle. Daryl returns to his well-to-do Chicago family and lifestyle with a growing discontent. He leaves his fiancee for an extended multiyear pilgrimage through working-class Paris, a coal mine in Wales, and culminating in Tibet. Sent by a monk to a solitary mountain retreat, Daryl, who has read voraciously as an attempt to find meaning in his life, begins shredding the books into the fire. Having found a sense of peace and meaning, Daryl is now able to enter into a relationship with a former acquaintance who has become a Paris prostitute.

This theme of men's quest for wholeness and identity through a solitary pilgrimage that then permits them to develop some form of intimacy with women is a pervasive one. Even those identity stages characterized by giving to others center around acts of *doing* rather than *being* in relationship. Erikson's stage of generativity in mid life involves taking a leadership role and producing for the next generation (Gilligan, 1982). Relationships are heavily flavored by achievement rather than a mutual process of understanding.

Whereas developmental schemes for men neatly partition identity and intimacy, for women this compartmentalization is artificial. Personal strength is measured through the ability to be consistently caring and giving to others. Bowen's (1978) own description of his establishment of a one-to-one relationship with his own family fits this model of becoming separate and then reconnecting. This view of independence with a "feminine awakening" in later adult life, when relationships become important, is also found in the stage theories of Erikson (1968). Contemporary adult development theories such as Levinson's (Levinson et al., 1978) describe a similar longitudinal pattern. Levinson's and Erikson's models of adult development are based on male experience. Levinson stated this explicitly in his book *Seasons of a Man's Life* (Levinson et al., 1978). These stage models for men share the common feature that relationships and intimacy only become a focus after there is a foundation of independent achievement. Once personal goals are attained, then there appears to be enough security to attempt intimacy while keeping engulfment anxieties in check.

For women, men's attention to relationship in mid life is often far too little and too late. Marriage, anticipated as a source of intimacy for women, is often a major disappointment during the early years (Gilligan, 1982). Men's stirring of recognition in their early 40s of their importance to their wives and children as husbands and fathers often occurs after they have been given up on by their wives as confidants and nurturers. Men, typically marrying in their mid 20s, have paid little attention to relationships as a meaningful part of their own well being until mid life. For men, this is often like walking into a play when the drama is two thirds over and no one is expecting them to arrive. During these decades, women have developed in their abilities to care for others and to understand themselves through these relationships, while men are materially engaged elsewhere.

FAMILY-OF-ORIGIN THEORY REVISED

Bowen's theory in particular, and object relations theory to a lesser extent, describes psychological health from a traditional masculine relationship perspective. Bowen's (1978) description of the well-functioning adult as operating from a position of goal directedness and separateness conflicts with Surrey's (1991) and Miller's (1976) views of healthy female development through reciprocal understanding of others. Bowen is explicit in his view that sensitivity to others' emotional states and their reactions to the self are characteristic of poor differentiation (Knudson-Martin, 1994). This, in effect, relegates the female process of identity formation to a permanently lower level on the differentiation scale. The object relations approach to family-of-origin therapy views growth as a matter of becoming increasingly autonomous. As Surrey (1991) pointed out: "Separation implies a process of 'internalizing' the attachment and lessening the need for the other or the relationship" (p. 61). The earlier state of dependence on others for emotional security is seen as developmentally less mature. By internalizing a representation of this earlier relationship, the ability to nurture oneself becomes available. Again, however, the healthy person is considered to be an autonomous person whose needs can be self-satisfied.

Object relations theory, despite its overt focus on relationships as key motivating forces, actually minimizes the importance of maintaining meaningful social connections. Bergman (1995) noted that object relations theory, rather than leading to a relationship-based concept of identity, in effect leads to a "self-out-of relation" model.

Developmental research suggests that spatial metaphors such as separation do not grasp the actual process of change in relationships with time. Infants develop a more intricate pattern of interaction with their mothers as they grow (Miller, 1991). Similarly, adolescents and parents redefine their connections rather than distancing from one another (Grotevant & Cooper, 1986). Differentiation is not a simplistic process of defining one's own psychological space but is a complex interaction of self-understanding, appreciating contradictions, empathizing, and struggling to validate one's own needs while caring for others.

The process and end results of differentiation are distinct for men and women. Developing a sense of identity for women includes empathically viewing situations from the perspectives of others as part of defining one's own values and goals. Knudson-Martin (1994) noted that the issue is not *whether* women use relationships for self-definition but *how* they use those relationships. Attachment solely for security is not differentiation. The process of differentiation is an ongoing reciprocity in which others' perspectives are "tried on," with active consideration of keeping that which fits while acknowledging, without discarding, those characteristics that are not assimilated. Maturity—particularly for women—involves "being able to listen to others while still hearing one's own voice" (Knudson-Martin, 1994, p. 36).

Differentiation, although it may take distinct forms for women, must occur for healthy development. Women whose entire being is defined through taking care of others experience subordination and subservience (Candib, 1995; Miller, 1976), which results in an angry, demoralized helplessness that is not well articulated or clearly linked to external events. The healthy alternative is not complete independence but a newly articulated self, maintaining fluid personal boundaries that permit engagement and caring while promoting personal values.

GENDER-SENSITIVE FAMILY-OF-ORIGIN THERAPY

The writings of Surrey (1991), Miller (1976), and others on women's identity development, together with the embryonic work on relationships and men's identity, provide a more variegated perspective on the intrapsychic dynamics of each gender. The family-of-origin therapist should recognize that there are distinct "his and hers" differentiation processes.

Bowen's writing reveals considerable ambivalence about emotional closeness. Bowen's (1978) position that differentiation requires intimacy in the form of one-to-one emotionally meaningful exchanges is not consistent with his measurement approach. On his scale of differentiation, the healthiest score of 100 is given to persons who are cognitively oriented, independent, and governed by clearly articulated goals (Luepnitz, 1988). This view of well-being conflicts with Bowen's (1978) other positions emphasizing the ability to stay engaged with others—even under conditions of high intensity affect. Personal freedom is not complete independence from one's family but the ability to remain mutually engaged while preserving one's own values.

To be relevant to the experience of women, family-of-origin theory must struggle with the more complex interaction between self and others that is part of female identity development. A self-in-relation model can be incorporated into both object relations and Bowenian family therapy. Object relations theory could recognize that internalized representations of relationships initially formed during early childhood are subject to ongoing refinement and a drive toward greater complexity. Continuous empathic engagement with others is an important experience for altering and developing one's understanding of the self through interaction with others. Bowen often described differentiation as being meaningfully engaged with others while simultaneously maintaining self-direction. Although Bowen has been criticized for his focus on the rational, intellectual, and autonomous self as the epitome of psychological well-being, this view does not accurately describe his writing. Bowen consistently maintained that being disengaged from others was as dysfunctional as being enmeshed. By more strongly emphasizing the feeling system, Bowen's theory more readily takes into account a self-in-relation (Knudson-Martin, 1994). The feeling system is not as well articulated in Bowenian theory as the emotional or intellectual systems. The emotional system deals with preconscious drives and visceral affective experience, and the intellectual system includes reflectiveness, self-monitoring, and decision skills. In contrast, the feeling system deals with conscious affective experience. It is considered to be a more highly developed function than simple emotionality. The feeling system provides important affective information—particularly as it pertains to relationships. By its very nature, intimacy and the choice to develop connections with specific others requires the ability to make sense of affective experience. The healthy individual has fluid exchange between the intellectual and feeling systems (Knudson-Martin, 1994) rather than a reliance on intellect to harness emotionality.

HISTORICAL DETERMINISM, DIFFERENTIATION, AND SOCIAL CONTEXT: AN INTEGRATION

Family-of-origin therapy includes an implicit determinism. History establishes patterns, locking individuals into perpetuating agendas founded in prior generations. Gender-based stereotypes, although heavily determined by social–political forces, can be rationalized through intergenerational legacies. This historical determinism, in turn, crystallizes these sex role patterns and may obscure their role in family pathology. More disturbingly, intergenerational ledgers (Boszormenyi-Nagy & Spark, 1973) and the tenet that one's level of differentiation is relatively fixed provide disturbing rationalizations for sexual abuse and family violence. The view that women and men form relationships on the basis of largely unconscious needs and similar levels of differentiation may contribute to a "she asked for it" rationale for spouse battering. This line of reasoning is evident in the following recently published discussion of systemic ethics and incest:

> The passive "victim'" soon becomes an active participant in incest encouraging its continuation in order to keep the family or marriage intact and to maintain the spe-

cial position, power, and even physical gratification that constitutes the victim's meager compensation . . . [many] incest victims will later become sexually promiscuous or set themselves up to become rape victims. (Wendorf & Wendorf, 1985; cited in Searight & Merkel, 1991, p. 27)

At the intrapsychic and immediate relational levels, family-of-origin theory will require reformulation to adequately address identity and relationship formation among men and women. The distinct pathways for men and women influence parenting, marriage, and interactions between adults and their families of origin.

At the same time, social and political realities also define and constrain women's roles as wives, daughters, and mothers. Among the different family approaches, family-of-origin therapy in particular has developed in a hermetic vacuum apart from the broader cultural and economic context of gender.

For example, family-of-origin therapists have had little to say about domestic violence and incest apart from intrapsychic and intergenerational explanations. Spouse battering is not behavior that can be entirely reduced to issues of differentiation or faulty introjected objects, although intrapsychic phenomena do play a role in domestic violence. The fact that over 90% of the victims of domestic violence are female indicates that these aggressive acts are not gender neutral. Domestic violence reflects the economic and social power imbalances of a patriarchal society as well as the differences in the internalized views of relationships held by men and women.

Economically, through greater earnings, men's financial control often places genuine constraints on a woman's choice to leave or stay in a relationship—particularly when children are involved. Women's ethic of care intersects with their knowledge that men have a poor record of financially supporting their children after separation. A woman's earning power is typically significantly less than her male partner's. In addition, in the case of physical abuse, the legal system's poor response to battering is a memory that a woman is likely to have carried away from her own upbringing through its inability to protect her mother from abuse. There is also a political–cultural norm that family life should not be subjected to state control, a view that is currently becoming increasingly popular in legislative circles.

Intrapsychically, men's fear of merger is likely to be a dynamic in violent episodes. Male gender identity becomes threatened when the separation of the early maternal bond is re-evoked. This oscillation between fear of engulfment and the pain of disjuncture often underlies the chaotic anger and fear observed in men during battering episodes (Goldner, Penn, Sheinberg, & Walker, 1990). Violence arises when a man experiences "unmasculine" feelings of dependency and helplessness; the response is an aggressive attempt to rid himself of these frightening feelings through excessive unilateral control of the woman threatening to abandon him. A very high proportion of serious violence occurs when a woman threatens to leave a relationship (Searight, 1997).

Therapists working with battered women are often frustrated that they stay in abusive relationships. Goldner et al. (1990) noted that many of these women come from extremely patriarchal families of origin. These women, in their history as daughters, have accepted responsibility for the climate of their marriage and current family. The ethic of care becomes activated as they repeatedly try to care for their distressed husbands.

GENDER "RULES" IN FAMILY-OF-ORIGIN THERAPY

The case example below highlights the interaction of sociopolitical, familial, and individual historical factors in gender role conflicts within marriage.

> Tom and Alice were each 35 years old, had been married for 8 years, and had three children, ages 6, 3, and 2. They started therapy because of increased conflict. The therapist immediately noticed how overwhelmed, exhausted, and irritable each spouse appeared. Alice had initiated the therapy because she was feeling isolated and trapped with the children. She was persistently critical of Tom's unavailability. She was very devoted to her children but felt that Tom gave her little support with them. Alice had stopped working outside of the home soon after their first child was born. She had been a successful advertising executive. She and Tom, she said, both felt that mothers should be home with their children. Alice stated that she and Tom had not directly discussed how many children they would have or their temporal spacing ("the babies just came").
>
> Tom was also exhausted. He was working 70 hours per week at two jobs. Tom's primary job was as an accountant for a large corporation. After getting off work at 4:30, he went to his second job as an accountant/bookkeeper for an expanding network of furniture stores. In addition to working until 10:00 each night, he often went to both offices to catch up on Saturdays and Sundays.
>
> Inquiry into Alice's family of origin revealed that she was raised in an affluent family in which her father had worked long hours and her mother stayed home with Alice and her sisters. Alice was encouraged by her father to go on to college and achieve occupationally, but always with the implicit message that mothers should be at home with their children. Tom was from a lower middle class family in which his father worked in a factory, often overtime, and his mother "always had dinner on the table when he walked in the door." Both Tom and Alice said that although they had not directly discussed it, they had expected to live out similar gender roles.
>
> Alice said that several years previously she had considered going back to work but soon learned that she would earn far less than before because of her time out

of the job market. Alice concluded that for the money it wasn't worth it because Tom could earn three times what she could make. Tom said that he was aware that Alice felt "worn down" by the kids but that to maintain their home and lifestyle, the family had to have the combined income of his two jobs. Alice agreed that their suburban home was important to her and the children. Tom also felt proud to be a good provider for the family and was particularly pleased that he had done better than his own father. However, Tom felt he had nothing left at the end of the day for his family.

As this example illustrates, current gender role patterns reflect a constellation of intrapsychic issues, family-of-origin rules about gender, and current economic realities. Importantly, this couple did not present gender roles as a problem for therapy. Instead, conflicts centered around the absence of mutual support.

Gender, like ethnicity, has a pervasive and often unquestioned set of rules that for many years have been implicitly supported by society at large. Avis (1985) argued that the family is the primary source of gender socialization; it is the mediator between the individual and larger society. These gender-based *Weltanschaugen* have, until recently, been off limits to therapists. Social and political issues have been seen as extraneous to the therapist's consulting room. In the past decade, feminist family therapists have made it clear that social and economic imbalances play a key role in marital and family life. The therapist who ignores these forces is engaging in a pathological form of collusion and denial.

All marital and family therapy involves the therapist's response to gender-based patterns of organization. Failure to examine gender roles is equivalent to accepting the status quo (Avis, 1985). In the case of Tom and Alice, the therapist invited both spouses to reflect on how their current division of roles had emerged.

For both Tom and Alice, their families of origin had provided them with templates of traditional gender roles. These expectations appeared to be enacted in their marriage with little reflection and no formal discussion. Both Tom and Alice viewed themselves as trapped with their respective responsibilities. Although family-of-origin histories contributed to their dilemma, current social and economic realities also placed constraints on role flexibility. The therapist, over several sessions, began to point out these unspoken rules governing the couple's division of responsibility. Tom and Alice's increased awareness of these issues reduced the blaming of one another and the sense of isolation that each experienced. They began to examine childrearing and financial obligations with the possibility of greater flexibility. An element of choicefulness surrounding their involvement with work and family contributed to a new awareness of their shared values as well as provided more options for achieving these ends. Tom gave up his second job and spent more time with the children and Alice. To offset the lost income, Alice took on a part-time job, and the couple critically examined their budget for unnecessary expenses.

CONCLUSION

Gender is a pervasive organizing principle for family life and individual identity. Shaped by family history and sociopolitical forces as well as by intrapsychic representations of men and women, gender carries a set of often unquestioned assumptions about relationships. Family-of-origin therapy historically has neglected gender as a distinct socializing influence. Although female–male differences around dimensions such as autonomy and intimacy create greater complexity in family-of-origin therapy, therapists who attend to gender will be more successful in helping their clients develop greater flexibility and understanding of these issues.

Chapter 6

Gay and Lesbian Relationships

Intimate, same-gender relationships are found across all cultural groups. However, their openness varies considerably, as does the social support for gay and lesbian relationships. For example, Denmark legalized marriage and divorce for same-gender couples in 1989 (Miller, 1995). In the United States, the 1969 Stonewall uprising in New York's Greenwich Village is often seen as the historical landmark launching the drive for gay and lesbian rights. A police raid on the Stonewall Inn, a gay bar, triggered 10 days of rioting by gays, lesbians, and transvestites (Arey, 1995). One eventual outcome of this movement was the removal of homosexuality from the list of psychiatric disorders in the mid-1970s.

Approximately 5% of the U.S. population is self-identified as gay, with about 2% self-identified as lesbian (Diamond, 1993; Janus & Janus, 1993). The frequency of gay and lesbian relationships in the population differs depending on how questions are posed. When persons who report both homosexual and heterosexual activity in adulthood are included, the figures rise to about 9% of men and 5% to 6% of women (Seidman & Reider, 1995).

The family of origin is a model or template that guides most adults in establishing family roles as parents, lovers, and partners. Gay and lesbian families do not have this foundation to guide their organization, either as a model or contrasting point of comparison. Although many heterosexual parents and partners choose to reject certain aspects of their own upbringing, the presence of a contrast at least provides a reference point. Gay and lesbian families are generating new forms of family life—often without a model or even a schema to react against. Guidebooks, magazine articles, and even much of the guidance of therapists about relationships derives from heterosexist models. The absence of tradition, a sense of direction, and cultural support may leave the gay or lesbian family in a quandary as they search for a meaningful pattern (Goodrich, Rampage, Ellman, & Halstad, 1988).

Fears of social consequences about a gay or lesbian relationship continue to generate a forced secrecy for many couples. Family censure, job loss, or anxiety about subtle retaliation or discrimination in the community or work place are very real reactions. Men and women both report having to pose as roommates or friends for family and coworkers. There is often a need to generate acceptable cover for the heterosexual world.

DEVELOPMENT OF GAY AND LESBIAN IDENTITY

The process of developing a gay or lesbian identity begins in late childhood or early adolescence. For all children, there is a greater awareness of sexuality as they develop. There are also typically periods of confusion about sexual identity. An eight-stage scheme for gay and lesbian identity development, adapted from McWhirter and Mattison (1984), was presented by Scrivner and Eldridge (1995). In the early phase, *sensitization*, many children who later define themselves as gay or lesbian may experience sexual attraction to the same sex (McWhirter & Mattison, 1984). However, these experiences are not fully figured or labeled in consciousness. Negative views of homosexuality may be uncritically internalized during this time. In the next stage, *identity confusion*, adolescents and occasionally young adults begin with a view of themselves as heterosexual. However, a growing number of thoughts, feelings, or actions generate confusion; the individual may ambivalently accept these or respond with denial. *Identity comparison* is then entered, in which adolescents and adults feel a strong sense of not fitting into the heterosexual world but have nothing with which to replace the void. *Identity tolerance* is characterized by the position "I probably am gay or lesbian" (Scrivner & Eldridge, 1995). Although gay or lesbian culture is not embraced during this stage, there is a growing awareness of a gay and lesbian community that may provide support. *Identity acceptance* occurs when there is increased interaction with the gay and lesbian community. This stage is important in providing a foundation of social validation for an identity that may not be accepted in heterosexist culture. The *first relationships* stage is then entered; the individual learns how to be in a same-sex relationship. Scrivner and Eldridge noted that these early gay or lesbian relationships often include possessiveness and anxiety around trust. In addition, difficulty traversing earlier stages of identity development (in particular, ambivalence around accepting a gay or lesbian identity) will result in additional emotional baggage being brought to this first relationship. Entering the seventh stage, *identity commitment and pride*, often includes a deepening involvement with the gay and lesbian community and a more solid commitment to being gay or lesbian even in the face of social adversity. Society may be viewed in dichotomous "us versus them" terms. Last, *identity synthesis* is characterized by a more integrated self, with gay or lesbian identity as only one facet. Although this stage includes pride in one's identity, it is without the dualism of the previous stage (Scrivner & Eldridge, 1995).

CHARACTERISTICS OF GAY AND LESBIAN RELATIONSHIPS

About 40% to 60% of gay men and 45% to 80% of lesbians report being in a long-term relationship (Peplau & Cochran, 1990). Kurdek and Schmitt (1987) compared social support among gay, lesbian, and heterosexual married and cohabiting couples and found important differences between homosexual and heterosexual couples in perceived sources of support. Gays and lesbians were less likely to experience support from family members than heterosexual respondents. Among gays and lesbians, friends were the primary source of socialization outside of their partner. In contrast, for heterosexual cohabitants, family members were considered to be more important sources of social support than friends. This pattern suggests that cohabitation per se may no longer be viewed negatively by family members but that same-sex relationships are not well received by the extended family (Kurdek & Schmitt, 1987).

Gender differences in identity and relationship formation, discussed in the previous chapter, are important for understanding gay and lesbian relationships. Previous research has found that lesbians, as compared with gay men, seek and form more stable relationships, value sexual fidelity, and desire companionship as well as affection. In addition, lesbian relationships are more likely to be enduring than those of gay men (Duffy & Rusbult, 1986).

Gay male relationships are briefer, less exclusive, and less likely to be monogamous than those of heterosexual men and women as well as lesbians (Duffy & Rusbult, 1986). However, most gay men report seeking enduring relationships with intimate communication and support. Financial independence and equal power sharing are valued (Keller & Rosen, 1988; Peplau & Cochran, 1990). Gay men also value social networks of friends independent of their primary relationship. Relationship satisfaction, as with heterosexual relationships, is related to flexible, nonstereotyped roles (Kurdek, 1995). Differences in decisional control in gay dyads appears to be related to age discrepancies between partners (Harry, 1984; Keller & Rosen, 1988). Several studies have found that gay partners in open, nonmonogamous relationships had been together longer than those in closed sexual relationships (Kurdek & Schmitt, 1986; McWhirter & Mattison, 1984).

Because lesbian couples tend to have longer relationships than gay men and because they seek therapy fairly frequently, there are more descriptions of relationship dynamics among lesbians than among gays. Lesbian dyads are more likely to be closed and monogamous. In addition, there is a strong norm of equality around household tasks, finances, and decision making. When compared with gay men, lesbians tend to report higher levels of relationship satisfaction (Kurdek, 1995). Many of these dimensions may be a function of gender rather than sexual orientation. Women are socialized into a relationship orientation, in which interpersonal skills are highly valued. Kurdek (1995) noted that married heterosexual men and gay men did not differ in their ratings of relationship satisfaction and that lesbian and heterosexual married women also reported equal relationship satisfaction. If satisfaction is assessed for the relationship as a unit, lesbian dyads may report higher levels of satisfaction than heterosexual dyads. However, when relationships are disassembled, the differences appear to be a function of gender rather than sexual orientation. Men and women, regardless of their sexual orientation, appear to have similar degrees of relationship satisfaction.

Sexual and affectional dimensions are often melded in lesbian relationships. Lesbian couples typically describe themselves as friends first before becoming sexual partners. This friendship often continues after the lesbian couple has split up and each partner has taken new lovers. Lesbian social networks value inclusiveness—not leaving others out or losing one relationship to form another. Ending a relationship to begin with a new partner may not be a common practice; the previous relationship, while changing in intensity, is often incorporated into the woman's network. There is a strong theme of unacceptable disloyalty in terminating a relationship. There is an ongoing challenge of doing what is necessary for one's own development while simultaneously not hurting another. If a member of the intimacy network appears hurt, left out, or angry, the woman reexamines and modifies actions until the distress is reduced (Goodrich et al., 1988).

CHILDREN OF GAY OR LESBIAN PARENTS

There are estimated to be between 1 and 5 million lesbian mothers and 1 to 3 million gay fathers in the United States (Patterson, 1992). Six to 14 million children have gay or lesbian parents (Patterson, 1992). These figures range widely, in part because many gay and lesbian parents are not open about their sexual orientation out of fear of losing custody of their children. Bell and Weinberg (1978) reported that about 10% of gay men and 20% of lesbians have children. Many lesbians have had children in the context of a heterosexual marriage, divorced, and then "come out" as lesbians. These children have been the most commonly studied and form the basis for empirical conclusions about growing up in a lesbian household. However, more recently, lesbian couples have had children through donor insemination or adoption. An early study of lesbian parents found little difference between young children (age 3) of lesbian mothers and those of heterosexual couples (Steckel, 1987). The differences that did exist included children of heterosexual parents seeing themselves as somewhat more aggressive and being perceived by parents and teachers as somewhat more bossy and domineering. Children of lesbian parents on the other hand saw themselves as more loveable and were seen by parents and teachers as more affectionate, responsive, and protective of younger children.

Sexual identity issues do not appear to be greater among children in gay or lesbian households. Among adolescents and young adult children of gay or lesbian parents, the proportion who identify themselves as gay or lesbian is about the same as in the general population (Patterson, 1992). The quality of peer and adult relationships also does not appear to be affected by parents' sexual orientation (Patterson, 1992). There are suggestions that children and adolescents may be somewhat better adjusted when they learn of their parents' sexual orientation during childhood rather than during adolescence (Patterson, 1992).

Although the vast majority of existing studies focus on lesbian rather than gay households, the overall pattern of findings challenge the psychodynamic view that normal development is dependent on being raised by heterosexual parents. It is likely that the important dimensions of healthy development with families are not parents' sexual orientation but instead the ability to provide a balance of support and promotion of independence, as suggested by Grotevant and Cooper (1986).

FAMILY-OF-ORIGIN ISSUES

The agonizing question of whether to tell family members about their sexual identity propels many gays and lesbians into psychotherapy. Often, the client has developed strategies for managing his or her identity with the family. These temporary solutions include emotional and geographic cut-offs, an unspoken rule that the client's personal and social lives are off limits for discussion, and disclosure to one family member such as a sibling with a strict agreement that no one else be informed (Brown, 1988). Many gays and lesbians will not present family-of-origin issues as a therapeutic agenda but instead will focus on a current lover or less specific issues, such as chronic depression or alcohol use. The lack of authenticity with the family of origin may be a significant contributing factor to these symptoms in the form of introjected homophobia or fear of disappointing parents.

When parents and siblings are informed of an individual's gay or lesbian identity, they actively attempt to understand that orientation within the context of their ethnic, religious, and value systems. An experience of alienation and confusion about how to view the son or daughter, brother or sister is likely to follow. Parents may ask themselves where they went wrong and launch a search for the cause of their son's or daughter's homosexuality. They may also grieve the loss of seeing their son or daughter in a heterosexual marriage and having grandchildren (Hancock, 1995). Family members may be justifiably worried about prejudice that the gay or lesbian relative may experience in a heterosexist culture. Parents of young men may voice anxiety about the AIDS epidemic. Research on coming out suggests a fairly consistent pattern in self-disclosure to family. The gay or lesbian adult discloses his or her identity first to siblings, followed by mothers, with fathers almost always last (Hancock, 1995). Fathers, in particular, may feel threatened by a gay or lesbian child and perceive themselves as a failed parent (Keller & Rosen, 1988).

After learning of their adult child's homosexuality, parents often feel anxiously lost about how to treat the homosexual couple. Many gays and lesbians find out that parents and siblings do not treat their partner with the same inclusiveness in the extended family as they do a heterosexual in-law by marriage. This creates a profound disappointment and a sense of not being accepted. It may feel as if the gay or lesbian relationship is not taken seriously or is trivialized by heterosexual family members. Including the significant other in family events such as weddings, funerals, holidays, and reunions may generate considerable anger and may provoke a cut-off after the gay or lesbian has come out to his or her family. Parents may profess outward acceptance of the gay or lesbian relationship, but their underlying anxiety with their child's orientation may emerge as they refer publicly to the partner as their child's roommate or friend. Although these reactions may reflect anger, homophobia, or a denial of the sexual dimension of the relationship, parents may simply have no models for responding to same-sex relationships (Hancock, 1995). This dimension becomes even more complicated when children are involved. In lesbian families, parents—particularly those of the nonbiological mother—may have difficulty accepting that they have a grandchild. Tension and jealousy also arise when one partner is out to his or her family but the other is not, as seen in the following example:

> Tom and Jim had been living together as a couple for the previous 5 years. Tom was a community activist lawyer and was very open about his gay lifestyle. Jim, a dentist, was more secretive and expressed concern that he would lose patients if he were openly gay. Tom's relationship with his parents was warm and close; he had been open with them about his homosexuality since his late teens. Tom's family lived

nearby—he usually saw them every week and spoke with them by phone every other day. Jim moved from his parents' home town to attend a college 1,500 miles away. Jim left his home town in part because of concern that his parents would learn of his gay lifestyle. Jim talked with his parents once or twice a year and had last seen his parents and siblings at his grandmother's funeral 2 years previously. Tom was puzzled by Jim's distance from his family but did not challenge it. However, Tom found himself increasingly under attack for his "overinvolvement" with his own family. Jim had been openly accepted by Tom's parents but responded ambivalently, often refusing to attend family gatherings and chiding Tom for not being free of "Mommy's apronstrings."

In couples therapy, several issues emerged for Jim. He was generally fearful of others knowing about his homosexuality and was afraid that Tom's family's openness would translate into spreading this information around their medium-sized community. Tom and Jim discussed this directly with Tom's family, who responded with sensitivity and a firm promise to respect Jim's privacy. After this issue had been satisfactorily addressed, Jim became more depressed and was often tearful in couples therapy as he described his intense jealousy of Tom's close family relationship and his profound sense of loneliness. Tom responded with considerable support, and with the therapist's guidance, Jim began to explore ways to reconnect with his family of origin.

The coaching model discussed earlier is often useful in helping gays and lesbians come out as well as in addressing issues of acceptance with their families of origin. The therapist can assist the client in developing a strategy for disclosure, predicting family members' reactions, and role playing anxiety-provoking conversations in therapy sessions.

GAY OR LESBIAN IDENTITY AND RELATIONSHIPS

In addition to coming out and family-of-origin issues, gays and lesbians entering therapy are likely to be struggling with identity and relationship issues that are inextricably intertwined. Self-in-relation theory will be very helpful to the therapist working with lesbians. Because women are socialized around an ethic of care, and family identity is attained through relationships with others, fusion is a common outcome (Klinger, 1991). Rather than the "ebb and flow of separation, connection and separation" (Klinger, 1991, p. 133) characteristic of the differentiated self, lesbian partners may become closely fused. The natural differences between men and women probably maintain a built-in level of distance in heterosexual intimacy. This biological gap between heterosexual men and women is further delineated by differences in identity content and formation, discussed in the previous chapter.

Lesbian relationships often feel "so right" partially because women's development emphasizes constant sensitivity to the welfare of others: "Since in a lesbian relationship the other is also a woman, each partner finds herself receiving a degree of attention unknown in her relationships with men or family members where women are expected to be unilateral givers" (Goodrich et al., 1988, p. 143).

Male identity is based on separateness; the boy is different from his mother (Chodorow, 1978). In gay relationships, the issues of power, control, and individuality will often oscillate with a deep, underlying, and often unrecognized desire for intimacy. Because emotion and dependency needs are often not recognized by men, the therapist may have to dig to get at the real issues. Intimacy is likely to be very anxiety provoking, and the overt content of relationship conflicts is likely to center on intellectualized rules or what is right or wrong rather than on fears of closeness and abandonment.

In gay male relationships, these differences in identity lead partners to maintain a degree of constant distance. Sex, in particular, is often kept distinct from emotional closeness. Thus, isolated sexual encounters with others may not be highly threatening to a primary relationship. At the same time, however, the ambiguity surrounding these encounters can be used to provoke jealousy in the long-standing partner.

Part of the process of commitment to a gay or lesbian coupled relationship is often a turning away from society at large. Passing becomes more difficult, and efforts at impression management often cease when a long-term relationship is entered. For both gays and lesbians, the loss of outside support and social status may promote an intense relationship focus in their new dyad. The intensity of this relationship—particularly for lesbians—may result in blurring of individual boundaries and a loss of self (Krestan & Bepko, 1980).

Even among those who experience less fusion in their primary relationships, the extended family of origin as the dominant social network among heterosexual families is often replaced by a friendship network among gay and lesbian couples. Because of the need for support in a heterosexist culture, the gay and lesbian network provides important validation for gender identities that are, at minimum, often misunderstood and, sadly, often persecuted. These affiliative networks are often like adopted kin but are unfortunately rarely given the status and respect of family among medical, legal, educational, and even mental health systems.

BOWEN'S THEORY AND GAY OR LESBIAN RELATIONSHIPS

Bowen's (1978) theory has been sharply criticized in its application to gay and lesbian relationships. The concept of triangles—including a third person to manage tension or anxiety in a dyad—is viewed as a pathological solution in family-of-origin therapy.

In lesbian and gay relationships, involving others in a dyadic relationship may not result in discord. Particularly among women in same-sex partnerships, resolving issues with multiple women simultaneously may be a therapeutic goal. Third parties may not be disruptive forces for detouring dyadic conflict but simply part of a more encompassing view of primary relationships.

Boundaries

Closely related to triangulation is the issue of the boundary-determined self, emphasized by Bowen (1978) as healthy. For those with more fluid boundaries, psychological health involves erecting stronger social barriers, with the ability to retreat behind them when necessary. Being able to access emotional support from a network of lesbians or gays is healthy when similar support is unavailable from the family of origin or society at large.

Many states and countries do not legally recognize same-sex marriages. The absence of legal marriage for gays and lesbians, while preventing a legitimation of the relationship, also eliminates barriers to ending the partnership. The common economic, legal, and social barriers to ending a marriage are often not present in gay or lesbian dyads (Blumstein & Schwartz, 1983). For lesbians, this absence of a legal boundary, together with the ethic of care, may create ambiguity around when a relationship begins and ends. In addition, the decline in frequency of sex in long-term lesbian relationships described by Loulan (1985), together with the extended family ties of the lesbian community, may make termination of a relationship unclear. Lesbians often maintain ex-lovers as part of their ongoing social network and may include them in holidays and continue to celebrate birthdays.

Family-of-origin theory conflicts with many of these presumptions. In general, family-of-origin theory implies that healthy intimate relationships are exclusively monogamous, that friendships are asexual and secondary to a dyadic relationship, and that intimate partnerships have a firm boundary delineating them from their social context (Goodrich et al., 1988). Gay men define relationships less in terms of sexual exclusivity than do heterosexual men. Sexual monogamy may not be required in a gay dyad. It is likely that companionship and intimate sharing, rather than sexual monogamy, are important defining features of enduring gay relationships. These patterns suggest that the boundary emphasis of family-of-origin theory may need to be reinterpreted for gays and lesbians.

Fusion of Identities

Fusion of identities has been a particular concern in therapy with lesbian couples (Krestan & Bepko, 1980). Bowen (1978) viewed fusion as an emotionally driven process that makes people extremely reactive to others; the result is a sense of feeling controlled but being unable to detach from another. Fused individuals are very dependent on others' wishes to guide their behavior. For women, maintenance of relationships is a high priority and a value guiding daily decision making. When two women become intimately involved, these same value systems may cause the relationship to appear undifferentiated. This poses a clear challenge to reformulate the Bowenian concept of the "I" position as synonymous with health: "This earth would be a safer, more habitable place if more than only the female half of the race were trained to nurture relationships, to respond to the feelings and opinions of others, and to foster the well-being of others" (Goodrich, Rampage, Ellman, & Halstad, 1988, p. 147).

CONCLUSION

This book is being written in a cultural context of greater sensitivity to diversity. However, many heterosexual therapists may not attend to the implicit biases that mental health practitioners often bring to treatment of gays and lesbians. The therapist must recognize that gays and lesbians often approach therapy with a painful history of being viewed as a deviant by family, coworkers, and often previous therapists. Failure to recognize this experience constitutes harmful denial. At the same time, the therapist may go overboard in the opposite direction and uncritically accept issues that would be addressed with heterosexual clients. For example, the absence of exclusivity in relationships may be erroneously accepted as status quo for a gay dyad. A more useful approach would be one of open-ended inquiry into what closed or open means to each partner and how their current relationship pattern evolved.

This chapter has attempted to provide descriptions and research about common dimensions of gay and lesbian relationships. It is dangerous to take these descriptions into the therapy room as prototypes. Gays and lesbians are of multiple ethnicities, family backgrounds, religions, and personalities. A "one size fits all" perspective erases important uniqueness in gay and lesbian clients' lives (Greene, 1994b). Referring to the gay or lesbian couple as a unique and distinct entity is about as meaningful as describing a unique heterosexual couple.

Family-of-origin influences are likely to interact with current extended family relationships as well as stage of gay or lesbian identity development. Apart from the coming out process, little has been written about the relationship between gays and lesbians and their parents and siblings. Continued discrimination may make gays and lesbians particularly prone to cut-offs with their family of origin. Those who conceal their orientation, who do not cut themselves off but remain engaged often devote considerable effort to passing. Concealing a fundamental part of his or her identity may leave the gay or lesbian adult in a chronically unfulfilling pattern of impression management with extended family.

The United States is in the midst of a new generation of children being raised by parents who are openly gay or lesbian. Although research on these families is in its infancy, children of gays and lesbians appear to be psychologically healthy and well adjusted (Patterson, 1992). Finally, family-of-origin concepts such as differentiation, boundaries, and even the centrality of the dyad require reconceptualization to be more meaningful to the relationships and experiences of gays and lesbians.

Chapter 7

Ethnic and Cultural Diversity

The family of origin is the medium through which ethnic and cultural norms are communicated. Much of this communication is nonverbal—that which is *not* done or even considered (e.g., marrying outside of one's ethnic background)—or in the form of ritual and symbolism (e.g., the Irish Catholic wake). In the comparative discussion of ethnic groups that follows, it will be helpful to attend to the following dimensions: individualist versus collectivist orientation; definition and boundaries of family membership; openness and directness of emotional expression; emphasis on intellectual, cognitive understanding of experience; conflict management style (overt vs. covert); views of marriage; roles of men and women (e.g., traditional gender roles vs. androgyny); styles of socializing and rearing children (e.g., permissive vs. authoritative); and importance of family loyalty.

The Bowenian concept of differentiation is heavily influenced by culture. Bowen's (1978) focus on separateness may be seen as overemphasized among cultural groups that value family cohesiveness, such as Asians and Mediterranean Europeans. An individualist emphasis is found in the United States and among persons of northern European background. This central tension between the individual versus the family (and even the surrounding community) as the defining context for understanding human behavior is a culturally relative continuum.

ROLE OF ETHNICITY AND CULTURE IN SHAPING FAMILY WORLDVIEWS

The social norms of ethnic and cultural groups vary widely. They include such basic family dimensions as expression of emotion versus intellectualization, the amount of interpersonal distance encouraged or permitted, and the level of personalness versus formality in dealing with outsiders. Important for those conducting family therapy, culture is a pervasive lens that mediates and dictates experience and determines what is perceived in the outside world as well as how personal experience is labeled. A good example of this is the experience of depression among Asian Americans. On the west coast of the United States, patients of Asian background frequently went to physicians with complaints of heaviness in their chest. They were routinely referred on to cardiologists and typically had a negative cardiac work-up (Kleinman, 1988). However, more recently it was discovered that heaviness in the chest is a way that depression is experienced and expressed among Asian Americans. Rather than being an affective state of sadness or sense of guilt and hopelessness accompanied by cognitive symptoms, depression is often a somatic experience among Asians (Kleinman, 1988).

An ethnic group has been defined as those who conceive of themselves as alike by virtue of common ancestry—real or fictitious—and who are so regarded by others (McGoldrick, 1982). Ethnicity is a sense of commonality transmitted by the family over multiple generations. Giordano (1973) pointed out that ethnicity is also a form of belonging, a connection to a social network, a shared history and identity that provides a sense of security. Because these cultural values are unlabeled, they are often not subject to refutation or critical reflection. They are the lenses that we have been socialized with; they make us see one specific dimension and not others. Often, family and cultural values are not dictates but the absence of something. A family may never directly convey, "Don't talk about your feelings." Instead, implicit rules are communicated through a refusal to acknowledge affective experiences and events. When emotion is hinted at, the subject is simply changed.

CULTURE AND THERAPY

These cultural differences have been recognized in medicine for some time, and considerable literature is devoted to them. Cultural groups have been found to differ widely in terms of their experience of pain, what is labeled as a symptom, and how they communicate about their pain and symptoms. For example, Italian American and Jewish patients are often seen by physicians as exaggerating the intensity of their symptoms (Zola, 1966). White Anglo-Saxon Protestant (WASP) patients tend to be very future oriented about pain or illness. They believe in technology and science as forces that can cure illness. Cultural groups also vary in terms of their beliefs about the cause of illness and pain. Irish American patients, for example, often have some religious convictions, and supernatural meaning is attributed to the cause of their symptoms. Italian Americans tend to be significantly less reflective about physical distress. They simply want their distress to go away (McGoldrick, 1982; Zborowski, 1969). In addition, attitudes toward helpers, both physicians as well as mental health professionals, are shaped by ethnic worldviews. WASP patients are very likely to see the mental health professional as a technician. It should be no great surprise from a cultural perspective that so many therapists experience WASP parents as bringing in their child with a mandate to "fix the kid." WASPs see therapists as technologists or "doers." Jewish families are actually more likely to be congruent with the more common view of therapists as explorers of feelings and as persons who assist in labeling experience and promoting self-understanding. The expectations for therapy as well as the desired goals for therapy are also likely to be affected by ethnicity.

In medicine, a dramatic example of ethnic differences is provided by Hispanic Americans' views of blood transfusions (Hayes-Bautista, 1978; Kleinman, 1988). Hispanic patients will often refuse them—not because of reluctance about medical treatment, but because they believe that the essence of the person is in the vital fluids. By drawing out blood and putting it into someone else, the physician is in effect transferring that person's personality to someone else. In Hispanic lore, there are a number of descriptive accounts of people who have had dramatic personality changes as a result of blood transfusions.

PREJUDICE AND ETHNICITY

There is sometimes a reluctance to address ethnic issues because of stereotyping or concern that undue emphasis will be placed on how people are different (McGoldrick, 1982). The United States views itself as a melting pot country in which citizens often place considerable value on being American before being Black, Hispanic, Jewish, or Italian. For many readers, discussions of ethnicity may prompt memories of negative stereotyping, ethnic slurs, and jokes that were often very painful (McGoldrick, 1982). The exploration of ethnic differences is probably particularly frightening in that these labels have been used to deprive people of equality. Blacks, Jews, Hispanics, and others have all suffered from this prejudice. There is also a danger of overgeneralizing—as an example, consider the statement, "Oh he is Irish, he must be able to drink like a fish" (McGoldrick, 1982). However, after one hears enough presentations of families with different ethnic origins, some consistencies do tend to emerge. Often, because of the stress on equality in U.S. society, therapists have a built-in reaction that a focus on ethnic differences leads to prejudice. The study of ethnicity in the context of family therapy is not meant to be an experience leading to greater prejudice but instead is designed to highlight plurality and diversity. By being able to reflect on cultural values that therapists and clients adhere to, therapists can be more differentiated and choiceful about which values they want to retain and which they may respect in others but do not want for themselves. Ideally, therapists can engage families in a similar reflective process. In general, clients seem to be open to this sort of examination if it is done sensitively. It does not blame them. In a sense, issues may be in part a product of culture in the way that classical psychoanalytic theory views people as a product of their family or childrearing.

Another assumption that often goes unquestioned is that therapists do under-stand ethnicity, that it seems to be common sense. However, as is seen later in this chapter, a number of dimensions of family life are not usually appreciated as being culturally based. Often therapists do not ask the family what their ethnic origins are because of assumed knowledge about African Americans, Hispanics, or Irish Catholics. Many people in the United States, actually about 50% of them, come to know another culture by marrying into it (McGoldrick, 1982). In addition, many people have close friends of different ethnic backgrounds.

ACCULTURATION

Psychological anthropology continues to dispute the importance of the individual versus society in acculturation. Individualistic approaches emphasize the person as a distinct, separate unit apart from the social context (Johnson, 1993). The sociocentric perspective views the individual as interwoven into a larger social landscape, with fluid boundaries between the person and the social context. The surrounding culture exerts a strong pull for the individual to fit with his or her surroundings.

The acculturation process highlights the tension between sociocentric and ego-centric perspectives (Alarcon & Foulks, 1995). When a person enters a new cul-ture, acculturation pulls for new behaviors that help the person to fit into the dominant society. However, when this process is impeded because certain values of the original culture are not accepted by the dominant culture (e.g., veils worn by Islamic women in the United States), there is a danger of pathologizing the immigrant's behavior.

Acculturation, while modifying family influence, does not appear to eliminate it. Sabogal, Marin, Otero-Sabogal, Marrin, and Perez-Stable (1987) found that although Hispanic Americans' perceptions of an obligation to provide material, emotional support to family members declined with acculturation, as did family members' salience as identity models, acculturation did not alter perceived sup-port from the family. Sabogal et al. noted that among Hispanic Americans who were highly acculturated, there was still greater emphasis on relationship to the extended family than among non-Hispanics.

From a Bowenian perspective, immigrants' successful differentiation from the dominant culture and preservation of their own values may be seen as being nonre-active to the demands of the new culture. However, the maintenance of subcultural norms within the dominant culture may lead to pathologizing. Alarcon and Foulks (1995) noted that among Mexican Americans, there are often exaggerations of the dominant culture's traditional gender expectations among both men and women. As a result, Mexican American women may be inappropriately labeled as histrionic and men as antisocial because of the latter's *machismo* behavior.

Family-of-origin therapists should be similarly cautious with regard to behavior that may appear overly dependent. The deferential advice seeking that many Asians and Arctic aboriginal peoples exhibit toward family elders is a cultural norm rather than an indication of pathological family functioning. Members of these cultural groups also may appear overly self-effacing and self-blaming. Again, this behavior, rather than being reactive or indicative of poor self-worth, is instead a form of politeness. In the sections that follow, culturally based differences transmitted by the family are examined for a series of distinct cultural and ethnic groups. Implications for therapy are also discussed.

NATIVE AMERICANS

It is not possible to talk about Native Americans as a unitary culture. There is considerable diversity among different tribal cultures—even among tribes living in the same geographic area, such as the American Southwest (Attneave, 1982; LaFromboise, Berman, & Sohi, 1994). About half of Native Americans in the United States reside in urban areas (LaFromboise et al., 1994; U.S. Bureau of Census, 1993). The Native American population also tends to be young, with a median age of 18 (Harjo, 1993).

Worldview

Although religions and spiritual issues are discussed in a separate chapter in this book, such a distinction is artificial in Native American cultures. Spiritualism occurs in the context of a unity of the natural and human worlds (LaFromboise et al., 1994). The concept of time, in particular, is an important distinction for non-Native American therapists. At a micro level, the therapist will experience a loss of rhythm in the flow of conversation. A White therapist of European background will often press ahead with the interview and raise new topics when the Native American client is silent. The therapist will then be caught off guard when the client breaks the silence to address a previous point. The therapist may misinterpret these extended pauses as resistance or repression, but they are more accurately viewed as reflectiveness and communicatively underscore the view that what is said is of importance (LaFromboise et al., 1994).

Mental illness is often seen as an absence of harmony with an interdependent natural human and spiritual world. The physical, mental, and spiritual worlds are viewed as inextricably linked. Human existence is a continuous process, with emphasis on the past and present. Adjustment to one's circumstances and the important events in life are often seen as a recurring reciprocal pattern (LaFromboise et al., 1994).

A value that is difficult for many people of European background to appreciate is the importance of sharing. Rather than piling up and hoarding individual possessions, Native Americans emphasize that wealth is to be shared with the community (Ho, 1992).

Emotions are well controlled. To the non-Native American therapist, there may be an erroneous view that the client is schizoid or cut off from his or her affective life. There is an element of determination or even fatalism underlying this countenance. However, this stems from a realistic appraisal that the forces of nature as well as many human events are not subject to personal control (Ho, 1992).

Family Life

There is considerable warmth and playfulness between parents and children, particularly among mothers. Ho (1992) suggested that this nurturant relationship thrives because of the shared sense of responsibility for the child among tribal members. Children are viewed as having unique personal identities, which are to be respected and cultivated. Controlling, authority oriented parenting is not as common as among people of European background (Ho, 1992). At the same time, there is built-in respect for authority figures such as parents. However, children are seen as learning appropriate behavior through personally experiencing logical consequences (Attneave, 1982).

Native American women in traditional societies often had greater parity with men than is the case in European cultures. The role of mother was highly valued, and many women obtained powerful roles within the tribe through their spiritual powers. Women's status often increased with age (LaFromboise et al., 1994). Acculturation has often eroded this equality. Contact with White institutions, such as the Indian boarding schools, has played a major role in imposing gender-based roles on Native American life.

The family is often a broadly defined kinship network that extends beyond nuclear boundaries. There is a tolerance for individual differences, including behavior that might be considered eccentric. Cut-offs from one's family are relatively rare. Grandparents often assume much of the responsibility for childrearing (Attneave, 1982). This extended kinship network provides a basic degree of monitoring and support so that children's autonomy can be cultivated. Several developments in the latter part of the 20th century eroded this family network among Native Americans. First, the involvement of the state and provincial child welfare systems in Native American families often resulted in children being placed in non-Native American families and siblings being separated. It is likely that differences in values and childrearing styles played a role in Native American parents' being perceived by the state as neglectful, with the result being removal of the children from the family. A second factor, which dates back to the 1800s, was the development of Indian boarding schools. These institutions were usually some distance from reservations and had the mission of acculturating Native American children into mainstream society. A third, more recent factor is the increased urbanization of Native Americans (LaFromboise et al., 1994). Urbanization has removed the protective social network from young Native Americans. In the urban setting, the pre-existing value of natural consequences and learning from one's mistakes occurs without the counterbalancing force of an extended community. Thus, drug and alcohol use as well as other social problems are likely:

> Mary was an 18-year-old woman from a Canadian Cree family, who was referred because of a long history of drug abuse and depression. She reported using marijuana, alcohol, and amphetamines in various combinations since she was 13 years old. Mary's parents separated when she was 3. Her father lived on a reservation with his girlfriend and Mary's three half siblings. Mary's mother lived "in town" about 30 miles from the reservation with Mary's sister and brother. Mary had a 2-year-old child, who had been removed from her care because she was born with drugs in her system. Mary described her pattern of bouncing back and forth from her mother's to her father's home. She stated that now she was no longer welcome back on the reservation because she had "given her child to the White man." Mary spoke in a detached matter-of-fact way about these events, with little apparent emotion.

Conflicting values between White, European norms and those of Native American parents may emerge in distress among Native American adolescents and young adults. Assimilation to mainstream American society is seen as an insult to one's Native American heritage.

Implications for Therapy

Although the relationship context of the Native American client is extremely important for personal identity, the therapist should gather this information in a slow and respectful manner. The Native American client or family is likely to be evaluating the therapist and his or her credibility as much as vice versa. Because of the important role of grandparents, aunts, and other relatives in childrearing, the therapist should not push for boundaries that are culturally incongruent (Attneave, 1982). The family-of-origin approach is often useful as an assessment model. However, historical information should be gathered at a slower pace, and the therapist should develop comfort in obtaining information in a piecemeal manner. A strategy that may engage Native Americans' pride in their heritage is to draw a genogram on a large piece of poster paper while family members assist in filling it in. Countertransference issues among therapists of European background often are rooted in a poor knowledge base. Stereotypes drawn from movies, a day spent on a reservation while vacationing, or reading New Age literature that has appropriated Native American concepts do not equip one to be a culturally sensitive therapist (Attneave, 1982).

AFRICAN AMERICAN FAMILIES

A Historical Perspective

African American families are very difficult to describe as a unitary category. In terms of their cultural background, there are significant differences between families who are recent immigrants from the Caribbean and those who have been in the United States for extended periods. Long-term African American residents of northern U.S. cities may differ from those who have migrated to northern U.S. cities from the southern states. For example, in the midwestern United States, it is very common to see African American families who migrated to large cities such as Chicago 30 to 50 years ago. By contrast, on the east coast of the United States, it is very common to see families from the Caribbean islands such as Jamaica or Haiti. Unfortunately, many of the descriptions of African American families written for therapists have focused exclusively on those residing in the northern inner cities.

The family structure of African American families has often been described as having its historical roots in slavery. It was common for friends or extended family to take in children from other slave families when the parents were sold or killed. Another factor influencing family structure has been the high mortality rate among African American men as well as an ongoing history of employment discrimination. Burgess (1995) noted that the mother–child dyad developed into a central feature of African American family life. Single mothers, however, typically did not live alone. Although slavery played a role in the development of a broader, community-based definition of family, this structure also had a predecessor in the African extended kinship network. This current network often includes fictive kin—"aunts" and "cousins" who are not blood-related, as well as godparents. Godparents often serve as surrogate or back-up parents when other relatives cannot care for a child.

Sociologists in the 1950s and 1960s presented a deficit-oriented view of the African American family. The writing of E. Franklin Frazier (1966) and Daniel Patrick Moynihan's (1965) *The Negro Family: The Case for National Action* typify this perspective. These influential works erroneously emphasized a matriarchal family structure as deficient. This position falsely assumed that the psychologically healthy family consisted of a two-parent household. Furthermore, Moynihan and others blamed the economic deprivation of many African American families on the absence of fathers in the home. There are a number of problems with this contention. First, African American men are often involved in family life, but their role definition may differ from the conventional one. Second, marriage as an institution often has a different meaning in the African American community. Marriage, economically, was not seen as a relationship in which the man was the primary breadwinner. Historically, the poor wages for African American men prevented them from being the primary financial provider for the family (Burgess, 1995). In addition, large numbers of African American women have been in the work force since the early part of the 20th century (Boyd-Franklin, 1989).

African American men have often been a hidden population as far as family therapists are concerned. The descriptions of African American men presented by urban ethnographers have been contradictory. Liebow's (1967) *Talley's Corner: A Study of Negro Street Corner Men* described African American men as engaging in intricate social performances designed to save face over their poor viability in the work place. For example, Liebow noted that a stepfather could often be warmer and more involved with a child than the child's biological father because the child was not the stepfather's responsibility to provide for. *Talley's Corner* presented a view of men coping with poverty and poor self-worth through a series of psychological maneuvers, including brief heterosexual relationships, designed to prevent confrontation with poor economic viability. A contrasting view of African American men as responsible wage earners with a deep sense of commitment to one another was presented by Duneier (1992), who noted that the stable, responsible working-class men he studied are often neglected by the media as well as by urban ethnographers searching for sensationalism.

Family Structure

African American family structures are varied. There are often subfamilies within a larger family system. A young teenager and her boyfriend and infant child may live with a larger family consisting of her mother, aunts, brothers, and sisters (Boyd-Franklin, 1989). Sometimes the family may consist of a mother and her children living with the mother's mother or aunt. Family members that many WASPS might not see for years (cousins, great aunts, etc.) are often considered integral parts of the family. These individuals may be part of the household or they may be relatives relied on in hard times (Stack, 1974). African Americans often do not really retire either; older adults maintain an active valued role at home. It is often the case that an adult's first experience of full-time parenting, where they have most of the childcare responsibility, occurs with their grandchildren.

Nonblood relatives are also very much a part of the family. About half a million African Americans live with families to whom they are not related by marriage, ancestry, or adoption. Adults who are friends or neighbors are often labeled as aunts and uncles, and unrelated children may be labeled cousins. Strong kinship bonds and extended family relationships have historically been very important. "Doubling up"—taking in other children and elderly adults—has a long history (Boyd-Franklin, 1989). There is also considerable pressure not to put up a child for formal adoption. Adoption agencies historically have not catered to non-Whites. In addition, abortion is frowned on; it is seen as a refutation of one's family heritage. An abortion by a 15-year-old girl generates far more criticism than her having a baby. Family reunions are frequently held to bring everyone together. These have particular value as a validating ritual and for maintaining contact among people who would otherwise not see each other on a regular basis.

The Family's Worldview

African Americans often respond to the spirit versus the letter of the law. Rules and social institutions exist to meet personal needs rather than as detached objectives (Greene, 1994a). The context and the ends often justify the means. Again, given the social discrimination African Americans have experienced and the segregationist laws that have maintained them in a disadvantaged position, this "subversive" orientation is understandable. The rational, intellectually oriented Bowenian therapist may have some difficulty with this worldview. An example that commonly occurs in my work setting is that an adolescent will come to a clinic for medical care, accompanied by an aunt or older sibling. Although the patient views the older relative as an appropriate parental surrogate, medical law and clinic policies do not; the parent or legal guardian must authorize nonemergency treatment. When the nurse indicates that treatment cannot proceed without parental authorization, the surrogate may step outside to use the phone and "remember" that he or she was given a note by the parent authorizing the visit.

It is common for adults, relatives, or friends to take in children when parents are unable to care for them. Some reasons for this include teenage mothers who may be developmentally unable to care for a child, the breakup of a relationship, or economic adversity. In these situations, children may be distributed among extended family until the parent (usually the mother) can take them back again.

With extended family members, these caretaking arrangements are often like ledgers. A friend of the mother takes care of the child for a while, and later the friend has an ally if needed for her own child's care.

These situations may lead to conflicts when the terms of the adoption are not spelled out. The informality and flexibility may lead to a series of unspoken family ledgers and obligations, as described by Boszormenyi-Nagy and Spark (1973). The biological parent and the parent who raises the child may disagree about childrearing. For example, an adolescent mother may have her own mother raise her child until she enters her mid-20s, at which point she establishes a relationship and wants her child to live in her new household.

The child, at this point, is 10 years old and has known her grandmother as her mother all of her life. In fact, the child may call the grandmother "mother" and the biological mother by her first name. Although the courts would generally side with the biological mother, these conflicts are rarely settled through formal legal proceedings. The impact on the child may resemble the torn loyalties activated during formal custody conflicts. There may also be conflicts involving the father's family. If paternal grandparents provide some financial support, they often make a claim to the child (Boyd-Franklin, 1989). In addition, the mother and her family may depend on this money but, at the same time, view the father negatively.

African American Women

Greene (1994a) provided a thoughtful analysis of the contradictions facing African American women. The perception of African American families as matriarchal stems in part from a longer history of egalitarianism in gender roles within the household. As noted earlier, there has been a long history of African American women in the work force. African American mothers have likely been blamed for family ills that are more accurately a function of social discrimination and lack of economic opportunity. A common theme for many women is the absence of support. The relative gender imbalance in African American communities may contribute to an acceptance of "sharing" men and infidelity. This, too, should be critically reflected on by the therapist when encountered. Although "man-sharing" may be a function of diminished self-worth, it may also be a practical issue of demographics (Greene, 1994a).

Grandmothers in African American families are central figures for the extended family; they often serve as a switchboard. These women can withstand a lot, but they suffer burnout and may enter therapy extremely depressed. African American women have been socialized into this excessive caretaking role. They may see themselves as having no choice but to take on parenting duties for incarcerated, drug involved, or young adolescent offspring. These burdens are "supposed to be" carried out and may be viewed in a spiritual light (Greene, 1994a).

> Gwendolyn was a 50-year-old African American woman who came to therapy with her four grandchildren, who ranged in age from 2 years to 11 years of age. Two of the children were from Gwen's daughter, who was in prison for drug sales, and the other two children were taken by Gwen after Child Protective Services had found them home alone for 3 days. Gwen also had a 20-year-old son at home. The referral to therapy had been made by the Juvenile Court, which had been involved because the 11-year-old boy had not been attending school. In the office, Gwen appeared irritable and angry and repeatedly spoke sharply to the 2- and 4-year-old children. She reported sleeping poorly, having little energy, and being chronically worried about finances. When asked about her reasons for taking the children, Gwen answered, "What else could I do? If I didn't take them in, the state would put them in a home. They can't take my grandchildren, they're family. It's God's way of helping me do what I didn't do for my own kids."

These women often have a hard time accepting support and are reluctant to engage in therapy directed toward their own needs. At the same time, they are often emotionally overwhelmed and physically exhausted.

Childrearing

Childrearing practices may seem harsh and overly controlling to European American therapists. Children may not be allowed outside of the house. Adolescents may be required to come home directly from school. Affection may appear limited, with strong rebukes more prevalent. There are several practical issues related to these practices. First, the world outside of the family is often viewed as threatening. Parents and grandparents often experience a strong mission to save their children from the drugs, gangs, and teen pregnancy that are highly prevalent in the inner city. Second, the history of discrimination and poverty among many African American families results in parents working to toughen up their children and to prevent them from going soft. Third, there is a view that dealing with children more harshly when they are young will prevent them from dealing with severe consequences of acting out in adolescence, such as being arrested or going to jail (Boyd-Franklin, 1989).

Therapeutic Issues

Mental health services are generally seen as White-oriented institutions and are the source of what may be labeled "healthy cultural paranoia" (Grier & Cobbs,

1968). Mental health agencies may be seen as another social welfare institution, which have been the source of discrimination. In addition, mental health care as it is conventionally known is not generally seen as a natural service to be sought out (Greene, 1994a). In the African American community, extended family members, churches, and even hairdressers are more natural sources for what European Americans perceive as mental health care. Often in mental health settings, African American families are agency referred and may feel considerable pressure to "share family business," which in and of itself violates African American values. It is not uncommon for families to present themselves as single-parent families, and the clinician will not learn for many months of the mother's live-in boyfriend (Boyd-Franklin, 1989). This information is often seen as "nobody's business but our own" and as "not the kind of business you tell on the street."

Intense and direct emotional expression is common. Often, however, there is an oblique quality to these expressions. The real issues are often not addressed directly to the actual source of the conflict but to third parties. Impression management—particularly when dealing with those outside of the extended family— is often a source of frustration to family therapists of European background. There may be a sense of not being able to grasp what is really going on. This apparent vagueness has a long history of adaptive value among African Americans in interacting with White institutions. There is, with good historical reason, distrust of therapists and social service agencies. This seeming obfuscation allows the family to avoid revealing information until the therapist can be sized up and trusted.

As noted earlier, the therapist should be attentive to the extended kinship network as a form of family structure. Thus, an aunt or grandmother may appear for mental health or medical care with the biological mother or the child (or both). It is best for the clinician to treat the senior woman with the same respect as the mother. Often, the biological mother, who may have had the child when she was 15 or 16, cannot provide basic information about the child's development. The grandmother, however, does know this information because she raised the child. This situation also arises in other settings, such as when the child is registering for school. It is a mistake for the clinician to shove the grandmother to the background because she may, from the point of view of daily responsibilities and attachment, really be the parent. As noted earlier, the child may call her "Mamma" or "Big Mamma," and the biological mother is often called by her first name (Boyd-Franklin, 1989). The clinician will often observe that the grandmother will describe a child's problem and that the interaction of the biological mother and the child is more like that of a pair of siblings.

The non-African American mental health professional should raise issues of race directly, asking the client, "How do you feel about working with a _____ therapist?" The therapist should not say that he or she understands the family's experience because that is probably not true. Instead, the therapist should present a willingness and interest in understanding their experience.

Early interventions may focus on structural reallocation of family tasks. Child and adolescent problems often arise because of the absence of clearly spelled-out responsibilities between a grandmother and mother or an older sibling and mother around parenting (Minuchin & Fishman, 1981). Family-of-origin work should probably not be a first-line intervention. Attempts to gather this historical information will often be met with silence or vagueness. These inquiries are often experienced by the family as prying (Boyd-Franklin, 1989). It is usually helpful to wait until some structural or behavioral intervention has been successful. After this initial success, family issues and legacies, such as multigenerational teenage pregnancies, are more likely to be openly discussed.

The family-of-origin therapist should be aware that there are often extensive family secrets. These may include secrets about a child's paternity or a parent's whereabouts. For example, a teenage girl may have a baby and while the baby is very young establish a relationship with a man who behaves like a father to the child. The child is raised believing that this man is his biological father. In other instances, there are secrets around parental abandonment. Often children are protected from the reasons that the mother could not raise them, and often this may be because the mother is involved with drug use or is incarcerated. The therapist needs to earn the family's trust before this information will be shared (Boyd-Franklin, 1989).

HISPANIC FAMILIES

In the United States, Hispanic Americans are a culturally diverse group. The primary countries of origin include Puerto Rico, Cuba, and Mexico. However, there are a number of immigrants from Central and South America as well. Although there are certain cultural characteristics that these groups have in common, there are noteworthy differences as well.

"Character" and *Personalismo*

A potential value conflict between White European society and Hispanic Americans is that self-worth, rather than being based on achievements, is rooted in one's character. Personal success is defined in terms of being honorable and respectful in one's behavior rather than in terms of material acquisition. This *personalismo* is seen as being rooted in the stagnant socioeconomic situation of many Latin American countries (Garcia-Preto, 1982).

In his study of Puerto Ricans, the anthropologist Oscar Lewis (1966) presented this example of the importance of character as a determinant of self-worth:

> I swear that I'm not afraid of any *boss*. If a *boss* curses me or pushes me around I give it right back to him. Let him fire me if he wants to! I won't starve. Once I was working in a shoe factory and a girl named Carmen took some pairs of *Medium* size shoes and sewed them *Small*. When I went to check my work I saw she had thrown two or three pieces of hers in with mine. The *boss* blamed me and said I was stupid. I said he was the stupid one, he and his whole family, and I told him I was an employee, not a slave, because slavery had been abolished long ago. He said I shouldn't answer back and I said, "If you speak to me like that I'll answer back. I don't take that kind of thing from anybody. Not from my own mother."
>
> He told me to punch the clock and get out. I told him I'd punch out when I finished my day's work at four-fifteen and not a minute earlier. And that's what I did. But before I left, I proved to him that Carmen had been the one who had done the bad work. Then he asked me to forgive him. "I forgive the dead, not the living." I told him. None of the other girls dared talk to the *boss* like that. (Lewis, 1966, pp. 213–214)

Cuban value structure varies somewhat from that of other Hispanic immigrant groups. Although *personalismo*—individual integrity and dignity—is important, many immigrant Cuban families also place great value on achievement and formal education (Bernal, 1982).

Among Mexican Americans, *personalismo* may be exhibited through an outward presentation of calm and self-control. This outward demeanor may often be preserved at the expense of emotional expressiveness. Emotionality may be indirectly shown through somatic means, drinking, and angry diatribes toward those representing social exploitation (Garcia-Preto, 1982). A common somatic expression of emotion among Puerto Ricans is the *ataque*. *Ataques* appear as dissociative states in which the person falls on the floor and flails his or her limbs (Abad & Boyce, 1979; Lewis, 1966). This has been interpreted as a culturally acceptable means of affective expression in a culture that places a strong value on self-control.

Family Structure

The family as a unit is very broad and includes nonblood relatives such as godparents and informally adopted children. Children may be temporarily turned over to godparents, aunts, and grandparents for periods of time during family stress. Marriage is seen as a large-scale uniting of two clans rather than as a relationship of two individuals (Chilman, 1982). Hispanic households are governed by shared values, including a respect for authority, a well-defined family hierarchy, a strong sense of connection to immediate community and extended family, and a strong religious orientation (Bernal, 1982; Garcia-Preto, 1982).

Children are most often seen as unique self-directed persons. They are expected to be compliant and "seen but not heard" (Garcia-Preto, 1982). Gender roles are often fairly rigid, with adult women being exclusively in charge of the domestic sphere and men expected to provide financially and make decisions about the family's interactions with extrafamilial persons and agencies. Respect for elders is a paramount value, particularly for children. A serious affront would be for a child to call an adult by his or her first name or make direct eye contact (Chilman, 1993).

Among Puerto Rican and Cuban families in the United States, there is often a cultural tension. Adolescents have come to a country with greater emphasis on individualism and less value on family loyalty. A parental reaction to the Americanization of Puerto Rican youth may be to clamp down and become more authoritative and controlling. This response often results in further disobedience by the adolescent. In the Caribbean an extended family kinship network buffers these conflicts, but this degree of support is often lacking in the United States mainland (Garcia-Preto, 1982).

Gender Roles

Traditional gender roles have been described as rigidly manifested among Hispanic Americans. Men are characterized by *machismo*, an emphasis on strength, reserve, and hypersexuality. Women are viewed as morally superior, spiritual, and as deferring to rules (Vasquez, 1994). This view is likely to be more common among Hispanics of lower socioeconomic status and has been moderated by immigration and women's entry into the work force. In the past, descriptive accounts of Mexican American families have typically highlighted the mother as a "self-sacrificing, ever-fertile woman without aspirations for herself other than to reproduce" (Chilman, 1993, p. 152). Fathers have been characterized as authoritarian and disengaged from the family's daily activities. Research, however, has found less role rigidity and greater egalitarianism than these so-called classic descriptions suggest (Chilman, 1993; Hawkes & Taylor, 1975).

A research study of Mexican American women found that depression was associated with separation and divorce as well as with the lack of a confiding, supportive relationship (Vega, Kolody, & Valle, 1986). This is likely to be exacerbated by immigrant status. Mexicans are likely to come from extended kinship networks that are important sources of social support. Immigration often results in a cut-off from this network, which is likely to contribute to depression.

Immigration and Acculturation

For Puerto Rican and Cuban immigrants, coming to the United States mainland was often viewed as a temporary move, which became an extended stay. Among Cuban immigrant families to the United States, cut-offs from extended families of origin often occurred. For some, immigration occurred in the context of major political differences within families, whereas for others it occurred with a promise of families returning to Cuba when "things settled down" (Bernal, 1982). However, political realities are such that this hoped-for return to Cuba never took place. During the assessment process, it is useful to ask questions about immigration (Bernal, 1982): Who in the family was for and against it? Was the move an escape from other family issues (e.g., intrusive in-laws)? Did family members precede them in the United States? Did the extended family move all at once or did the move occur in stages?

Migration often brings to a halt, accelerates, or adversely affects normal family life-cycle changes. Finding employment or learning a new language and functioning within a new culture often took place at the same time adult children were "launched" or adolescents and parents were negotiating for greater degrees of independence. The strains associated with migration may result in arrested family development.

Unlike Mexican Americans and Puerto Ricans, who can and do regularly return to their country of origin, Cubans have been forcibly cut off. Confounding this situation further is the fact that in the late 1950s and early 1960s many Cubans, particularly middle and upper class families, entered this country with the anticipation of returning to Cuba. They often did not seriously attempt to integrate into mainland United States society. The family functioned in a time warp in which they were de-Cubanized and cultureless (Bernal, 1982). This cultural limbo, however, was often challenged by adolescent children identifying with U.S. mainland culture or with the Cuban culture of the 1950s through interactions with extended family members left behind. Another strategy, perhaps more common among larger extended families who immigrated together, is pseudo-Cubanization. The family functions as if they are still in Cuba immediately prior to immigration (Bernal, 1982).

Therapy Issues

With respect to interactions in therapy, Hispanic Americans are often deferential to authority but may be hesitant to reveal family issues. There is often a push to "do something" in treatment. The therapist may have difficulty maintaining him- or herself outside of the family's emotional field. At the same time, however, the therapist should recognize that the slower paced, detached, and inquiring style of the traditional Bowenian therapist will not be well received by many Hispanic clients. A useful initial approach is a structural intervention that respects existing roles and family boundaries while reorganizing duties. There is a tendency in family-of-origin therapy to view families organized around three generations or extended networks of relatives as inherently disturbed. Review of the writings of Bowen and Framo suggest that an adult who has daily contact with a parent would be viewed as overinvolved and poorly differentiated. It is important for the therapist to remember that with the exception of British American and Northern European families, extended family networks are very common and have a long history.

In working with families from Hispanic backgrounds, the therapist will often find it helpful to obtain a picture of who is currently considered to be part of the family. With this understanding, the therapist may proceed with developing a reallocation of duties and responsibilities among family members. For example, in a three-generation female-headed household, there may be conflict between a child's mother and grandmother about discipline and rules. A Bowenian therapist may see the solution as placing the mother in charge and removing the grand- mother from the disciplining scene. However, this intervention reflects an ethno- centric view of family health. Three-generation and other extended family structures become problematic because of a lack of role clarity. For example, in one household, the grandmother was alone with the children from about 3:00 p.m. until 6:00 p.m., when the mother came home from work. On her arrival home, the mother would attempt to take charge of the children but would be sabotaged by her mother. The sabotage centered around the grandmother's reluctance to relinquish control to her more lenient daughter. The daughter would "bend" the rules that had been established earlier in the day, and the grandmother would protest to her daughter that she was too easy on the children. The initial structural intervention clarified the time that each adult was in charge. The grandmother's rules were in force from the time the children came home from school until 6:00 p.m., when the mother came home from work. Each adult was encouraged to enact any conse- quences for the children during their watch. This reduced the conflict considerably.

The family's status with respect to citizenship and immigration is also impor- tant. Particularly in the southwestern United States, many Hispanic families include unauthorized immigrants. The tension associated with being discovered and deported further exacerbates the family's anxiety and sense of temporariness. The therapist should also assess the degree of acculturation of the family as a unit as well as that of individual family members.

ASIAN AMERICANS

Asian Americans are a very diverse group. This diversity extends to language, culture, and religion and is nicely illustrated by Chao's (1992) description of lunchtime at a Denver community mental health center:

> We were sitting in a makeshift kitchen where the staff crowded in for lunch. The speaker was Laotian. A H'Mong coworker placed a straw basket packed with sticky rice in the center of the table; a Japanese counselor added short-grained rice from a rice cooker; a Chinese American clinician added a bowl of long-grained rice. The different varieties of rice silently spoke to the different philosophical, ethnic, cultural, historical, and religious traditions represented around that table. And yet, we were all considered to be "Asian." (Chao, 1992, p. 158)

Asian is a term that is overly inclusive and homogenizes a number of genuine differences existing between Japanese, Philippinos, Chinese, Laotians, Cambodians, Pacific Islanders, and Koreans. These nationalities do not have a shared culture, religion, or language. Half of all immigrants entering the United States are Asian (Takaki, 1989). Whereas Chinese, Philippinos, Japanese, and Vietnamese are currently the largest Asian groups in the United States, there is increasing immigration by Indonesians, Laotians, Cambodians, Khmer, and H'Mong. These latter groups have received little attention in the mental health literature (Bradshaw, 1994).

Interdependence as a Central Value

Early immigration of Asians to the United States centered around Chinese laborers. People from other Asian cultures immigrated to the United States over time, but with a disproportionate number of men relative to women. Among the Japanese and Chinese, many of the early female immigrants were sold into prostitution. After governmental restriction of selling women into prostitution, a number of Japanese women were sent as "picture brides" (Bradshaw, 1994).

It is difficult to describe Asian American values apart from the value of interdependence with one's family, work setting, and community. Whereas American culture emphasizes standing out through individual initiative and achievement, Asian culture highlights "standing in" through a web of connections with others (Shweder & Bourne, 1982). A value on outwardly harmonious relationships with others underlies the apparent passivity, fatalism, deference to authority, and conformity of Asian Americans. This worldview clashes with Western psychology in general as well as with Bowenian concepts such as differentiation, which place a greater emphasis on individual autonomy than is seen in Asian culture. A web of often unspoken obligations maintains Asian individuals in an ongoing interdependence with their larger social network. Individual actions that are too selfish or that otherwise violate social norms evoke a social response involving sanction and threats to withdraw support (Feiler, 1991).

Communication is often indirect and may seem somewhat evasive and tangential to the Western ear. Ambiguous social situations, such as therapy, may trigger considerable anxiety because the absence of clear role definition provides no guidelines as to expected behavior. Anxiety in these situations stems from making an error, and the Asian client may become quite vigilant as he or she tries to discern what is expected (Shon & Ja, 1982). Direct expressions of anger—particularly toward others—are seen as a serious affront and are particularly inappropriate for women. Fatalism, obedience, and self-restraint are highly valued. Japanese psychotherapies, such as *Morita, Naikan,* and *Zen* place emphasis on self-discipline, gratitude toward one's larger family, and a corresponding sense of shame for ingratitude (Bradshaw, 1994).

Definitions of insider, outsider, public, and private are complicated; *public* may mean extended family or it may include the community. The sense of duty or obligation experienced by members of a family does not have a well-articulated Western equivalent. Terms such as *dependency* and *obligation* do not capture the underlying meaning and felt experience of this aspect of Asian life.

Filial piety—the honor, reverence, and outward respect experienced for and shown toward parents, grandparents, and other adult relatives—is a paramount dimension of family life (Shon & Ja, 1982). Filial piety also extends to extrafamilial authorities, such as teachers, work supervisors, and therapists. This sense of loyalty may be misunderstood by therapists of non-Asian background and misconstrued as denial, avoidance, or familial enmeshment. Openly complaining about, being critical of, or being angry toward a family member is a major violation of filial piety. The family-of-origin therapist will have to reconsider his or her approach, with attention to somatic expressions of psychological issues as well as family metaphors and rituals. One example of a metaphor is the presence of family "ghosts"—members who may have died under trying circumstances (e.g., drowning when fleeing Vietnam). These spirits are, in many respects, real family members who have not yet been laid to their proper rest (Chao, 1992). Therapy may include rituals to complete this cycle.

Being critical of one's parents—even when they are not physically present—is culturally incongruent. Techniques such as Gestalt therapy's empty chair procedure (in which the client openly confronts a parent in absentia) are likely to arouse incredible anxiety among Asian American clients. This respect for parents and extended family should not be regarded as evidence of resistance but should be understood as culturally normative.

Concepts such as differentiation from one's parents are more helpfully translated into accommodation and new forms of interdependence. A common response among Asian American clients who do verbalize concerns about siblings, parents, or in-laws is that the client needs to work on better accepting the situation. Although this agenda may seem inconsistent with the goals of family-of-origin therapy, it is in reality a search for strategies and perspectives for maintaining family engagement while alleviating personal distress. Although the emphasis on interdependence in Asian families may conflict with Western perspectives of mental health, consider also that extended social support networks have often been associated with lower rates of psychopathology. Recent studies with Asians and Asian Americans suggest that they may have less psychological disturbance than European Americans in the United States (Sue, Sue, Sue, & Takeuchi, 1995).

Male–Female Relationships

Historically, marriage has not been seen as a relationship for emotional intimacy. The companionate marriage that is the model of marital well-being in the United States has only recently been given attention in industrialized Asian countries such as Japan. In many Asian societies, such as China, arranged marriages are still practiced. Parents are seen as appropriately having considerable input into the choice of marital partners (Ingoldsby, 1995; Meredith & Abbott, 1995). Even in the absence of arranged marriages, there is often a businesslike interaction between husbands and wives. Feiler (1991) described attending a lavish Japanese wedding and reception in which the bride and groom did not touch each other except to exchange rings. Love was not mentioned.

Asian women are regarded in contradictory terms by Americans. Although characterized as demure, shy, and erotic, they are also seen as manipulative and untrustworthy. However, Asian women are also viewed as asexual automatons— a perspective conveyed by newsreel footage and magazine photos of Asian women hard at work tilling fields or laboring in factories (Bradshaw, 1994).

Although women have historically been perceived as subordinate, views of male–female relationships vary somewhat across differing Asian ethnicities. Chinese couples often feature men attempting to give women the perception— albeit illusory—of control through outward agreement, although men have the final word. Vietnamese men perceive a greater sense of authority and dominance in relation to their wives, and Laotian and Khmer relationships show even greater power imbalances. Extramarital relationships among men and forced sex within marriage may be viewed as male prerogatives (Bradshaw, 1994). Even in affluent societies such as Japan, there are fairly rigid gender roles. Men are often relatively uninvolved in the domestic sphere. Japanese workers spend 11.5% more time on the job than their American counterparts. Until recently, nearly 75% of Japanese workers were on the job during weekends (Hinkelman, 1994). Socializing for Japanese businessmen often takes the form of drinking or playing golf with coworkers. Women are charged with raising children, with particular emphasis on preparing them for the rigorous entry exams for schools (Feiler, 1991).

Therapy Issues

There is a fairly solid body of research supporting a reluctance by Asian Americans to use mental health services and to admit to psychological distress. Because of the strong ties to family, seeking mental health services is more than an individual act—it is a reflection on the nuclear and often the extended family. Thus, problems may be fairly far progressed before an individual or family formally seeks services.

Cultural beliefs are also likely to influence the therapy process. Whereas the North American mental health community views the psychological and biomedical domains as fairly distinct, this dualism is not nearly as extreme among Asians (Kleinman, 1988). Psychological problems are also more likely to be seen as character defects—specifically, a lack of willpower. Verbal expressiveness is highly valued among North American psychotherapists. However, among many Asians, silence is an indication of respect (Bradshaw, 1994). Asian clients often have treatment goals that differ from those of Western therapists. Asian clients look to therapy to strengthen their will and help them be better, more obedient sons, daughters, or spouses. This goal often conflicts with family-of-origin therapy's emphasis on individual well-being and self-directedness as treatment objectives. However, the approach to assessment discussed in chapter 2 is often culturally congruent with Asian clients. The emphasis on placing the individual client in a family context is one that Asian Americans see as very relevant. The client is likely to be able to provide considerable factual information about family members over multiple generations. However, it may be very difficult for the therapist to determine how the client feels about different family members as well as which relationships are close and which are conflictual. Intimacy itself often has a different meaning and value among Asian Americans. Family roles are seen as those involving duties and obligations rather than affective experiences. Distress among Asian Americans is likely to be linked to a sense of shame or guilt in relation to a parent or a conflict between Asian and American values and behavioral expectations:

> A Japanese American social work student was seen in consultation. The student was training in a family service agency. The student's practicum supervisor had referred the young woman with the following description: "She can't seem to relate

to people—particularly when working with couples or families. She is polite, pleasant and respectful, but won't take charge of the interview, reflect feelings, or confront when necessary." The student exhibited a similar demeanor with the therapist. The therapist provided her with published descriptions of Asian families in a mental health context. By discussing issues such as respect for authority, the role of affect in therapy, and cultural views of men and women, the student was able to explore and understand the role of these issues in therapy. At the same time, she began to recognize that this respectful, sensitive approach was helpful with a wide range of families but might need to be complemented with more directness when families were highly conflictual or in crisis.

As this case illustrates, therapists of differing cultural and ethnic backgrounds should be aware of how their own social norms may impact treatment of clients from various cultural groups. In this example, expanding the therapist's technical repertoire was an easier process when her cultural heritage was taken into account.

ARAB AMERICANS

Increasingly, Arab immigrants from countries such as Syria, Jordan, Palestine, Iraq, Egypt, and Lebanon are entering the United States. Although some of these immigrants are Muslim, others are Christian. In coming to the United States, many Arabs have considerable difficulty finding employment. This is particularly true for professionals, who experience a substantial decline in social status and lifestyle when they are unable to obtain comparable positions in this country (Budman, Lipson, & Meleis, 1992).

Upper class Arabs who have come to the United States from Iraq and Iran may have plans to return if there are changes in the government. It is difficult for these immigrants to become rooted in the United States because it is viewed as a temporary refuge until the political climate in their home countries becomes more hospitable. However, there is considerable ambiguity about if and when a return will occur. In particular, families with children are in a cultural limbo. Adolescents often identify with Western dress, music, and dating patterns, which clash with traditional Islamic values.

Family Worldview

Individual identity is deemphasized in Arab culture compared with the United States. Meeting social obligations and being part of a group—be it a community or family—is the primary definition of person within Arab culture (Budman et al.,

1992). Individual initiative and goals are pursued only if they are congruent with family needs and expectations.

Persons of Middle Eastern background are likely to be more outwardly emotionally expressive than Westerners. Men and woman readily exhibit outward displays of anger, sadness, and happiness. Social greetings between members of the same sex may include hugging and kissing (Jalali, 1982). Communication within families is often indirect; family members often implicitly know what is expected of them. There are few direct confrontations or demands between children and parents or husbands and wives.

Traditional family structure is patriarchal, with sons, their wives, and their children often living in a large compound. Fathers typically have substantial authority over family decisions. There is an implicit agreement that, in return for providing materially for the family, the father will receive obedience and respect. The woman's established role in the family is to manage the home and children. Obedience toward her husband is expected. However, women hold covert power. Close emotional ties with children are developed, and the mother may serve as a mediator between the father and child, often indirectly softening his authoritarian stances. The son's close relationship with his mother continues after his marriage, and a man's competing loyalties to his parents and his wife are a common source of conflict. Brothers often assume a patriarchal role in relation to their sisters. In cases of divorce or death of a husband, a brother assumes the role of protector over his adult sister (Jalali, 1982).

The adolescent period of individuation is considerably muted compared with adolescence in the West. The separation of adolescents from their parents is of far less magnitude than described by family-of-origin theorists. Because roles are determined in early childhood, latitude for self-expression is far more limited. Although there are fluctuations in how attachment to one's parents takes place, there is no major emancipation process as in the West. Young men have the mission of assisting their father, and women's marriages are largely oriented toward maintaining and enhancing family honor (Budman et al., 1992).

Marriage is viewed as a relationship for the purpose of having children. Devotion to one's children is a strong value in Arabic culture. However, marriage is viewed differently than in the West. The companionate marriage, in which spouses have an emotionally intimate relationship, is not the model in Middle Eastern countries. Marriages are often arranged, with husband and wife having little prior contact before the wedding.

Patterns of socializing further illustrate the utilitarian view of marriage. Couples often do not socialize as a unit. When groups of married couples come together for recreational purposes, men go off as a group and women socialize as a group. Women look to female peers, mothers, and sisters for emotional closeness, and men tend to bond with male friends and brothers.

Arab families are unlikely to see therapy as a modality for addressing problems. Mental illness is often expressed physically through fatigue or pain (Budman et al., 1992; Kleinman, 1977). These symptoms often are usefully understood as a metaphoric expression of interpersonal conflict. Because of this, little has been written about therapy with individuals of Arabic background. However, given the increase in immigration from Arab countries and the number of Arabic children growing up in this county (and the resulting stresses), family conflicts are likely to arise.

EUROPEAN AMERICANS

Among Americans of European background, there is considerable ethnic diversity. The European countries from which many Americans originally immigrated have very heterogenous customs, psychological worldviews, and family dynamics.

German Americans

German Americans are often fiercely independent. Productive activity is a paramount value, and free time is usually spent in accomplishing household tasks. In traditional gender role relationships, the husband may spend his weekends and evenings maintaining the car or yard or renovating a house, while the wife is cleaning, cooking, and doing laundry. Although these activities sound typical for an American family, German Americans tend to approach them with intensity. In my city, St. Louis, a running joke is that German women scrub their front walks with toothbrushes while their husbands manicure the lawn with hand shears.

With this emphasis on control and activity, German Americans may appear emotionally constricted. Emotionality is seen as an irrational and chaotic phenomenon that should be kept in check. Repression and denial are fairly common intrapsychic defenses. As a result, people of German background often have difficulty when dealing with stressors around painful events such as sudden death or loss, especially situations that evoke strong affect.

Childrearing often centers around obeying rules and completing assigned tasks, with an absence of playfulness between parents and children. Although there is a deep underlying attachment between husbands and wives and between children and parents, this is often difficult for the non-German outsider to perceive because of the family's stoicism. Members stay connected through an almost ritualized schedule of eating, church-going, and recreation, which occur at regularly appointed times and days. Relationships between parents may have a businesslike appearance. The marriage may appear to the outsider more like a work partnership than a relationship that includes any sort of intimate romantic sharing (Winawer-Steiner & Wetzel, 1982). A number of people have described a rigid role distinction within German families, with the father being authoritarian and stern and the mother being more subservient and deferential. Parental roles show a rigid compartmentalization of function, with mother being the nurturer and father the disciplinarian. Fairness is in general a much stronger value for parents than is warmth (Winawer-Steiner & Wetzel, 1982).

German Americans value personal independence and their ability to take care of themselves and their immediate families. Seeking outside help is difficult for members of this ethnic group. Dependence is poorly tolerated. Cancer may be too far advanced for chemotherapy before a German American shows up at a doctor's office. Similarly, when German Americans experience psychological problems, these are likely to be very serious by the time they seek outside mental health assistance.

> Frank, an 85-year-old German American man, was referred to a therapist by a visiting nurse. Frank was reporting difficulty swallowing, was very preoccupied with his health, and constantly complained of being weak. His wife had died 10 years earlier. Frank reported some concerns about whether he and his wife had been close. He stated that they often spent their evenings seated side-by-side in matching easy chairs watching television. Although Frank maintained contact with his only child—a daughter—as well as with his grandchildren, he stated that typically they spoke briefly on the phone about mundane daily activities. He said that he had stopped talking to his daughter about his health concerns because she usually changed the subject abruptly. To the therapist, Frank appeared anxious. Frank would often bring in scrapbooks, which featured commendation letters from superiors and awards that he had won at work. He always brightened up when speaking about how he had "whipped into shape" a division within a large company. He became visibly anxious, with observable shortness of breath when he mentioned his fear of going to a nursing home. The underlying theme of losing his independence exacerbated his anxiety and actually incapacitated him further, so that placement was a greater likelihood. The more Frank attempted to control his symptoms through more detailed monitoring, the worse he felt.

Because of the legacy of World War II, there is still some reluctance among older German Americans to acknowledge their ethnic heritage. There was a period in the United States in which discussion of German heritage was discouraged and German Americans were often suspect and seen as spies or collaborators with the enemy (Winawer-Steiner & Wetzel, 1982). Thus, the therapist may encounter an uneasy silence or a response such as "We're all Americans now anyway" when ethnicity is raised. As noted above, health problems are often a medium of communicating distress. However, the clinician may become frustrated by these expressions of illness because nothing seems to be done about the health problem. Nevertheless, German Americans will want something done in therapy. Thus, the family-of-origin therapist should attempt to address immediate distress through a direct behavioral intervention. With this as a foundation, facilitating more direct and frequent communication between family members will often counter the individual isolation that is an underlying theme among German Americans.

Italian Americans

Italian Americans tend to be emotionally expressive, and exhibiting a range of strong feelings is normative. From a WASP perspective, Italian Americans seem to be fighting all the time. In Irish or German families, these conflicts would be the basis of a significant cut-off. But within the Italian family, 5 minutes later everyone is happy again. Another aspect of this emotionality is that often it does not seem to be grounded. There may be an intense emotional expression, including yelling and screaming. Several hours later, the family and friends may come back together as if nothing had happened previously. The ethnocentric therapist may make the mistake of pathologizing these expressions as histrionic. In addition, the seeming failure to process and resolve these disputes to a point of closure is likely to be puzzling and frustrating to the therapist.

Among Italian Americans, individual identities are rooted in a social network; what's important is who one knows, not what one does. Personal independence or achievement is accepted if it does not conflict with one's primary duty and loyalty to the family (Rotunno & McGoldrick, 1982). Italians have two words for walls— one for the internal walls of a building and one for the walls on the outside of a building. This is an apt metaphor for the Italian family's distinction between what goes on within the family and what can be shown to outsiders. Within the family, a wide range of emotions is acceptable, and feelings are often expressed with intensity and directness. However, when dealing with persons outside the family, significantly more control is required. It is almost like a theater in which anything goes backstage, but onstage one must play a role. The role centers around the pre-eminent value of loyalty to the family (Rotunno & McGoldrick, 1982).

Particularly among families from the more rural and less cosmopolitan regions of southern Italy, households are more likely to be traditionally organized. Gender role stereotypes are common, with women being more responsible for domestic chores and men for financial support. However, both fathers and mothers are involved with their children and extended network of relatives. Work is not seen as a vehicle for individual achievement but as a necessary way of supporting the family. Families will often have businesses together so that work and family life do not have to be exclusive.

Marriage is viewed as a permanent commitment with associated and historical legacy. In addition, marriage is not a pairing of two people but instead is the uniting of two large clans (Rotunno & McGoldrick, 1982). Extended family members often see themselves as having a right to have considerable input into one's choice of a marriage partner.

Therapy is not likely to be readily sought out. Psychological symptoms are likely to be expressed somatically (Zborowski, 1969). Even when difficulties are labeled as emotional, Italian Americans are likely to seek help through the extended family or the church. Therapists should be attuned to the likelihood that emotional conflicts stem from difficulties reconciling individual goals or values with family loyalty. Movement toward greater independence from the family of origin through marriage outside of the community or through educational and career achievement will often be profoundly threatening to the family. The high degree of ethnic emotionality, together with this threat, will likely provoke considerable reactivity on the part of family members. The goal for the therapist is to help the individual seeking these goals to stay engaged and renegotiate his or her relationship with family members. The therapist should be alert to the likelihood of cut-offs or the adult's giving up his or her goals in response to family pressure.

Irish Americans

Among Irish Americans, there is an expectation that much of life will be demanding and unpleasant. This is probably related to the significant poverty that characterized Ireland (McGoldrick, 1982). Irish Americans tend toward stoicism. Feelings that individuals have toward each other, particularly among family members, are managed indirectly. These expressions may take the form of humor and at times sarcasm. Irish American Catholics tend to be talkative and often convey important issues through stories. To the non-Irish observer, these stories may seem vague or disconnected, but they often contain important themes such as the untrustworthiness of men or the harshness of life. Repression and denial are common defenses. Irish Americans do not manage strong affect well, particularly in relation to outsiders. They tend to "underground" their feelings, particularly anger. There is generally an emphasis on presentation of a good front to outsiders. Thus, it may take the therapist some time to understand what is actually going on within the family. Family ties may not appear evident to the outsider. Family members have a sense of duty to one another out of a largely unlabeled experience of what one is supposed to do as a family member. Individual pride and outward praise for a family member's accomplishments are discouraged (McGoldrick,

1982). Those on the receiving end of an award or compliment will rapidly discount it.

Women are the predominant influence in Irish family life. They are viewed as stable, self-sacrificing, and able to handle a wide range of challenges. Men, on the other hand, have been characterized as relatively disengaged from ongoing family life. Men are often characterized as rambunctious little boys who are not responsible. Marriage is not seen as a source of emotional intimacy. Given the above characterization, distance between men and women is expected. Conflicts and differences are often not directly addressed but lead to an alienated distancing between husband and wife (McGoldrick, 1982).

Warmth toward children may not be apparent to the outsider because it often takes the form of teasing. There is often a strong competitiveness between the children in Irish families. Appearances are also important, with considerable emphasis being placed on being polite and respectable. Guilt induction, often with religious or moral overtones, is a common mode of discipline. In contrast to many of the other ethnic groups described, the extended family is not usually a source of closeness. Cut-offs, together with a strong respect for privacy, result in the nuclear family's being isolated. Reaching out to the extended family for support at crisis points is not as common among Irish families (McGoldrick, 1982).

Irish Americans tend to view mental health problems as a source of shame and guilt. Although conjoint family therapy with a behavioral or strategic emphasis may be helpful for child-focused problems, the more exploratory family-of-origin approach is unlikely to be met with cooperation when families are convened conjointly. Bowenian-style coaching, however, in which one person is worked with individually, can be very useful (McGoldrick, 1982). The isolation of family members from one another and the presence of cut-offs can be addressed by helping the Irish American client alter his or her behavior in one-to-one interactions. The therapist should be aware, however, that many of these cut-offs may have their origins several generations back.

Jewish Families

Jewish families are defined through both religion and ethnicity—the two dimensions are so strongly interwoven that they cannot be disentangled. Thus, Jewish families are discussed in this chapter as an ethnic group. The majority of American Jews come from Eastern Europe (Herz & Rosen, 1982). Recently, large numbers of Jews from the former Soviet Union have also immigrated to the United States.

People of Jewish background express feelings, but they also place a high value on analyzing their emotional expressions. Carping, criticism of others, and complaining are all acceptable. This is a common manner of discourse. For the therapist from a WASP background, the carping and criticism may sound harsh, but a useful analogy is watching television with the sound turned off. The words often are not terribly meaningful. The carping and complaining is simply a mechanism for conveying concern to family members.

Intellectual accomplishment and financial success are important values in Jewish households. As such, pleasure is not an end in itself but should be associated with some goal or achievement (Herz & Rosen, 1982). In part, this attitude may stem from the long history of persecution that Jews have experienced such that suffering is an expected part of life. Family loyalty is very important, as is ethnic loyalty. One important Jewish myth described by Friedman (1982) is the myth of the *shiksa*. Shiksas are non-Jewish women, who seduce Jewish men into marriage. They are viewed with distrust if not downright paranoia and are seen as threats to the man's ethnic and religious origins as well as to his family.

Intermarriage is seen as an affront to one's family and to one's ethnic background and may provoke a cut-off. Marriage, in general, is viewed as a uniting of two families. Parents routinely render strong premarital opinions about an adult child's choice of a mate. Until recent years, there have been fairly pervasive gender stereotypes among Jewish couples. Women's success was measured by how well they married (i.e., by their husband's financial achievement). Fathers often worked excessively, and their physical presence at home was minimal (Pogrebin, 1991). Men's self-worth is closely tied to their ability to provide well for children and spouse. Wives have been socialized to care for their husbands while simultaneously expecting to be cared for (Featherman, 1995). Boundaries between parents and children are fairly fluid. This fluidity also extends to married adults and their parents and siblings. Even the choice to have children is based on an implicit commitment or the experience of guilt in relation to parents ("My mother kept telling me how all her friends had grandchildren but that her stingy daughter wouldn't give her any"). Parenting often combines pressure to succeed with a high level of support, at times bordering on indulgence (Herz & Rosen, 1982).

Family-of-origin work is well received by Jewish individuals, couples, and families. This style of treatment, with its emphasis on analysis of historical patterns, is congruent with Jewish expectations of therapy. Therapy is expected to be a long-term process in which emotions are important but also in which considerable energy is spent toward understanding what these feelings mean. Complicated formulations that include multiple perspectives are particularly compatible with the intellectualism and cognitive complexity of Jewish clients. The characters played by Woody Allen, who have typically been in analysis for decades, are little more than an exaggeration of this value. Although Jewish clients approach treatment from a Bowenian perspective, there are situations in which this may be a hindrance.

For example, Jewish families may divert the therapist from appropriate action by their emphasis on talk and analysis. Issues such as limit setting with children or with aging parents are very difficult to keep in focus because the family wants to process limits from multiple vantage points rather than simply taking action (Giordano & Carini-Giordano, 1995). A key conflict that is likely to contribute to distress among Jewish clients involves separation and appropriate boundaries in relation to the family of origin. Common patterns include balancing educational and financial success with obligation to one's parents or spouse and the maintenance of appropriate boundaries around the marriage in relation to the family of origin.

WASP Families

In terms of ethnic origins, WASP families reflect the structure of British families. They tend to be very distance sensitive. Families are sets of individuals. There is considerable emphasis on personal space and individual identity. Of all the family structures that have been discussed, the WASP family emphasizes the individual against a collectivist backdrop. WASP families are the model of family life that is seen as traditionally American. They are often portrayed as the "normal" family in movies, television, and advertisements. It is often difficult for many therapists from a WASP background to see WASPs as having a set of cultural rules like other ethnic groups.

Persons of British (WASP) background, because of their individualist emphasis, are reluctant to involve others when challenged or overwhelmed. There is an emphasis on logic and rationality. Intense displays of emotionality are uncomfortable to observe and are often dismissed as hysterical. Emotions are often seen as uncontrollable, unpredictable forces—something to be tamed or kept in check. Given that WASP values predominate in the United States, it should not be surprising that the mental health community has readily adopted cognitive therapy. The cognitive approach of Beck (1976) and the rational–emotive approach of Ellis (1962) are very congruent with the WASP view of therapy as a technical process. In addition, these therapies emphasize cognition as a force to manage affect.

WASPs have a very pragmatic orientation to life. Family dinners, for example, are often opportunities to review individual members' activities rather than enjoy the food. Hard work, clear goals, and organization are seen as the keys to a satisfying life. There is an emphasis on hobbies, work, and other forms of activity over human relationship. Because of the built-in value of independence, difficulty managing emotional cut-offs is very common.

Denial, secrecy, and minimization (sweeping it under the rug) are common strategies for managing difficult issues. In cases of sexual abuse or alcoholism, there is often greater anger toward the party who uncovers or confronts the problem than concern about the affected family member. Because of the emphasis on personal responsibility and self-control, WASPs who are victimized often feel that they brought it on themselves (Schmidt, 1995).

With this emphasis on self-control, independence, and self-reliance, activity becomes a common way of managing external stress. WASP families, particularly men, have a difficult time being dependent and emotionally close. This is a common complaint in marital therapy with WASP families. Typically, a wife will say, "I don't feel close to my husband, he doesn't share." The husband often responds, "Close, what do you mean? We sleep together, we eat together, how much closer can you get?" Marriage is viewed as a contract between two people. If one party does not fulfill the contract sexually, financially, or otherwise, divorce is perfectly acceptable. There are often polite relationships between spouses and their in-laws but no real sense of closeness. Again, this pattern generally mirrors how outsiders are dealt with—politely, yet kept at a distance (McGill & Pearce, 1982).

Childrearing is seen as a set of techniques—a scientific enterprise. It is not surprising that childcare books have been so successful in the United States. These expert-authored guides provide a technical rationale for parenting success. Peer group activity by children and adolescents is strongly supported. Sports, clubs, and classes in dance and foreign languages all support the values of competition, achievement, and doing. These activities are often action oriented, with social interaction secondary. As McGill and Pearce (1982) noted, these childhood activities often serve as the basis for the golf quartets, bridge clubs, and other recreational groups that WASPs engage in as adults. These activity groups usually foster superficial yet constant relationships.

Stein and Pontious (1985), in their description of Midwestern farm families, noted that receiving health care is not for the purposes of well-being or improved life satisfaction but so that one can work. Surgeries are timed to occur during winter months, when farming demands are lower. Mental health care among Midwestern farmers was seen as impractical and as a source of stigma. The preferred coping style for psychological distress was to deny and minimize its impact. Keeping up appearances is an important value. In interactions with mental health professionals, the work ethic often takes over. For example, one WASP man that I was treating asked whether he would get over his problem twice as fast if sessions could be 2 hours instead of 1. The relationship aspects of therapy tend to be downplayed, and dependence on others is not well tolerated.

WASPs are likely to enter treatment with the goal of increasing personal control. Expectations of treatment are that it is technologically oriented, goal directed, and will help resolve a specific issue. Bowenian coaching and family-of-origin work is particularly well-suited to persons of British or WASP background (McGill & Pearce, 1982). It is intellectually oriented and somewhat didactic in practice. The concept of the well-differentiated adult—independent and self-directed, with a clear set of goals—is an almost exact fit with the WASP ideal. However, Bowen (1978) emphasized the complementary importance of meaningful engagement with family members. This latter dimension is often lacking in WASP families. Isolation, emotional sterility, and a sense of stoic loneliness often predominates. Bowen's coaching methods, emphasizing the establishment of one-to-one relationships with members of the family of origin, counteract this disengagement. In addition, once clients understand how these patterns emerged in the family of origin and are able to alter these interactions, they may be able to translate these insights into their marriage and relationship with their children. The cognitive emphasis of Bowen's approach also prevents the overload of strong affect that WASPs fear.

CONCLUSION

Family-of-Origin Theory Across Cultures

Although family-of-origin theorists view the individual as a product as well as an ongoing member of a social context, they have paid little attention to the role of ethnic and cultural factors. Emotional and intellectual functioning, as well as separateness and togetherness, are useful in understanding persons in their family system, but culture exerts a powerful influence on the normative balance of these dimensions. The major theoreticians of historical and depth-oriented approaches to treatment have usually been White men of European background.

As noted earlier, WASP therapists in general are likely to underplay ethnic and cultural differences. With the exception of McGoldrick (1982, 1995), family-of-origin therapy has featured an absence of reflection on the cultural relativity of values (Schmidt, 1995). The Bowenian polarities appear to be relevant across all cultures. Different ethnic groups can be placed at differing points on the emotional–intellectual and separateness–togetherness continua. Outward emotionality is far more common among Italian Americans and other ethnic groups from Mediterranean Europe. Northern Europeans and those of British and Irish descent tend to be far more intellectualized. The relative emphasis on separateness while staying socially engaged that is viewed as the model of health in Bowen's theory is more problematic cross-culturally.

In all but Western society, individuals are highly connected to their family context. The family of origin is often the most important context for adults—more salient than marital partner or vocation. Even among European cultures, there is considerable variability in the normative degree of physical and psychological distance that adults have with their families of origin.

However, some type of differentiation process appears to take place in all cultures. Support for this position comes from family research and anthropological studies of adolescents. The process of separation from parents occurs in some fashion in all cultures, but the course, context, and meaning of the adolescent's move toward autonomy varies. In many societies, rather than a lessening of parental and extended family influence, early adulthood is characterized by a redefining of relationships.

Assimilation and Acculturation

As noted in discussing several of the specific ethnicities, a complicating factor is the immigration process itself. Within a family, members may differ in the extent to which they have assimilated (absorbed the dominant culture's values) or acculturated (selectively taken on the dominant culture's values). In addition, the immigration process itself often includes a historical legacy. A sense of obligation, or ledger, may create an indebtedness among immigrant families. Unless these issues are directly probed by the therapist, the presenting family difficulties may not be adequately understood. Obligations incurred several generations previously may be called in. When a family immigrates, the debt may take the form of requiring an immigrating family to take with them a child from an overburdened mother, a child from an extramarital liaison, or a mentally ill relative. The guilt over leaving members behind or the sense of obligation to pay back funds required for the immigration may be carried over into a financial obligation by the immigrant family.

Cross-cultural marriages are often rooted in ethnically based differences of the spouses. The Italian American man finds the British American woman to be solid, predictable, polite and dignified, unlike his brash, intrusive, and hysterical family of origin. She, in turn, is drawn to his ability to be spontaneous, free with his feelings, and socially affable. At the same time that this complementarity draws spouses to one another, it can be the source of many conflicts. In the above example, the intensity and emotional expressiveness of the Italian husband may at times be overwhelming for his wife, who shuts down and withdraws. He may, in turn, accuse her of being cold, rigid, and unfeeling. The blame and anger in these marriages can rapidly be defused by the culturally sensitive therapist who is able to describe the unspoken ethnic worldviews that are being enacted by each spouse.

The Therapist's Ethnicity and Cultural Heritage

Attention to the therapist's own ethnic and cultural background is an important element of family-of-origin work. Much of what therapists label as resistance stems from a cultural disjunction between the therapist's views of health and the content of therapy itself and the family's ethnic worldview (Giordano & Carini-Giordano, 1995). Although psychodynamically oriented therapists have traditionally been aware of countertransference issues, these have usually involved intrapsychic rather than sociocultural dynamics. Many therapists are of upper middle-class background and often emphasize universalism (Giordano & Carini-Giordano, 1995) and the homogeneity of American culture. For therapists wishing to develop a deeper understanding of distinct cultures, there is a growing body of non-mental health literature that is extremely useful. Sources include ethnographic studies and sociological work, as well as novels, short stories, and movies that depict different ethnic groups.

Chapter 8

Religion, Spirituality, and the Family

There appears to be a rekindling of interest in spirituality in the United States. For many, this resurgence is likely to stem from a dissatisfaction and accompanying malaise with materialism as well as individualism. Much of religion and spirituality comes from a realm of experience that stands outside of psychology and family dynamics. Although it exerts a salient role in family life, spirituality cannot be understood in terms of boundaries, emotionality, and concepts such as differentiation. However, religious traditions do differ around the extent to which the individual is emphasized versus being viewed as an interdependent member of a holistic universe.

For example, Christianity in general and the Protestant faith in particular stress individual accountability for moral transgressions and individual activity (good works) as important dimensions. Islam emphasizes the importance of adhering to a specific code of conduct, with an emphasis on avoiding transgressions. A holistic perspective in which people are united with one another and the natural world is a tenet of many Asian and Native American beliefs. These religions, rather than stressing personal accountability, highlight a harmonious balancing of the individual with his or her surroundings. This distinction between an indexical (person-centered) and referential (collectivist) orientation (Falkenhain & Lowry, 1995) is a useful distinction for the family-of-origin therapist to consider when including an individual's or family's religious life in the assessment process.

Although there is a growing literature on ethnic and cultural diversity in family therapy and mental health, there has been relatively little direct attention to religion. Religion is occasionally addressed in discussions of family transitions such as marriage and death. The norms for several of the cultural groups described in the previous chapter are strongly influenced by religion. For example, with the growing influence of Islam in the Middle East, religious dimensions have become interwoven with Arabic culture—particularly around issues such as marriage, divorce, and gender roles.

135

Several recent articles have appeared addressing the role of religion in family therapy (Prest & Keller, 1993; Stander, Piercy, MacKinnon, & Helmke, 1994). Yet little attention has been devoted to the role that religion plays in shaping fundamental family values that, like ethnicity, are often transmitted across multiple generations. Although religion is formally communicated through the teachings of institutions such as the synagogue, church, or mosque as well as through rituals and holy days, the family plays a fundamental role in interpreting religion for daily life. In addition, culture interacts with religion and how it is interpreted. For example, Catholicism is perceived and understood differently in Irish, Italian, and Hispanic cultures. Religion's importance to Americans is evident through surveys showing that two thirds view religion as an important part of their lives (Bergin, 1991; Religion in America, 1985). Therapists, as a whole, are somewhat less religious than the general population. Of four different mental health professions surveyed, marriage and family therapists were the most likely to report regular attendance at religious services. Despite the importance of religion to Americans at large, only 29% of mental health professionals surveyed viewed religious content as an important dimension of therapy (Bergin, 1991).

As Bergin's (1991) survey suggests, spirituality and religion are usually removed from the realm of therapy. Spiritual dimensions are often seen as soft and subjective in a field that is attempting to establish itself as scientific. The somewhat detached and intellectualized approach to treatment described by Bowen and Framo may have difficulty incorporating the unseen, unverifiable assumptions of religion. Bowenian theory, through its links with central nervous system functioning and sociobiology, attempts to relate its principles to empirical knowledge. Religion, by its very nature, deals with unseen phenomena that guide individual, marital, and family life through beliefs and values that are experienced but often not well articulated. As Prest and Keller (1993) pointed out, family therapy concepts such as boundaries, differentiation, reactivity, and even rules have been reducible to measurement and even quantification. However, dimensions such as divine intervention, grace, and spiritual energy fall outside the realm of verification through sensory data.

Another factor contributing to the banishment of religion from therapy is that it often has been viewed as an oppressive force that has been emotionally harmful. Clients frequently describe being obsessed with anxious guilt around conflicts regarding religious teachings and experiences such as masturbation, premarital sex, or impure thoughts. The doctrines of certain fundamentalist Christian and Muslim sects that have supported physical punishment of children, women's subservience to men, and scrupulosity have been seen as antithetical to sound mental health. Even mainstream American religious faiths such as Catholicism and many Protestant denominations emphasize one's underlying obligation to be sensitive and responsive to other's needs—including family members, neighbors, and one's fellow human beings in general. This interpersonal commitment has often been seen as oppressive to individuals and in opposition to the prevailing mental health philosophy, which emphasizes personal fulfillment through being true to oneself. Therapists in Western countries have often admonished clients to "take care of yourself" and to cast off the yoke of social obligations. A frequent therapeutic question to clients is "Who are you doing this for?" The client who responds with "my wife/husband/mother/father/son/daughter" is immediately exhorted to think about "what do you need to do for yourself?"

Doherty (1993, 1995) recently pointed out that family and marital therapy, in particular, are embedded in a moral matrix. Although being nonjudgmental has been the revered stance among psychotherapists, this acceptance of all manner of behaviors even when they have moral consequences often leads to a moral nihilism. A young mother who leaves her husband and 3-year-old child to "find out who she is" may be supported in this quest by her therapist. This support is often provided automatically and reflexively without considering the impact of the mother's choice on her child. In contrast to Japanese models of psychotherapy, which often include a social obligation to others, American therapies are rooted in the values of individualism and self-interest (Bellah, Madsen, Sullivan, Swidler, & Tipton, 1985). By working in a value-free vacuum, therapists have little to guide them when they encounter dilemmas involving moral behavior. In fact, many therapists routinely say that these issues fall outside of psychotherapy and should be handled by the clergy. This compartmentalization often results in a cost–benefit analysis when addressing issues such as an adult's responsibilities to one's parents, spouse, or children. Rather than the tally sheet questions— "What are you getting out of this relationship?; Are you getting enough out of your marriage to warrant what you're putting in?"—therapy should incorporate a respect for maintaining relationships because of one's reverence for family and marriage as institutions. Many couples who may appear less than compatible or who exhibit ongoing conflict may be implicitly guided toward divorce by a therapist who does not appreciate the couple's religious heritage. Many religions such as Judaism and Catholicism view marriage as a sacred institution. This respect for marriage, which has been handed down intergenerationally, is a constant presence that can weather considerable day-to-day discord between husband and wife.

Perhaps a stronger moral challenge to the therapist comes from religious faiths that have taken absolutistic stances on issues such as gender roles and discipline of children. Most marital and family therapists would agree that compartmentalized traditional gender roles and corporal punishment of children are psychologically harmful. Families of Islamic as well as certain Christian fundamentalist faiths may, however, operate from these positions. Doherty (1995) suggested that these dilemmas may be addressed from a therapeutic position midway between absolutism and complete relativism. In the case of physical discipline of children, a combination of openness to understanding the family's religious beliefs, which includes consultation with church elders (Dixon & Kixmiller, 1992), together with factual, legal, and psychological information about the adverse impact of this practice will be helpful.

Because religion is often inextricably intertwined with culture and ethnicity, its unique role is often not directly apparent to the mental health professional. One window into religious practices is the treatment of death. The view of an afterlife, rituals surrounding the death, the importance of family members at these times, and the management of emotionality all provide valuable information about how religions view human nature. Thus, in discussing many religious belief systems, an emphasis will be placed on the role and meaning of death.

In the discussion that follows, the terms *spirituality* and *religion* are often used synonymously. Religion usually refers to institutionalized values and beliefs that are associated with a particular doctrine. Spirituality is an internalized, personal, and subjective experience of a higher power (Stander et al., 1994). Personal spirituality may stem from adherence to a religion, or it may be unrelated to institutional theology. Certain religions appear to support and encourage a personal experience of a higher power, as in some Native American belief systems, whereas others are more tied to formal doctrine. In this chapter, the terms *religion* and *spirituality* are generally used interchangeably except in discussing belief systems in which a personal subjective perspective predominates.

NATIVE AMERICAN SPIRITUALITY

Native American spirituality is diverse, reflecting the array of tribal communities in North America. As a result, it is not possible to describe these belief systems in a unitary way. Because of the work of missionaries and assimilation with the larger U.S. culture, many Native Americans practice forms of Christianity. Although Christianity may be practiced in a "pure" form, Native American spirituality often encompasses Christianity alongside traditional beliefs.

In general, Native American spirituality emphasizes the unity of human beings and nature. Spiritual practices are directed toward maintaining an interconnected balance between individuals and their ecological surroundings. Ceremonies often celebrate seasonal variations and their impact on nature. Harvest and hunting seasons, as well as times of migration, are common foci of celebrations. The spirit world is composed of animals, plants, and human-like beings (Attneave, 1982).

Medicine persons are still invoked in healing the sick. Illness in an individual is seen as an imbalance or disconnection between that person and their surroundings. In some Native American cultures, the sick individual is believed to be expressing distress or imbalance in the larger community. The medicine woman or man often invokes the spirit world to restore this balance. LaFromboise, Berman, and Sohi (1994) pointed out that many spiritual representations are female, for example, the Animal Mother of the Northwest Coast Indians, who is the mother of game animals.

Death is seen as entry into a different realm of being. Some tribal groups believe in forms of reincarnation, and others believe that the spirits of the dead can be contacted directly or through the medicine man or woman. Dreams are sometimes believed to be communications from the spirit world.

Often, these spiritual systems are used to account for and treat contemporary psychological problems. For example, Native American adolescents and young adults exhibit one of the highest death rates of any U.S. ethnic group. Suicides, homicides, and motor vehicle accidents account for most of these premature deaths, and alcohol and drugs often play a role (Grossman, Putsch, & Inui, 1993). However, these deaths are often seen to be mediated by *spirit sickness*. The Salish community of the Pacific Northwest views spirit sickness as an illness similar to depression and as stemming from ghosts of deceased family and community members:

> After my mom passed away, my sister didn't want to let go, she talks a lot about my mom. She was feeling sorry for herself. My sister is spirit sick . . . She'd stay at home, cried a lot in bed, sang her [spirit] song. I didn't hear it. They say the spirit can get angry, hurt the ones you love most.
>
> Have you heard about snatching? If the person died and [you] don't really want to let them go—if your soul is out there, you need help from religion. (Grossman et al., 1993, p. 595)

The sadness associated with spirit sickness may lead one to drink. In addition, the Salish believe that the dead may attempt to snatch the living; this explanation is often used to account for suicides and violent deaths among surviving youth after a family or community member has died.

Spirit dancing, a traditional Native American healing ritual, was described by Grossman et al. (1993) as one way to disrupt a deceased relative's control over the living. Catholicism, adopted by many Salish, is also seen as a power for healing spirit sickness. Spiritual practices are seen as healthier ways of treating the hallucinations and dreams associated with bereavement than is drinking, which is a way of simply suppressing these experiences.

ISLAM AND FAMILY LIFE

There are over 800 million Muslims in the world. Media coverage in this country has created an image in which Muslims are seen as Arabs or Iranians. This generalization is not supported by demographic date (Nanji, 1993). The country with the largest Muslim population is the Southeast Asian country of Indonesia. It is estimated that there are 2 to 3 million Muslims in North America (Nanji, 1993).

Islam is practiced in two forms—Shiism and Sunnism. Shiites practice a more fundamentalist and mystical form of Islam. The Shiites are growing in numbers, particularly in the Arab world. Shiites await a leader to bring them salvation for the Last Days (Schoeps, 1968) and often rely on a literalist and, at times, esoteric interpretation of the Koran, the Islamic holy book. Iran and Iraq are strongly influenced by Shiite doctrine. There is a view that through self-denial and turning one's will over to God, a transcendent state of unity will occur.

Islamic faith is founded on the unity of religion with all walks of life. The practice of prayer five times a day, the embodiment of Islamic values in law, and the significant role of Islam in defining marriage make it difficult to separate religious life from daily life and experience. The Shariah, Islamic law derived from the the the Koran and the Sunnah, provides a set of guidelines to regulate daily activities (Nanji, 1993). This fusing of religion with law, family, and larger social values is often inappropriately labeled as fanaticism by American society, which is founded on a separation of church and state.

Islam includes a number of dictates about gender-specific behavior. Islamic faith views women as being seductive and a source of temptation. This is epitomized in the saying, "Whenever a man encounters a woman, Satan is also present" (Maas & Al-Krenawi, 1994). In Islamic law, a man may obtain a divorce by saying to his wife "I divorce thee" three times with a witness present. In a divorce, the children are kept in the custody of their father.

At the same time, however, Islamic law actually includes considerable attention to women's rights. Divorce is permitted with attention to equitable financial support for divorced or widowed women. In the United States and other Western societies, Muslim women have entered the work force. This is but one of the traditional boundaries between public and private spheres of life that have been broken down. Styles of relating to men and women, distinctive dress, and gender roles within the family have become areas of tension with migration to non-Islamic societies. These changes have in turn altered the practice of Islam itself through women's increased involvement in the mosque.

Interfaith marriages are generally discouraged and can trigger considerable family-of-origin conflict. Muslim men can more readily marry a non-Muslim than can Muslim women. In the latter case, the man would be expected to convert to Islam.

A major source of tension among Muslims in Western countries centers around separation and individuation in adolescence. Behaviors of experimentation—drinking alcohol, smoking cigarettes, dating, and youthful heterosexual contact—are violations of traditional Islamic values. Although Muslim families often do value the work ethic and achievement through education, American culture is typically viewed as too permissive with respect to childrearing practices and tolerance of immoral behavior. The likelihood of interfaith dating and marriage—particularly by young Muslim women—is a source of considerable anxiety among parents.

AFRICAN AMERICAN SPIRITUALITY

Psychiatrist Robert Coles (1994), in a study of children's experiences of school desegregation, found that spirituality was an important element in African American families living in the southern United States. While seated at the kitchen table in one household, Coles had this exchange with one of the children's mothers:

> She asked me about the questions I'd been putting to her, to her husband, to Ruby—and again, I patiently tried to explain to her that it was important to know how Ruby's appetite was holding up, and whether she was sleeping soundly, and what she said or did under various sets of circumstances. She nodded, and then told me, reassuringly, that she appreciated quite well my interest in her daughter and realized that I was trying to see how her mind and body were responding to an extremely stressful time—but she did want to say something to me that had been on her mind off and on. I waited for her to speak, but to no avail. I decided to encourage her, and when I did, I heard this: "You're the doctor, I know. I shouldn't be asking you questions. You know what to ask children. But my husband and I were talking the other night, and we decided that you ask our daughter about everything except God."
>
> She stopped and looked down at the floor. I was at a loss for words. To be honest, I didn't really understand, at the time, what she was talking about—and so I started doing what people like me so often do! I worried about her "mind," her "psychiatric status," her "educational level." . . . I fumbled for words, and when they didn't come easily, I resorted to the old familiar ploy, the verbal tic, the arrogant mannerism people like me have at their disposal: "Would you explain what you mean?" She had no trouble doing so, quite concisely: "God is helping Ruby, and we thought you'd want to know that." I must admit: I decided to let the matter drop. I was a doctor, I was studying children caught up in social stress, in a racial crisis, and best to stick with my notion of how to go about that study. I changed the subject—

asked yet again about Ruby's eating and sleeping habits, her comments about her school work. Never again did Mrs. Bridges broach the subject of God in that way to me. (Coles, 1994, pp. 135–137)

African Americans' cultural heritage is diverse and includes spiritual beliefs from Christian churches as well as a broadly based spirituality (Knox, 1985). Because of racism after the Civil War, African American churches separated and formed their own congregations. The African Methodist Episcopal (AME) church and distinct Baptist churches for the African American community arose from this separation. Other denominations, such as Jehovah's Witnesses, Seventh Day Adventists, Lutheran, and Roman Catholicism, are also found in the African American community (Boyd-Franklin, 1989).

African American church services tend to be emotional and include singing of spirituals, dialogues with the preacher, and group interaction. The churches also provide a wide range of community services, including food pantries, day camps, after-school recreation, and counseling. Single mothers often rely heavily on the church to help with children. Many African American mothers will say "I raised my children in church" (Boyd-Franklin, 1989).

The church is the primary source of mental health care among African Americans. They are far more likely to take personal and family problems to a pastor than to a mental health professional. Although faith in God is seen as an important way to address psychological symptoms, pastors often provide conventional advice that is similar to that provided by therapists. Pastors in the African American community are often better able to harness the immediate social network of the distressed person than a therapist is. Boyd-Franklin (1989) recommended that, when appropriate, the therapist contact the family's pastor and even include him or her in a therapy session.

Spirituality is a very strong influence, even among African Americans who have no formal religious ties. There is a strong belief in a higher power that can solve personal problems, including financial, interpersonal, and psychological distress (Knox, 1985). Even formal religious concepts are often recast in a personal spirituality. Beliefs in bands of angels that are personally watching over someone and reading particular sections of the Psalms to increase personal control over good forces are examples of the immediate intimate application of Christianity among African Americans (Snow, 1993).

This spirituality may extend to incorporate witchcraft, hexes, and voodoo (Knox, 1985). Hexing is used to seek revenge on someone who has harmed a person or to obtain control over another's behavior. A common way for a hex to be placed on another is to put "goofy dust" in their food. Candles and oils may be used to protect oneself against hexes (Snow, 1993). Root doctors are indigenous practitioners who can both impose and remove hexes. Snow's study of alternative healing in the African American community found that a fusion of Christianity and spiritualism was a very common foundation for beliefs in herbal healing. Respondents noted that herbal treatments could be found in the Bible.

The Nation of Islam ("Black Muslims") has a number of adherents in the United States. The Nation of Islam grew during the 1960s and 1970s under the leadership of Elijah Muhammad. Islamic teachings are synthesized with Black Nationalist values. Members of this faith are unlikely to avail themselves of formal mental health services. Black Muslims operate from a particular set of gender guidelines, which include patriarchal dimensions (Edwards, 1968). In contrast to Christian families, African American Muslims discourage female employment and view the woman's role as caretaker to children and home. Children raised in the Black Muslim tradition are rarely subjected to physical punishment, although it is used for serious infractions. Use of alcohol and tobacco are forbidden. Women do not use cosmetics or hair straighteners (Edwards, 1968). Education for children is highly valued, and the Nation of Islam operates its own schools. There is considerable suspicion of White Americans, who are viewed as having had a corrupting influence on African American society. Boyd-Franklin (1989) noted that family conflicts often arise when a young adult converts to the Nation of Islam. The customs, dress codes, and isolation of many adherents from nonbelievers can create conflicts between the family of origin and young adults. These issues become more intense when grandchildren become involved.

Boyd-Franklin (1995) argued that, as in Coles's (1994) example, many African Americans suspect Whites of being antispiritual. I consulted to a predominantly African American residential youth facility. Periodically, administrators and therapists would, with some uneasiness, suggest that prayer and reading the Bible were often equally, if not more, effective interventions than psychotherapy. This was accompanied by nervous laughter. After some reflection, I readily agreed that for many young people spiritual guidance made more sense than formal mental health treatment. Therapists may make the mistake of viewing African American spirituality as a rationalization, excuse, or form of resistance to treatment. Although it is not advisable to engage in spiritual guidance beyond one's training, therapists should recognize that therapy and spirituality are often parallel and intermingling pathways to similar ends.

Death within African American families often results in a major gathering of the extended family. Unlike White Americans of European background, who typically hold funerals within 2 to 3 days of death, African Americans may wait up to one week after a family member's death to allow the entire family to convene. The funeral, while focusing on the deceased, also serves an important function in reaffirming ties among the living. During the funeral itself, intense emotion including moaning, wailing, crying, and even fainting (Boyd-Franklin, 1995) may occur. However, there is often a norm that emotionality and outward mourning is contained within the funeral and family gatherings held immediately afterward. These expressions are frequently not acceptable after this immediate mourning period. As a result, the African American family may become stuck in their mourning and may not proceed through the grief process. In addition, deaths of cousins, uncles, and informal (non-blood) relatives may still have a very current quality about them as they are related to the therapist. Clients may also continue to have dreams, visions, and experiences in which they feel the presence of a long deceased relative:

> Jammeka, a 19-year-old African American woman, was seen by a therapist becasue she had been increasingly depressed over the previous 3 months, with frequent crying episodes, suicidal ideation, and disturbed sleep. Eight months earlier, Jammeka had lost a baby to a sudden, unknown illness. Although the illness had similarities to sudden infant death syndrome, the death was mysterious. Jammeka suspected that the infant had been "called home" to join her own mother, who had died a year earlier. Jammeka showed the therapist a number of photos of the baby, dressed in a white gown and laid out in an ornate tiny coffin. The pictures often included a smiling Jammeka accompanied by her boyfriend, sister, cousins, and friends—all smiling while encircling the baby's coffin. Although guilt ridden, Jammeka said at the funeral she had felt a sense of relief that her mother would not be alone now. However, several months afterward, she began having visions of her deceased infant calling out to her.

Views of death often reflect a fusion of Christian and African spirituality. Death represents the beginning of life in a new form. Among the elderly, deaths may be consciously postponed until a significant life event (holiday, reunion) has come to pass. Christianity and African spirituality are often compatible in their views that death is a way of obtaining a new life. Death is a very real part of daily life among African Americans—the next life frees one from the sorrow, discrimination, and toil of current existence. Deaths may be good, as in the end of suffering for an elderly person, or bad, such as through violence (McGoldrick et al., 1991). Even in the latter case, there is often a sense of fatalism or determinism but at the same time a view that the deceased is being released to a better place.

Within African American churches, funerals serve as a significant emotional catharsis—prayers and hymns are often selected toward this end. However, after the funeral, there is an expectation that emotionality will be constrained. This norm, in part, contributes to sustained and complicated bereavements among African Americans. Another factor contributing to disrupted mourning in the inner city is the occurrence of a number of violent deaths in rapid succession.

Often because of gang activity, many young African Americans can readily describe sudden deaths of cousins, brothers, uncles, and friends—all within the span of 1 to 2 years. Mourning for one loss is disrupted and left incomplete by another death.

PROTESTANT DENOMINATIONS IN THE UNITED STATES

The WASP value orientation has been strongly influenced by the Protestant religious tradition. Self-sufficiency and hard work are reflected in Lutheran, Presbyterian, and Methodist church teachings. Calvinism emphasizes an individualist orientation, in which one is judged by one's deeds. This action orientation occurs at the expense of emotionality. Mainline Protestant church services are typically staid and reserved, particularly when compared with African American churches. Individual parishioners often have minimal interaction with one another before, during, or after services. Sermons tend to be intellectually oriented; at times, they may resemble college lectures. Protestants in particular do not have a mechanism for absolution of sin. Sin, though often seen as an inherent part of the human condition, also becomes enacted through behavior. The Methodist tenet "by their fruits ye shall know them" holds people personally responsible for whatever goes wrong in their lives. When someone is sexually or physically abused, there is often an implicit message that the victim brought the assault on him- or herself (Schmidt, 1995). Although most Protestant denominations view faith in God as important for salvation, the influence of Calvinism emphasizes good works and even material success as salient for receiving God's grace.

Fundamentalism has become a prominent influence within many Protestant faiths. Although it is impossible to describe overarching principles that unite fundamentalist Christians, there are frequently shared values. Individuals are held accountable for their actions. However, there is also an emphasis on being able to forgive those responsible for transgressing against a fellow church member. Many fundamentalist sects have rigid gender distinctions, with men often being in positions of control and privilege within the church community as well as in the family. Taylor and Fontes (1995) provided a thoughtful discussion of how sexual abuse is managed among Seventh Day Adventists. They noted that the emphasis on victim responsibility and forgiveness for the perpetrator often borders on denial. Conversion to fundamentalism by one parent in the family often leads to a type of authority-based control that extends to the spousal relationships and to childrearing. This may lead to conflicts that are difficult for therapists to address. Fundamentalists have often been critical of the secular values espoused by many therapists. At the same time, fundamentalism is a response to the growing individualist emphasis among many liberal Protestant churches and usually includes a strong belief in a person's responsibility to fellow church members and family.

ROMAN CATHOLICISM

Catholicism is not practiced as a unitary faith. Within Catholicism there is considerable diversity associated with different ethnic backgrounds, migration patterns, and the synthesis or assimilation of Catholicism with native spiritual systems.

Italian Americans, as well as Hispanics, tend to view God in a personal way, much like a close family friend. Church holidays are valued more for pageantry and the opportunity for extended family gatherings than for spiritual significance (Rotunno & McGoldrick, 1982). Italian Americans also value the church as a source of temporal continuity and family tradition.

Irish Catholics have a more formal and removed relationship with God. Irish Catholicism was strongly influenced by Jansenism. Jansenism emphasized that the human body and pleasure were related to sin. Self-denial and asceticism became the ways that one knew God. God is a strong authority who punishes sinfulness, which is an inherent part of the human condition (McGoldrick, 1982). In the United States, Irish Catholicism has been maintained through schools run by Irish nuns and priests.

Emotional suffering may be seen as the way that one comes to know God:

> Evelyn, a 35-year-old Irish Catholic woman, was being treated for depression. Evelyn had experienced sexual abuse as a child, which she could only talk about briefly in treatment. She then focused on how she was responsible for it by being "so stupid." Evelyn was treated with medication and with psychotherapy, which included both family-of-origin and cognitive–behavioral approaches. Despite some awareness of the patterns associated with her depressions, Evelyn seemed stuck and could not move through her sense of sadness and guilt. The therapist began to explore Evelyn's religious beliefs during treatment. Evelyn expressed the feeling that she was closer to God when she was "in the desert" with her emotional pain. She compared her experience to that of Christ suffering on the cross. The therapist became aware that by alleviating Evelyn's depressive symptoms he was, in effect, cutting off her lifeline to God. The therapist began to label this fear and to discuss some of the assumptions underlying Irish Catholicism. With open discussion of these experiences, which had previously been felt yet unlabeled, Evelyn was able to view her depressive symptoms differently. She began to read spiritual books and had a number of discussions with her priest about experiencing God's presence in new ways.

Italian and Latin American Catholics have a more benign view of God. God is seen as a revered family friend who can bestow protection and assist the family with individual needs. In the movie *Saturday Night Fever*, one son accuses his mother of turning God into a personal telephone operator when she says that she is going to church to pray for her other son (a priest) to call her.

These differing perspectives of Catholicism have, at times, led to conflict. In the earlier part of this century, the Catholic church in the United States was dominated by Irish clergy, whose guilt-oriented ascetism was often experienced as oppressive by Italian immigrants (Rotunno & McGoldrick, 1982).

Catholicism also takes different forms among Americans of Latin American or Caribbean descent. The religious and spiritual life of Hispanic Americans is very much present-centered. Likewise, Catholicism among Hispanics is less likely to be future oriented (Garcia-Preto, 1982). Although there may be outward respect for the priest and other Catholic clergy and religion, Hispanics often practice Catholicism in a personal way. The priest is not seen as a necessary intermediary to one's relationship with God. Personalized relationships with preferred saints are an important part of this practice. This personal relationship with God often includes having a shrine in the home. God is seen as an approachable figure who may be accessible for personal trials and needs. At the same time, God is a significant authority for whom respect and reverence is necessary (Cervantes & Ramirez, 1992).

Many native Hispanic cultures featured witchcraft or spiritualism, which often is practiced in a parallel form or loosely integrated with Catholicism. Synthesized belief systems among Hispanics often emphasize harmony and interdependence. Family misfortune, including psychiatric symptoms, are seen as the work of evil spirits, which arise when there is an imbalance in interpersonal harmony. These spirits are often seen as arising from spells that a resentful or angry family member has placed on another (Cervantes & Ramirez, 1992). This interdependence extends to the mind–body dualism. Psychiatric illness is often attributed to spells, which are manifested through alteration of bodily fluids or other physiological changes. *Curanderismo* is a set of spiritual beliefs that includes folk medical care. *Curanderismo* includes a view of a unified mind and body as well as an emphasis on the integration of the individual with the social and physical environment. The distinction between physical and emotional illness is much less of a division than in European belief systems. One becomes spiritually, emotionally, or physically ill because of an imbalance or lack of harmony with one's surroundings. The *curandera* is a conduit between the higher spiritual power and the individual or family. The context of healing may include sacred words, chants, or therapeutic imagery. The *curandera* is attempting to achieve reintegration through the higher power. Visionary and auditory experiences may be part of this spiritual illness and healing and should be distinguished from hallucinations (Cervantes & Ramirez, 1992).

Brujas and *brujos* (female and male witches) are other forces that can change one's behavior suddenly and uncontrollably. However, these sinister forces can be counteracted by appeals to angels and saints. In many respects Mexican American spirituality is highly congruent with the view of the family as an interactive system because it emphasizes "the connecting of group balance with transcendent balance, familial responsibility with broader universal awareness, and familial goals with existential purpose" (Cervantes & Ramirez, 1992).

Although spirituality among Hispanic Americans includes some shared conceptual elements, there are also differences. *Curanderismo* is more common among mestizos of Mexican background, whereas Cubans and Puerto Ricans practice *santeria,* a fusion of Caribbean–Christian and Spanish beliefs (Cervantes & Ramirez, 1992).

Cuban and Puerto Rican folk healing often includes a synthesis of Roman Catholicism with African beliefs. *Espiritismo* has been transplanted to the U.S. mainland by Puerto Rican and Cuban immigrants (Bernal, 1982). This practice includes the exorcism of spirits by a medium. Charms and amulets are used in this regard. At the same time, some spiritists believe that one person can put a spell on another such as a wife or husband. Roman Catholic saints are often invoked to protect one from these spells.

Among Puerto Ricans, spirits are seen as playing an etiological role in personality disorders and psychoses. In spiritism, the healer attempts to elicit the spirits that are harming the individual (Garcia-Preto, 1982). Once contacted, the healer tries to convince the spirit to stop harming and begin helping the afflicted individual.

ASIAN RELIGIONS

Confucian philosophy has had a pervasive influence on social order in many Asian countries, even among those that later departed from Confucian teachings. Concepts such as gender-based hierarchies often were carried over by immigrants to the United States. The Confucian tradition is more practical than spiritual (Bradshaw, 1994). Rather than addressing issues of transcendence, Confucianism focuses more on prescriptions for daily social exchanges and roles.

In Confucianism, birth order was associated with specific social expectations. Gender roles were well defined, with women viewed as subservient to men. Marriages were often arranged by parents, with the daughter typically not meeting her husband until the wedding (Bradshaw, 1994).

The Confucian framework prescribes three distinct roles for women, which become salient at different points in the developmental cycle. In childhood and adolescence, the woman takes the role of a dutiful daughter. As an adult, she is to be an obedient wife, and in old age she becomes a member of the oldest son's household (Shon & Ja, 1982). Women's authority is often direct. In traditional societies, they were typically the primary nurturer and supporter, and they were the mediator between the father and the children.

The success with which individuals adhere to Confucian principles is a reflection on the immediate family and broader kinship network. Confucian doctrine emphasizes ongoing reverence and respect for one's parents. The elderly are treated with the utmost respect and are usually incorporated into one of their children's households (Shon & Ja, 1982).

Among Chinese who are adherents of Confucianism, death is an important transition. Respect for the deceased—particularly parents—is paramount, and funerals can be elaborate, costly displays of devotion. Deceased parents are often the focus of household shrines. Ancestors are believed to bring protection and security to their relatives' household (Schoeps, 1968). Emotional outpourings are expected at the funeral, but control is expected afterward. Chanters and professional mourners are sometimes present to assist the soul's entry into the afterlife (McGoldrick et al., 1991).

In contrast to the practical, common-sense approach of Confucianism, which emphasizes maxims for daily life, Buddhism provides a belief system that transcends life's current challenges (Schoeps, 1968). Buddhists believe in an ongoing continuum of existence that includes past, present, and future lives. The soul's reincarnation in subsequent lives is part of this belief. Determinism and acceptance of one's fate preclude overt, intense, emotional expressions. Buddhism, even among those who do not directly practice the faith, has become an influential belief system among the Japanese (Bradshaw, 1994).

The Shinto religion is influential in Japan and may coexist with Buddhism. In Shintoism, spirits are believed to inhabit rocks, trees, and other natural objects. There is a deep reverence for nature, with little attention to afterlife or social rules. Family life cycle transitions—a birth, certain birthdays, and adulthood—are marked by visits to Shinto shrines (Feiler, 1991).

Belief in communication with the spirits of deceased persons is common. This view may not be directly tied to religious doctrine per se but may indirectly reflect a perception of existence as continuous. Reliance on shamans and other native healers is common, particularly among Laotian and Cambodian refugees. Altars to ancestors are common in the homes of immigrants from Southeast Asia. Ancestor altars are usually maintained by the family's oldest son but may be kept by any family member (Chao, 1992). Thus, the deceased family members are maintained in the living family members' daily experience. Immigration to the United States has created conflicts regarding ancestor worship; some Asian Americans may feel embarrassment about the practice and maintain the altar in a private part of the home (Chao, 1992).

Christianity has been influential in a number of Asian countries, such as Korea and Vietnam (Bradshaw, 1994). Some immigrants were sponsored by Christian denominations and became members of these churches once they came to the United States. Christian fundamentalist movements have become increasingly visible in Southeast Asian communities in the United States as well as in Asia. The holistic perspective of Eastern religions has often been able to accommodate or assimilate mainstream Catholic or Protestant faiths (Schoeps, 1968). However, Christian fundamentalist theology may be at odds with Buddhism or other Eastern religions. Fundamentalist doctrine may view practices such as ancestor altars as heathen. These religious schisms can create considerable conflict within families who practice Eastern religions and would view the removal of an ancestor shrine as offensive and not showing proper respect (Chao, 1992).

JUDAISM AND THE FAMILY

Characteristics of Jewish families were described in chapter 7. Several additional aspects of Judaism are highlighted in this section.

Historically, the American Jewish community has been diversified among Orthodox, Conservative, and Reform groups. These distinctions are not absolute categories but do describe some important differences in Jewish practice and belief systems (Epstein, 1990). Orthodox Jews abide fairly strictly by Jewish law. Rabbis have a very prominent role within Orthodox communities. Dietary rules and dictums forbidding work and travel on the Sabbath are closely maintained. The Reform movement sought greater integration of Jewish and non-Jewish society. Reform Jews have reinterpreted many Jewish rituals and traditions in the context of modern norms. For example, bat mitzvahs for girls have been practiced within the Reform movement for a number of years (Pogrebin, 1991). Conservative Jews occupy a position somewhere between Orthodox and Reform Jews. Although there is still an emphasis on tradition and scholarship as well as acceptance of rabbinic law, there is room for interpretation in light of the changes within modern society. A fourth movement, Reconstructionism, views Judaism as a culture or civilization in which religion is one part, along with literature, art, and language (Epstein, 1990). In the United States, reconstructionism may be found among feminist Jewish congregations, in which participants discuss spirituality as it relates to social activism, sexual orientation, and ethnicity. There is also a group of secular Jews, who may not formally practice a religious faith but experience a cultural bond to Jewish issues such as a commitment to Israel as a homeland (Featherman, 1995).

The Jewish faith is often celebrated through rituals conducted in the home as well as in the synagogue. Passover and Hanukkah are two examples of holy days with important rituals that are celebrated by the family at home (McGoldrick et al., 1991). The Holocaust continues to exert considerable influence on contemporary Jewish life. Many American Jews have extended family members who died in concentration camps. The Holocaust has also contributed to a legacy of shared suffering among American Jews and is remembered with painful respect.

This strong familial value, together with an emphasis on religious heritage, is particularly evident when a Jewish young adult becomes involved with a gentile. Friedman (1982) noted that some parents have engaged in the 7-day traditional mourning period (*shiva*) for an adult child who married out of the faith. This concern has been related to a shared history of persecution of the Jewish community and concerns about the Jewish faith being diluted by outsiders. Children born of non-Jewish women are not considered Jews and need to convert if they are Orthodox or Conservative. This requirement varies among Reform Jews.

Gender-role division has been frequently described in accounts of Jewish marriages. Male dominance is still common within Orthodox groups. Orthodox services involve segregation of men and women. In traditional communities, women are characterized as hard working, self-sacrificing, and submissive to God and their husbands (Featherman, 1995).

The afterlife is deemphasized in the practice of the Jewish faith as compared with Christianity. Funerals are often simple, and burial usually takes place within 24 hours of death. Arguments and other verbal discourse are common during the funeral and mourning period. The emphasis on accomplishments extends to the funeral, which is often a review of the deceased's achievements and their importance to the family (McGoldrick et al., 1991). Yiddish prayers are said daily by the family for a year after death, particularly in Orthodox families. The unveiling or dedication of the gravestone is an important ritual marked 1 year after the death (Herz & Rosen, 1982).

SPIRITUALITY, RELIGION, AND FAMILY SYSTEMS

Many family rules stem from religious or spiritual belief systems. Family-of-origin therapists should be aware of the importance of these belief systems as values—often unlabeled—that guide individual and daily decision making. Given the relative absence of guidelines for therapists for addressing religion and spirituality, and the diversity of the belief systems in the United States, therapists should raise the issue of religion in the context of a student desiring to learn. The family's religious background, the importance of spirituality, and intergenerational conflicts around religious issues should be examined in the assessment phase.

Because spirituality is a highly individualized experience, the client should be encouraged to describe religious values and meanings until the therapist can grasp them. Without taking a stand, the therapist can, by careful listening, describe sources of conflict between religious beliefs and family dynamics as current life choices that create distress for the client. Hearing these issues sensitively labeled is often a freeing experience for the client. The therapist's ability to define the client's own spiritual values and how they clash, fit, or complement with those of their family of origin provides the client with a foundation to address these dilemmas on his or her own.

Religion as a mechanism or focus of triangulation has been described in several recent articles (Griffith, 1986; Rotz, Russell, & Wright, 1993). A not uncommon dynamic is for one spouse to present him- or herself as spiritually superior to the other. This spiritually one-up position (Rotz et al., 1993) often implies that the other spouse is inferior and the source of marital problems: "If she would just take religion as seriously as I do and live by God's word, our marriage would be fine" is a position that may be presented to the therapist. At times, spiritual superiority may paradoxically coexist with morally disturbing behaviors such as incest, spouse battering, or marital infidelity. The religiosity may appear to be a reaction formation or rationalization in relation to these acts. At other times, preoccupation with the inadequate spirituality of a spouse may be a means for managing anxiety around intimacy and prevents meaningful one-to-one interactions (Bowen, 1978).

Another form of triangulation that occurs involves the growing number of pastoral counselors or family therapists who clearly identify their religious orientation to the public. The spouse who views him- or herself as spiritually correct (Rotz et al., 1993) may deliberately seek a therapist who shares that affiliation as a means of maintaining a one-up position in the marriage. Like any third party, the church or synagogue as an institution and the priest, minister, or rabbi as an individual can become triangulated into marital conflicts. Clergy frequently report that they are recruited by parents to deal with a drug abusing or recalcitrant adult son or daughter. The minister may become involved with a wife who complains about her emotionally abusive or disengaged husband. For a period, the wife's involvement with the minister may serve to reduce the rising tension in the marriage and stabilize the relationship.

As noted in this chapter's opening section, deaths are events in which spirituality becomes particularly important. Bowen (1976) described death as an event that sends emotional shockwaves throughout the family; it is unrelated to grief or mourning and is typically an underground experience that goes on for months or years.

Though not addressing religion per se, Bowen (1976) argued that funerals should be experiences that bring surviving family members into intimate one-on-one contact with one another as well as with the deceased. He also felt that the family-based funeral, including burial by the family, was the most therapeutic approach to death. Private, closed-coffin funerals are antiseptic rituals that prevent meaningful personal contact. Involvement of young children in the funeral, including direct contact with the deceased, is recommended (Bowen, 1976).

Bowen's (1991) view of funerals fits well with contemporary African American traditions. However, it is certainly more demonstrative and expressive than many Protestant and some Catholic families' mourning processes typically entail. Bowen viewed funerals as a time in which family members could make one-on-one contact with each other as well as with the deceased. He expressed concern about the technologically focused approach to death, which prevents healthy emotional closure

CONCLUSION

Religion and spirituality, although they are extremely important forces in shaping family and individual identity, are in many respects outside the realm of traditional therapy. Spirituality, which probably includes Bowen's emotional, intellectual, and togetherness forces, also embodies transcendent dimensions that theories of individual and family therapy do not address. The therapist should maintain a respectful reverence for this dimension of family life. Although including religion in family therapy is a conceptual and emotional challenge for which therapists are often ill-prepared, an openness to spiritual dimensions will provide a much richer picture of family life.

Chapter 9

Diversity in Practice

Family life cannot be adequately understood in a vacuum. Until recently, family therapy, despite its emphasis on social context, has paid little attention to the social matrix within which family life takes place. Ethnicity, gender, religion, and sexual orientation all convey a series of largely unspoken rules that organize current relationship patterns. The family of origin is the primary medium by which these worldviews become transmitted to individuals.

In comparison with other family theories, family-of-origin therapy offers a unique vantage point in that it highlights the role of intrapsychic representations of family life in identity development and relationship formation. As is evident in the examples that follow, therapy clients cannot be neatly categorized like the chapters of this book. In real life, the social context within which individuals function is a variegated interplay of gender, ethnicity, and orientation. Each of these perspectives may be more salient at a particular point in development.

For clients to come to an acceptance and deeper understanding of diversity, they must often undertake a somewhat confusing multistage journey. Initially, clients who begin to examine cultural or gender rules often experience increased anxiety. Their fundamental worldview is under siege. Most people acquire knowledge about diversity through life experience. Friends, significant others, and spouses trigger an awareness that "our way" is not the "only way." This collision of worldviews can be frightening and anxiety provoking. For those who grapple with this turmoil, there may be a sense of being cast adrift in a sea of relativism. If many worldviews are as valid as one's own, how can a decision be made? How does one decide on values to guide one's life? How should one live? This period, too, is often very anxiety provoking. The end point of this initially jarring process is a thoughtful examination of the diverse sources of one's own identity and family templates. This principled relativism includes a sensitive appreciation of others' diversity as well as the social forces shaping their own

155

background (Salner, 1986). At the same time, the individual is aware of actively choosing certain principles from which to operate.

Many psychotherapy clients are stuck in an early stage of upheaval and make personal attributions that are more usefully understood as reflecting unspoken rules about gender or ethnicity. By including diversity as a topic in the therapy hour, clients can be helped to depersonalize many seemingly personality-based conflicts.

> Nancy and Julie requested therapy for help in conflict resolution. They had been relationship partners for 6 years. Nancy came from an Eastern European Jewish family, and Julie had been raised in an Italian Catholic family. Nancy's family was aware of their lesbian relationship, but Julie's parents and siblings always referred to the couple as "roommates." Nancy celebrated major Jewish holidays and periodically went to services at temple. Julie would describe her anger at the Catholic church's negative view of homosexuality and say that she no longer practiced the faith. However, on visits to her parent's home, Julie always felt obliged to attend mass. Nancy's parents lived in the same city as the couple, whereas Julie's parents lived about 2 hours away. In the previous 2 years, Julie and Nancy had become involved in an escalating cycle of intense argument—usually over minor matters— followed by distancing and eventual reconciliation. Nancy had initiated therapy and appeared painfully bewildered by the increased conflict. Julie appeared to be undisturbed by the pattern and did not consider it a problem. ("We clear the air and then go on.") She did admit to feeling that Nancy was pushing her to come out to her own family. Julie said she did not think her parents could take it if she did and that they would "haul me off to a priest for confession."

The therapist was struck by several issues. First, Nancy's desire to process the couple's differences were compatible with her Jewish ethnicity. Julie's style of clearing the air and getting on with things was a common Italian American pattern, in which emotion is discharged without addressing underlying differences. Julie's issues with her family of origin, including her religious and ethnic heritage, were largely unlabeled, although the emotional tension associated with these dilemmas was clearly rising.

The therapist was able to label their differences in problem-solving styles in a nonjudgmental manner. Nancy was able to appreciate that Julie often did not want to process their differences but that she heard Nancy's feedback and privately considered it. At the same time, Julie verbalized a recognition that she and Nancy should be able to develop plans to keep their differences from escalating. Nancy also realized that she had been pushing Julie to be more out about her lesbianism even though Julie was not comfortable with this. The therapist pointed out that the coming out process was unique to each individual. The therapist urged Nancy to respect Julie's boundaries. Through discussion of spiritual issues, Julie recognized that she was not yet ready to abandon Catholicism. Although she was angry about the church's official stance on lesbianism, there were aspects of her faith that were meaningful. Julie made a decision to join a gay and lesbian Catholic organization and attempt to integrate Catholicism with her sexual orientation.

DIVERSITY AND FAMILY STRESSORS

The family life cycle is likely to interact with diversity as well. Religious differences between a couple may not be important until a child is born; the desire to baptize the child or send him or her to religious training may trigger previous issues. Having gay or lesbian parents may not be an issue for a child until he or she enters elementary school and recognizes that classmates' parents are heterosexual. For other children, this issue may lay dormant until early adolescence, when sexuality and the peer group become dominant. Gender as an organizing influence often does not become a focus among married couples until a child is born. Whereas household tasks may be divided equally in the prechildbearing period, the balance may shift afterward, with the mother becoming almost exclusively responsible for the child.

Ethnicity is a particularly pervasive influence during the separation and individuation tasks of adolescence and young adulthood. This period may define who is in the family as well as relationship obligations to the family at different phases and may differ according to ethnic background. WASPs—with their achievement orientation and built-in individual distance—separate readily. However, among ethnic groups stressing the responsibility of young adults to parents (e.g., Italian Americans), separation is difficult. As noted in chapter 8, death also has various meanings among different ethnic and religious groups. Individuals without an extended support network (WASPs, German Americans, or recent immigrants) may well experience a number of ill-defined psychosomatic complications following the death, particularly a sudden death, of a family member.

> Catherine, a 28-year-old woman of German American background, started therapy 1 month after she miscarried 20 weeks into her first pregnancy. Catherine, who came alone for the session, said that therapy was her husband's idea. Catherine's only complaint was that she was unable to get much housework done because she felt tired. She stated that her husband was increasingly frustrated about her lack of productivity at home. Discussion of her early upbringing revealed a Midwestern farm family with a strong work ethic. She reported that

both her mother and father put in about 70 hours per week on the family farm. Catherine had been raised in the Lutheran church. Her church affiliation continued to be very important to her as an adult.

Although Catherine had completed college and had worked in a small business, her primary goal had been to get married and have children. Her husband, John, was of a similar ethnic and religious background and was a salesman—often away for 3 to 4 days at a time.

When the therapist asked Catherine about the miscarriage, she, fighting back tears, said, "I should be over it by now." Catherine's parents had phoned and sent flowers at the time of the miscarriage but had not contacted her since then. Catherine's husband was supportive for the first 2 weeks but recently had been telling her that she "should be over it" and it was time to "get on with life." Catherine herself was confused and embarrassed by her daily crying spells and overwhelming sadness. She was also self-critical for not being able to "fulfill her responsibilities as a wife" at home. Catherine stated that she had rigorously adhered to all her doctor's prenatal recommendations during the pregnancy. Although her doctor and husband had tried to assure Catherine that she had done nothing wrong, Catherine held herself responsible for the miscarriage. "It must be my fault; I was carrying the baby. Who else's fault could it be?"

When the therapist inquired about support from her church congregation, Catherine said that the pastor had consistently conveyed his supportive concern for her over the past month. However, she went on to describe how some women in the congregation told her that the "unborn child was in a better place now." They were already encouraging her to try again despite her physician's insistence that she wait at least 6 months before getting pregnant.

The therapist began to label Catherine's emphasis on work and productivity as understandable given her German farm family background. The therapist went on to point out how women often were socialized to hold themselves responsible for family misfortune even when there was no evidence (e.g., of Catherine's having been negligent during the pregnancy). The natural process of recovery from a miscarriage was explained to her. Catherine was told that her sadness and reduced energy was normal in this situation. Over time, the therapist also encouraged Catherine to discuss her views of God with her pastor. Catherine had a view of God as a punisher of sin who primarily valued good works. Catherine was encouraged to ask her pastor for Biblical readings that emphasized God's love. Conjoint sessions with her husband were added. It became apparent that the housewife role was, by itself, not satisfying for Catherine. The couple agreed that Catherine would delay becoming pregnant for a while and return to work. The couple negotiated an equitable balance of household duties.

As this example illustrates, crises often interact with religious, ethnic, and gender role issues and may place unrecognized limits on the individual's and couple's coping skills.

THERAPIST DIVERSITY

One of Bowen's (1978) great contributions to the field of family therapy was highlighting the importance of the therapist's own family in the treatment process. In addition to making family-of-origin theory more real, developing an understanding of one's own family dynamics helps the therapist maintain a differentiated stance during the treatment hour (Wells, Scott, Schmeller, Hillmann, & Searight, 1990). Family-of-origin work allows the therapist to empathically engage with individuals and couples while not overidentifying with them.

The therapist's own ethnic and religious background shapes the assumptions that are brought to the therapy process. Similarly, social expectations of gender roles and heterosexism shape the therapist's clinical and personal worldviews. By reflecting on and labeling these largely unspoken assumptions, therapists can reduce their own emotional reactivity and minimize the influence of personal "hot spots" in treatment.

For example, therapists of WASP background may be readily overwhelmed by the intense emotionality of the Italian American family. These therapists have reported a paralysis—an inability to process information or think clearly—in the presence of intense affect. Similarly, the Jewish therapist's emphasis on understanding and integration of emotionality may be frustrated by the symptom focus of the WASP parent who asks the therapist to "fix the kid."

Therapists of many backgrounds may become uncomfortable with religious and spiritual issues. However, they are an important dimension of the lives of many clients. The values and moral guidelines provided by religious faith overlap considerably with the domain of psychotherapy. Value dilemmas and moral decisions, although historically viewed as separate from therapy, are often a central part of client distress. Therapists' ethnic and religious backgrounds may not be evident to clients, but gender is always evident. Therapists should critically reflect on their own views of gender roles as transmitted by their family of origin and as enacted in daily life. A female therapist raised in a "traditional" family and who has undergone her own struggle for equality may find it difficult to accept another woman's decision to stay home and raise children. The therapist may, without recognition, subtly push the client to look outside of her home for greater satisfaction. For the heterosexual therapist, continued self-examination of assumptions about normal relationships will be necessary to be helpful to gay and lesbian couples.

There are always at least three families present in the consulting room—the client's family, the therapist's family, and the new family created by bringing both families together (Kramer, 1985). Each family brings with them a myriad of social and cultural influences that affect their daily lives and the treatment process. Including diversity as a meaningful part of therapy enriches the experience, choices, and empathic capacity of clients.

References

Abad, V., & Boyce, E. (1979). Issues in psychiatric evaluations of Puerto Ricans: A sociocultural perspective. *Journal of Operational Psychiatry, 10,* 28–30.

Adams, G. R. (1985). Family correlates of female adolescents' ego identity development. *Journal of Adolescence, 8,* 69–82.

Adams, G. R., Dyk, P., & Bennion, L. (1987). Parent–adolescent relationships and identity formation. *Family Perspectives, 21,* 249–260.

Adams, G. R., & Jones R. N. (1983). Female adolescents' identity development: Age comparisons and perceived child rearing experience. *Developmental Psychology, 19,* 249–256.

Ainsworth, M. D. S., Blehar, M. C., Waters, E., & Wall, S. (1978). *Patterns of attachment: A psychological study of the Strange Situation.* Hillsdale, NJ: Erlbaum.

Alarcon, R. D., & Foulks, E. F. (1995). Personality disorders and culture: Contemporary clinical views (Part A). *Cultural Diversity in Mental Health, 1,* 3–17.

Alexander, J. F., & Parsons, B. V. (1982). *Functional family therapy.* Monterey, CA: Brooks/Cole.

Alexander, J. F., Warburton, J., Waldron, H., & Mas, C. H. (1985). The misuse of functional family therapy: A non-sexist rejoinder. *Journal of Marital and Family Therapy, 11,* 139–144.

Allgeier, E. R., & Allgeier, A. R. (1981). *Sexual interactions* (3rd ed.). Lexington, MA: Heath.

Anderson, S. A., & Sabatelli, R. M. (1992). The Differentiation in the Family Systems Scale (DIFS). *The American Journal of Family Therapy, 20,* 77–89.

Apter, T. (1990). *Altered loves: Mothers and daughters during adolescence.* New York: St. Martin's Press.

Arey, D. (1995). Gay males and sexual child abuse. In L. A. Fontes (Ed.), *Sexual abuse in nine North American cultures* (pp. 200–235). Newbury Park, CA: Sage.

Attneave, C. (1982). American Indians and Alaska Native families: Emigrants in their own homeland. In M. McGoldrick, J. K. Pearce, & J. Giordano (Eds.), *Ethnicity and family therapy* (pp. 55–83). New York: Guilford Press.

Ault-Riche, M. (1988). *One woman's family of origin* [Videotape]. Topeka, KS: Meninger Clinic.

Avis, J. M. (1985). The politics of functional family therapy: A feminist critique. *Journal of Marital and Family Therapy, 11,* 127–138.

Barnett, R. C., Marshall, N. L., & Pleck, J. H. (1992). Men's multiple roles and their relationship to men's psychological distress. *Journal of Marriage and the Family, 54,* 356–367.

161

Bartholomew, K. (1990). Avoidance of intimacy: An attachment perspective. *Journal of Social and Personal Relationships, 7,* 147–178.

Bartholomew, K., & Horowitz, L. M. (1991). Attachment styles among young adults: A test of a four category model. *Journal of Personality and Social Psychology, 61,* 226–244.

Bartle, S. E., & Sabatelli, R. M. (1989). Family system dynamics, identity, development and adolescent alcohol use: Implications for family treatment. *Family Relations, 38,* 258–265.

Barton, C., & Alexander, J. F. (1981). Functional family therapy. In A. S. Gurman & D. P. Kniskern (Eds.), *Handbook of family therapy* (pp. 403–443). New York: Brunner/Mazel.

Baruch, G. K., Biener, L., & Barnett, R. C. (1987). Women and gender in research on work and family stress. *American Psychologist, 42,* 130–136.

Beck, A. T. (1976). *Cognitive therapy and the emotional disorders.* New York: International Universities Press.

Bell, A., & Weinberg, N. (1978). *Homosexualities: A study of diversity among men and women.* New York: Simon & Schuster.

Bellah, R. N., Madsen, R., Sullivan, W. M., Swidler, A., & Tipton, S. M. (1985). *Habits of the heart: Individualism and commitment in American life.* Berkeley: University of California Press.

Bentovim, A., & Kinston, W. (1991). Focal family therapy. In A. S. Gurman & D. P. Kniskern (Eds.), *Handbook of family therapy* (Vol. 2. pp. 284–324). New York: Brunner/Mazel.

Bergin, A. E. (1991). Values and religious issues in psychotherapy and mental health. *American Psychologist, 46,* 394–403.

Bergman, S. J. (1995). Men's psychological development: A relational perspective. In R. F. Levant & W. S. Pollack (Eds.), *A new psychology of men* (pp. 68–90). New York: Basic Books.

Berman, W. H. (1988). The relationship of ex-spouse attachment to adjustment following divorce. *Journal of Family Psychology, 1,* 312–328.

Bernal, G. (1982). Cuban families. In M. McGoldrick, J. K. Pearce, & J. Giordano (Eds.), *Ethnicity and family therapy* (pp. 187–207). New York: Guilford Press.

Bernard, J. (1972). *The future of marriage.* New York: World.

Block, J., & Block, J. H. (1980). The role of ego control and ego-resiliency in the organization of behavior. In W. A. Collins (Ed.), *The Minnesota Symposium on Child Psychology: Development of cognition, affect and social relations* (Vol.13, pp. 39–101). Hillsdale, NJ: Erlbaum.

Blumstein, P., & Schwartz, P. (1983). *American couples.* New York: Morrow.

Bogdan, J. (1986). Do families really need problems? *Family Therapy Networker, 10,* 30–35, 67–69.

Boszormenyi-Nagy, I., & Spark, G. (1973). *Invisible loyalties: Reciprocity in intergenerational family therapy.* New York: Harper & Row.

Bowen, M. (1976). Theory in the practice of psychotherapy. In P. Guerin (Ed.), *Family therapy* (pp. 42–90). New York: Gardner Press.

Bowen, M. (1978). *Family therapy in clinical practice.* New York: Jason Aronson.

Bowen, M. (1991). Family reaction to death. In F. W. Walsh & M. McGoldrick (Eds.), *Living beyond loss: Death in the family* (pp. 79–92). New York: Norton.

Bowlby, J. (1977). The making and breaking of affectional bonds. *British Journal of Psychiatry, 130,* 201–210.

Bowlby, J. (1980). *Attachment and loss: Vol. III. Loss of sadness and depression.* New York: Basic Books.

Boyd-Franklin, N. (1989). *Black families in therapy: A multisystems approach.* New York: Guilford Press.

Boyd-Franklin, N. (1995). Therapy with African American inner city families. In R. H. Mikesell, D. D. Lusterman, & S. H. McDaniel (Eds.), *Integrating family therapy: Handbook of family psychology and systems theory* (pp. 357–374). Washington, DC: American Psychological Association.

Bradshaw, C. K. (1994). Asian and Asian American women: Historical and political considerations in psychotherapy. In L. Comas-Diaz & B. Greene (Eds.), *Women of color: Integrating ethnic and gender identities in psychotherapy* (pp. 72–113). New York: Guilford Press.

Bray, J. H., & Harvey, D. M. (1992). Intimacy and individuation in young adults: Development of the young adult version of the Personal Authority in the Family System Questionnaire. *Journal of Family Psychology, 6,* 152–163.

Bray, J. H., Williamson, D. S., & Malone, P. E. (1984). Personal authority in the family system: Development of a questionnaire to measure personal authority in intergenerational processes. *Journal of Marital and Family Therapy, 10,* 167–178.

Brett, C. A., Brett, A. S., & Shaw, S. S. (1993). Impact of traumatic incidents on family of origin functioning: An empirical study, *Journal of Contemporary Psychotherapy, 23,* 255–266.

Brooks, G. R., & Gilbert, L. A. (1995). Men in families: Old constraints, new possibilities. In R. F. Levant & W. S. Pollack (Eds.), *A new psychology of men* (pp. 252–279). New York: Basic Books.

Brown, L. (1988). Lesbians, gay men, and their families: Common clinical issues. *Journal of Gay and Lesbian Psychotherapy, 1,* 65–77.

Bruch, H. (1977). Psychological antecedents of anorexia nervosa. In R. A. Vigersky (Ed.), *Anorexia nervosa* (pp. 1–10). New York: Raven.

Budman, C. L., Lipson, J. G., & Meleis, A. I. (1992). The cultural consultant in mental health care: The case of Arab adolescents. *American Journal of Orthopsychiatry, 62,* 359–370.

Burgess, N. J. (1995). Looking back, looking forward: African American families in a sociohistorical perspective. In B. B. Ingoldsby & S. Smith (Eds.), *Families in multicultural perspective* (pp. 321–334). New York: Guilford.

Calhoun, J. B. (1962). A behavioral sink. In E. Bliss (Ed.), *Roots of behavior* (pp. 295–315). New York: Paul Hoever.

Candib, L. (1995). *Medicine and the family: A feminist perspective.* New York: Basic Books.

Canfield, B. S., Hovestadt, A. J., & Fenell, D. L. (1992). Family of origin influences upon perceptions of current family functioning. *Family Therapy, 19,* 55–60.

Caplan, P. J., & Hall-McCorquodale, I. (1985). Mother-blaming in major clinical journals. *American Journal of Orthopsychiatry, 55,* 345–353.

Capps, S. C., Searight, H. R., Russo, J. R., Temple, L. E., & Rogers, B. J. (1993). The Family of Origin Scale: Discriminant validity with adult children of alcoholics. *The American Journal of Family Therapy, 21,* 274–277.

Carlson, N. R. (1981). *Physiology of behavior* (2nd ed.). Boston: Allyn & Bacon.

Carter, B., & McGoldrick, M. (1989). *The changing family life cycle: A framework for family therapy* (2nd ed.). Boston: Allyn & Bacon.

Carter, E., & McGoldrick-Orfanidis, M. (1976). Family therapy with one person in the family therapist's own family. In P. J. Guein (Ed.), *Family therapy: Theory and practice* (pp. 220–231). New York: Gardner Press.

Cassidy, J. (1988). Child–mother attachment in self and six year olds. *Child Development, 59,* 121–134.

Cervantes, J. M., & Ramirez, O. (1992). Spirituality and family dynamics in psychotherapy with Latino children. In L. A. Vargas & J. D. Koss-Chioino (Eds.), *Working with culture: Psychotherapeutic interventions with ethnic minority children and adolescents* (pp. 103–128). San Francisco: Jossey-Bass.

Chao, C. M. (1992). The inner heart: Therapy with Southeast Asian families. In L. A. Vargas & J. D. Koss-Chioino (Eds.), *Working with culture: Psychotherapeutic interventions with ethnic minority children and adolescents* (pp. 157–181). San Francisco: Jossey-Bass.

Chilman, C. S. (1993). Hispanic families in the United States: Research perspectives. In H. P. McAdoo (Ed.), *Family ethnicity: Strength in diversity* (pp. 141–163). Newbury Park, CA: Sage.

Chodorow, N. (1978). *The reproduction of mothering: Psychoanalysis and the sociology of gender.* Berkeley: University of California Press.

Coles, R. (1994). *Harvard diary: Reflections on the sacred and the secular.* New York: Cross Road Publishing.

Cooper, C. R., Grotevant, H., & Condon, S. (1983). Individuality and connectedness in the family as a context for adolescent identity formation and role taking skill. In H. Grotevant & C. Cooper (Eds.), *Adolescent development in the family* (pp. 43–60). San Francisco: Jossey-Bass.

deShazer, S. (1985). *Keys to solutions in brief therapy.* New York: Norton.

Diamond, M. (1993). Homosexuality and bisexuality in different populations. *Archives of Sexual Behavior, 22,* 291–310.

Dicks, H. V. (1967). *Marital tensions.* New York: Basic Books.

Dixon, D. N., & Kixmiller, J. S. (1992). Home based family therapy with the religious, abusive family. *Journal of Mental Health Counselling, 14,* 243–247.

Doherty, W. J. (1993). I'm okay, you're okay, but what about the kids? *Family Therapy Networker, 17,* 46–53.

Doherty, W. J. (1995). *Soul searching: Why psychotherapy must promote moral responsibility.* New York: Basic Books.

Douglas, S. J. (1995). *Where the girls are: Growing up female with the mass media.* New York: Random House.

Duffy, S. N., & Rusbult, C. E. (1986). Satisfaction and commitment in homosexual and heterosexual relationships. *Journal of Homosexuality, 12,* 1–23.

Duneier, M. (1992). *Slim's table: Race, respectability and masculinity.* Chicago: University of Chicago Press.

Edwards, H. (1968). Black Muslim and Negro Christian family relationships. *Journal of Marriage and the Family, 30,* 604–611.

Ellis, E. (1962). *Reason and emotion in psychotherapy.* New York: Lyle, Stuart.

Epstein, I. (1990). *Judaism.* New York: Penguin Books.

Erikson, E. H. (1968). *Identity: Youth and crisis.* New York: W. W. Norton.

Fairbairn, W. D. (1952). *An object relations theory of the personality.* New York: Basic Books.

Falkenhain, M., & Lowry, J. L. (1995, August). *Religion and the family's world view: Implications for therapy.* Paper presented at the 103rd Annual Convention of the American Psychological Association, New York.

Featherman, J. M. (1995). Jews and child sexual abuse. In L. A. Fortes (Ed.), *Sexual abuse in nine North American cultures* (pp. 128–155). Thousand Oaks, CA: Sage.

Feeney, J. A., & Noller, P. (1990). Attachment style as a predictor of adult romantic relationships. *Journal of Personality and Social Psychology, 58,* 281–291.

Feiler, B. S. (1991). *Learning to bow: Inside the heart of Japan.* New York: Ticknor & Fields.

Fine, M., & Hovestadt, A. J. (1984). Perceptions of marriage and rationality by levels of perceived health in the family of origin. *Journal of Marital and Family Therapy, 10,* 193–195.

Finkelstein, L. (1987). Toward an object-relations approach in psychoanalytic marital therapy. *Journal of Marital Family Therapy, 13,* 287–298.

Framo, J. L. (1976). Family of origin as a therapeutic resource for adults in marital and family therapy: You can and should go home again. *Family Process, 15,* 193–210.

Framo, J. L. (1977). In-laws and out-laws: A marital case of kinship confusion. In P. Papp (Ed.), *Family therapy: Full length case studies* (pp. 167–182). New York: Gardner Press.

Framo, J. L. (1982). *Explorations in marital and family therapy.* New York: Springer.

Frazier, E. F. (1966). *The Negro family in the United States.* Chicago: University of Chicago Press.

Freud, S. (1961). Civilization and its discontents. In J. Strachey (Ed. and Trans.), *The standard edition of the complete psychological works of Sigmund Freud* (Vol. 21, pp. 59–148). London: Hogarth Press. (Original work published 1930)

Friedman, E. H. (1982). The myth of the shiksa. In M. McGoldrick, J. K. Pearce, & J. Giordano (Eds.), *Ethnicity and family therapy* (pp. 494–526). New York: Guilford Press.

Garcia-Preto, N. (1982). Puerto Rican families. In M. McGoldrick, J. K. Pearce, & J. Giordano (Eds.), *Ethnicity and family therapy* (pp. 164–186). New York: Guilford Press.

Garner, D. M., & Olmsted, M. P. (1984). *Eating Disorder Inventory (EDI) manual.* Odessa, FL: Psychological Assessment Resources.

Gilligan, C. (1982). *In a different voice: Psychological theory and women's development.* Cambridge, MA: Harvard University Press.

Giordano, J. (1973). *Ethnicity in mental health: Research and recommendations.* New York: National Project on Ethnic America of the American Jewish Committee.

Giordano, J., & Carini-Giordano, M. A. (1995). Ethnic dimensions in family treatment. In R. H. Mikesell, D. D. Lusterman, & S. H. McDaniel (Eds.), *Integrating family therapy: Handbook of family psychology and systems theory* (pp. 347–356). Washington, DC: American Psychological Association.

Goldner, V. (1985). Feminism and family therapy. *Family Process, 24,* 31–47.

Goldner, V., Penn, P., Sheinberg, N., & Walker, G. (1990). Love and violence: Gender paradoxes and volatile attachments. *Family Process, 29,* 243–364.

Goodall, J. (1979). Warfare and cannibalism among Gombe's chimpanzees. *National Geographic, 155*(5), 593–621.

Goodrich, T. J., Rampage, C., Ellman, B., & Halstad, K. (1988). *Feminist family therapy: A case book.* New York: Norton.

Greene, B. (1994a). African American women. In L. Comas-Diaz & B. Greene (Eds.), *Women of color: Integrating ethnic and gender identities in psychotherapy* (pp. 10–29). New York: Guilford Press.

Greene, B. (1994b). Ethnic-minority lesbians and gay men: Mental health and treatment issues. *Journal of Consulting and Clinical Psychology, 62,* 243–251.

Grier, W. H., & Cobbs, P. (1968). *Black rage.* New York: Basic Books.

Griffith, J. L. (1986). Employing the God–family relationship in therapy with religious families. *Family Process, 25,* 609–618.

Grossman, D. C., Putsch, R. W., & Inui, T. S. (1993). The meaning of death to adolescents in an American Indian community. *Family Medicine, 25,* 593–597.

Grotevant, H. D., & Carlson, C. I. (1989). *Family assessment: A guide to methods and measures.* New York: Guilford Press.

Grotevant, H. D., & Cooper, C. R. (1986). Individuation in family relationships. *Human Development, 29,* 82–100.

Guerin, P. J., & Pendagast, E.G. (1976). Evaluation of family system and genogram. In P. J. Guerin (Ed.), *Family therapy: Theory and practice* (pp. 450–262). New York: Gardner Press.

Haley, J. (1976). *Problem solving therapy.* San Francisco: Jossey-Bass.

Hancock, K. A. (1995). Psychotherapy with lesbians and gay men. In A. R. D'Augelli & C. J. Patterson (Eds.), *Lesbian, gay, and bisexual identities over the life span: Psychological perspectives* (pp. 398–432). New York: Oxford University Press.

Harjo, S. S. (1993). The American Indian experience. In H. P. McAdoo (Ed.), *Family ethnicity: Strength in diversity* (pp. 199–207). Newbury Park, CA: Sage.

Harry, J. (1984). *Gay couples.* New York: Praeger.

Hauser, S. T., Powers, S. I., Noam, G. G., Jacobson, A. M., Weiss, B., & Folansbee, D. J. (1984). Familial contexts of adolescent ego involvement. *Child Development, 55,* 195–213.

Hawkes, G., & Taylor, M. (1975). Power structure in Mexican and Mexican-American farm labor families. *Journal of Marriage and the Family, 37,* 806–811.

Hayes-Bautista, D. F. (1978). Chicano patients and medical practitioners: The sociology of knowledge paradigm of lay–professional interaction. *Social Science & Medicine, 12,* 83–90.

Herz, S. M., & Rosen, E. J. (1982). Jewish families. In M. McGoldrick, J. K. Pearce, & J. Giordano (Eds.), *Ethnicity and family therapy* (pp. 364–392). New York: Guilford Press.

Hinkelman, E. (Ed.). (1994). *Japanese business.* San Rafael, CA: World Trade Press.

Ho, M. K. (1992). *Minority children and adolescents in therapy.* Newbury Park, CA: Sage.

Holden, K. C., & Smolk, P. J. (1991). The economic costs of marital dissolution: Why do women bear a disproportionate cost? *Annual Review of Sociology, 17,* 51–78.

Hovestadt, A. J., Anderson, W. T., Piercy, S. P., Cochran, S. W., & Fine, M. (1985). A family of origin scale. *Journal of Marital and Family Therapy, 11,* 287–297.

Ingoldsby, B. B. (1995). Mate selection in marriage. In B. B. Ingoldsby & S. Smith (Eds.), *Families in multicultural perspective* (pp. 143–160). New York: Guilford.

Jalali, B. (1982). Iranian families. In M. McGoldrick, J. K. Pearce, & J. Giordano (Eds.), *Ethnicity and family therapy* (pp. 294–309). New York: Guilford Press.

Janus, S. S., & Janus, C. L. (1993). *The Janus report on sexual behavior.* New York: Wiley.

Johnson, F. (1993). *Dependency and Japanese socialization.* New York: New York University Press.

Jordan, J. V., Surrey, J. L., & Kaplan, A. G. (1991). Women and empathy: Indications for psychological development in psychotherapy. In J. V. Jordan, A. G. Kaplan, J. B. Miller, I. P. Stiver, & J. L. Surrey (Eds.), *Women's growth in connection: Writings from the Stone Center* (pp. 27–50). New York: Guilford.

Josselson, R. (1980). Ego development in adolescence. In J. Adelson (Ed.), *Handbook of adolescent psychology* (pp. 188–210). New York: Wiley.

Keller, D., & Rosen, H. (1988). *Treating the gay couple within the context of their families-of-origin.* Rockville, MD: Aspen Systems.

Kernberg, O. F. (1976). *Object relations theory and clinical psychoanalysis.* New York: Jason Aronson.

Kerr, M. E. (1985). Obstacles to differentiation of self. In A. S. Gurman (Ed.), *Casebook of marital therapy* (pp. 111–153). New York: Guilford Press.

Kerr, M. E., & Bowen, M. (1988). *Family assessment.* New York: Jason Aronson.

Kleiman, J. I. (1981). Optimal and normal family functioning. *American Journal of Family Therapy, 9,* 37–44.

Kleinman, A. (1977). Depression, somatization, and the "new cross-cultural psychiatry." *Social Science and Medicine, 11,* 3–10.

Kleinman, A. (1988). *The illness narratives: Suffering, healing and the human condition.* New York: Basic Books.

Klinger, R. L. (1991). Treatment of a lesbian batterer. In C. Silverstein (Ed.), *Gays, lesbians and their therapists* (pp. 126–142). New York: Norton.

Knox, D. H. (1985). Spirituality: A tool in the assessment and treatment of Black alcoholics and their families. *Alcoholism Treatment Quarterly, 2,* 31–44.

Knudson Martin, C. (1994). The female voice: Applications to Bowen's family systems theory. *Journal of Marital and Family Therapy, 20,* 35–46.

Kohut, H. (1977). *The restoration of the self.* New York: International Universities Press.

Kramer, J. R. (1985). *Family interfaces, transgenerational patterns.* New York: Brunner/Mazel.

Krestan, J., & Bepko, C. (1980). The problem of fusion in the lesbian relationship. *Family Process, 19,* 277–289.

Kurdek, L. A. (1995). Lesbian and gay couples. In A. R. D'Augelli & C. J. Patterson (Eds.), *Lesbian, gay, and bisexual identities over the life span: Psychological perspectives* (pp. 243–261). New York: Oxford University Press.

Kurdek, L. A., & Schmitt, J. P. (1986). Relationship quality of gay men in closed or open relationships. *Journal of Homosexuality, 12,* 85–99.

Kurdek, L. A., & Schmitt, J. P. (1987). Perceived support from family and friends in members of homosexual, married, and heterosexual cohabiting couples. *Journal of Homosexuality, 14,* 57–68.

LaFromboise, T. D., Berman, J. S., & Sohi, B. K. (1994). American Indian women. In L. Comas-Diaz & B. Greene (Eds.), *Women of color: Integrating ethnic and gender identities in psychotherapy* (pp. 30–71). New York: Guilford Press.

Lee, R. E., Gordon, N. G., & O'Dell, J. W. (1989). The validity and use of the Family of Origin Scale. *Journal of Marital and Family Therapy, 15,* 19–27.

Levinson, D. J., Darrow, C. N., Klein, E. B., Levinson, M. H., & McKee, B. (1978). *Seasons of a man's life.* New York: Alfred A. Knopf.

Lewis, J. M., Beavers, W. R., Gossett, J. T., & Phillips, F. A. (1976). *No single thread.* New York: Brunner/Mazel.

Lewis, O. (1966). *La vida.* New York: Random House.

Liebow, E. (1967). *Tally's corner: A study of Negro street corner men.* Boston: Little-Brown.

Loulan, J. (1985). *Lesbian sex.* San Francisco: Spinsters Ink.

Luepnitz, D. A. (1988). *The family interpreted: Psychoanalysis, feminism, and family therapy.* New York: Basic Books.

Maas, M., & Al-Krenawi, A. (1994). When a man encounters a woman, Satan is also present: Clinical relationships in Bedouin society. *American Journal of Orthopsychiatry, 64,* 357–367.

Mahler, M., Pine, F., & Bergman, A. (1975). *The psychological birth of the human infant.* New York: Basic Books.

Main, M., Kaplan, N., & Cassidy, J. (1985). Security in infancy, childhood and adulthood: A move to the level of representation. *Monographs of the Society for Research in Child Development, 50*(1–2), 66–104.

Mangrum, O. L. (1989). *Construct validation of the Family of Origin Scale.* Unpublished doctoral dissertation, Western Michigan University, Kalamazoo, MI.

Manley, C. M., Searight, H. R., Skitka, L. J., Russo, J. R., & Schudy, K. L. (1991). The reliability of the Family of Origin Scale for adolescents. *Adolescence, 26,* 89–96.

Manley, C. M., Searight, H. R., Wood, P., Skitka, L. J., & Russo, J. R. (1994). A latent variable model of the Family of Origin Scale for adolescents. *Journal of Youth and Adolescence, 23,* 99–118.

Marcia, J. E. (1976). Identity six years after: A follow up study. *Journal of Youth and Adolescence, 5,* 145–160.

Marcia, J. E. (1980). Identity in adolescence. In J. Adelson (Ed.), *Handbook of adolescent psychology* (pp. 159–187). New York: Wiley.

Maugham, W. S. (1944). *The razor's edge.* New York: Doubleday.

Mazer, G. E., Mangrum, O. L., Hovestadt, A. J., & Brashear, R. L. (1990). Further validation of the Family of Origin Scale: A factor analysis. *Journal of Marital and Family Therapy, 16,* 423–426.

McGill, D., & Pearce, J. K. (1982). British families. In M. McGoldrick, J. K. Pearce, & J. Giordano (Eds.), *Ethnicity and family therapy* (pp. 457–482). New York: Guilford Press.

McGoldrick, M. (1982). Irish families. In M. McGoldrick, J. K. Pearce, & J. Giordano (Eds.), *Ethnicity and family therapy* (pp. 310–339). New York: Guilford Press.

McGoldrick, M. (1995). *You can go home again: Reconnecting with your family.* New York: W. W. Norton.

McGoldrick, M., Almeida, R., Hines, P. M., Garcia-Preto, N., Rosen, E., & Lee, E. (1991). Mourning in different cultures. In F. Walsh & M. McGoldrick (Eds.), *Living beyond loss: Death in the family* (pp. 176–206). New York: W.W. Norton.

McGoldrick, M., & Gerson, R. (1985). *Genograms in family assessment.* New York: Norton.

McWhirter, D. P., & Mattison, A. N. (1984). *The male couple: How relationships develop.* Englewood Cliffs, NJ: Prentice-Hall.

Melitio, R. (1988). Combining individual psychodynamics with structural family therapy. *Journal of Marital and Family Therapy, 14,* 29–43.

Mendelsohn, H., & Ferber, A. (1972). Is everybody watching? In A. Ferber, H. Mendelsohn, & A. Napier (Eds.), *The book of family therapy* (pp. 431–444). New York: Science House.

Meredith, W. H., & Abbott, D. A. (1995). Chinese families in later life. In B. B. Ingoldsby & S. Smith (Eds.), *Families in multicultural perspective* (pp. 213–230). New York: Guilford.

Merkel, W. T., & Searight, H. R. (1992). Why families are not like swamps, solar systems, or thermostats: Some limits of systems theory as applied to family therapy. *Contemporary Family Therapy, 14,* 33–50.

Miller, J. B. (1976). *Toward a new psychology of women.* Boston: Beacon Press.

Miller, J. B. (1991). The development of women's sense of self. In J. V. Jordan, A. G. Kaplan, J. B. Miller, I. P. Stiver, & J. L. Surrey (Eds.), *Women's growth in connection: Writings from the Stone Center* (pp. 11–26). New York: Guilford.

Miller, N. (1995). *Out of the past: Gay and lesbian history from 1869 to the present,* New York: *Vintage.*

Mintz, S., & Kellogg, S. (1988). *Domestic revolutions: A social history of American family life.* New York: Basic Books.

Minuchin, S. (1974). *Families and family therapy.* Cambridge, MA: Harvard University Press.

Minuchin, S., & Fishman, H. C. (1981). *Family therapy techniques.* Cambridge, MA: Harvard University Press.

Minuchin, S., Rosman, B., & Baker, L. (1978). *Psychosomatic families.* Cambridge, MA: Harvard University Press.

Moos, R. H., & Moos, B. (1986). *Family Environment Scale manual.* Palo Alto, CA: Consulting Psychologists Press.

Moynihan, D. P. (1965). *The Negro family: The case for national action.* Washington DC: U.S. Department of Labor.

Nanji, A. A. (1993). The Muslim family in North America: Continuity and change. In II. P. McAdoo (Ed.), *Family ethnicity: Strength in diversity* (pp. 229–244). Newbury Park: Sage.

Nichols, M. P., & Schwartz, R. C. (1995). *Family therapy: Concepts and methods.* Boston: Allyn & Bacon.

Niedermeier, C. L., Searight, H. R., Handal, P. J., Manley, C. N., & Brown, N. Y. (1995). Perceived family functioning among adolescent psychiatric inpatients: Validity of the Family of Origin Scale. *Child Psychiatry and Human Development, 26,* 175–195.

O'Connor, B. P. (1995). Identity development and perceived parental behavior as sources of adolescent egocentrism. *Journal of Youth and Adolescence, 24,* 205–227.

O'Leary, J., Searight, H. R., Rogers, B. J., & Russo, J. R. (1992). *The Family of Origin Scale—Validity.* Unpublished manuscript.

Olson, D. H., Portner, J., & Lavee, Y. (1985). *FACES III manual.* St. Paul, MN: University of Minnesota—Family Social Science.

Onnis, L. (1993). Psychosomatic medicine: Towards a new epistemology. *Family Systems Medicine, 11,* 137–148.

Openlander, P., & Searight, H. R. (1983). Family therapy perspectives in the college counseling center. *Journal of College Student Personnel, 24,* 423–427.

Papero, D. V. (1990). *Bowen family systems theory.* Boston: Allyn & Bacon.

Parsons, T., & Bales, R. F. (1955). *Family, socialization, and interaction process.* New York: Free Press.

Patterson, C. J. (1992). Children of lesbian and gay parents. *Child Development, 63,* 1025–1042.

Peck, J. S., & Manocherian, J. R. (1989). Divorce in the changing family life cycle. In B. Carter & M. McGoldrick (Eds.), *The changing family life cycle: A framework for family therapy* (2nd ed., pp. 335–371). Needham Heights, MA: Allyn & Bacon.

Peplau, L. A., & Cochran, S. D. (1990). A relational perspective on homosexuality. In D. P. McWhirter, S. A. Sanders, & J. N. Reinisch (Eds.), *Homosexuality/heterosexuality: Concepts of sexual orientation* (pp. 321–349). New York: Oxford.

Pistole, M. C. (1994). Adult attachment styles: Some thoughts on closeness–distance struggles. *Family Process, 33,* 147–159.

Pleck, J. H. (1980). Men's power with women, other men, and society: A men's movement analysis. In E. Pleck & J. H. Pleck (Eds.), *The American man* (pp. 427–433). Englewood Cliffs, NJ: Prentice-Hall.

Pogrebin, L. C. (1991). *Deborah, Golda and me: Being female and Jewish in America.* New York: Anchor-Doubleday.

Pollack, W. S. (1995). No man is an island: Toward a new psychoanalytic psychology of men. In R. S. Levant & W. S. Pollack (Eds.), *A new psychology of men* (pp. 33–67). New York: Basic Books.

Pollack, W. S., & Grossman, F. K. (1985). Parent–child interaction. In L. L'Abate (Ed.), *The handbook of family psychology and therapy* (pp. 587–622). Homewood, IL: Dorsey.

Powers, S. I., Hauser, S. T., Schwartz, J. M., Noam, G. G., & Jacobson, A. M. (1983). Adolescent ego development and family interaction: A structural-developmental perspective. In H. D. Grotevant & C. R. Cooper (Eds.), *Adolescent development in the family* (pp. 5–26). San Francisco: Jossey-Bass.

Prest, L. A., & Keller, J. F. (1993). Spirituality and family therapy: Spiritual beliefs, myths, and metaphors. *Journal of Marital and Family Therapy, 19,* 137–148.

Quintana, S. M., & Kerr, J. (1993). Relational needs in late adolescence: Separation–individuation. *Journal of Counseling and Development, 71,* 349–354.

Reeves, P. C., & Johnson, M. E. (1992). Relationship between family of origin functioning and self-perceived correlates of eating disorders among female college students. *Journal of College Student Development, 33,* 44–49.

Religion in America (Report No. 236). (1995). Princeton, NJ: Gallup Organization.

Rolland, J. S. (1994). *Families, illness and disability.* New York: Basic Books.

Rotunno, M., & McGoldrick, M. (1982). Italian families. In M. McGoldrick, J. K. Pearce, & J. Giordano (Eds.), *Ethnicity and family therapy* (pp. 340–363). New York: Guilford Press.

Rotz, E., Russell, C. S., & Wright, D. W. (1993). The therapist who is perceived as "spiritually correct": Strategies for avoiding collusion with the "spiritually one-up spouse." *Journal of Marital and Family Therapy, 19,* 369–375.

Sabatelli, R. M., & Anderson, S. A. (1991). Family system dynamics, peer relationships, and adolescent psychological adjustment. *Family Relations, 40,* 363–369.

Sabogal, F., Marin, G., Otero-Sabogal, R., Marrin, B. V., & Perez-Stable, E. J. (1987). Hispanic familism and acculturation: What changes and what doesn't? *Hispanic Journal of Behavioral Sciences, 9,* 397–412.

Salner, M. (1986). The relationship of naive epistemology to formal epistemology: Implications for the teaching of human science methodology. *Methods, 1,* 125–152.

Schmidt, M. (1995). Anglo American culture and sexual child abuse. In L. A. Fontes (Ed.), *Sexual abuse in nine North American cultures: Treatment and prevention* (pp. 156–175). Thousand Oaks, CA: Sage.

Schmittroth, L. (Ed.). (1995). *Statistical record of women worldwide* (2nd ed.). New York: Gale Research.

Schoeps, H. J. (1968). *The religions of mankind.* New York: Anchor Books.

Scrivner, R., & Eldridge, N. S. (1995). Lesbian and gay family psychology. In R. H. Mikesell, D. T. Lusterman, & S. H. McDaniel (Eds.), *Integrating family therapy:*

Handbook of family psychology and systems theory (pp. 327–346). Washington, DC: American Psychological Association.

Searight, H. R. (1997). The Tarasoff warning and the duty to protect: Implications for family medicine. In L. K. Hamberger, S. K. Burge, A. V. Graham, & A. Kosta (Eds.), *Violence education for health care professionals.* New York: Haworth.

Searight, H. R., Graham, N., Rae, L., & Parker, N. (1989). Structured group therapy for at-risk infants and their mothers. *Journal of Contemporary Psychotherapy, 19,* 109–116.

Searight, H. R., Manley, C. M., Binder, A. F., Krohn, E. J., Rogers, B. J., & Russo, J. R. (1991). The family-of-origin of adolescent drug abusers: Perceived autonomy and intimacy. *Contemporary Family Psychology, 13,* 71–81.

Searight, H. R., & Merkel, W. T. (1991). Systems theory and its discontents: Clinical and ethical issues. *American Journal of Family Therapy, 19,* 19–31.

Searight, H. R., & Openlander, P. (1987). The new epistemology: Clarification and clinical application. *Journal of Strategic and Systemic Therapies, 6,* 52–66.

Seidman, S. N., & Rieder, R. O. (1995). Sexual behavior through the life cycle: An empirical approach. In J. Oldham & M. Riba (Eds.), *Review of psychiatry* (Vol. 14, pp. 639–676). Washington, DC: American Psychiatric Press.

Selvini-Palazolli, M., Boscolo, L., Checchin, G., & Prata, G. (1978). *Paradox and counterparadox.* New York: Jason Aronson.

Sennott, J. S. (1981). *Healthy Family Functioning Scale: Family members' perceptions of cohesion, adaptability, and communication.* Unpublished doctoral dissertation, Purdue University.

Shadish, W. R., Montgomery, L. M., Wilson, P., Wilson, M. R., Bright, I., & Okwumabua, T. (1993). The effects of family and marital psychotherapies: A meta-analysis. *Journal of Consulting and Clinical Psychology, 61,* 992–1002.

Shon, S. P., & Ja, P. Y. (1982). Asian families. In M. McGoldrick, J. K. Pearce, & J. Giordano (Eds.), *Ethnicity and family therapy* (pp. 208–228). New York: Guilford Press.

Shweder, R. A., & Bourne, E. (1982). Does the concept of the person vary cross-culturally? In A. J. Marsella & G. White (Eds.), *Cultural concepts in mental health and therapy* (pp. 97–139). Boston: Reidel.

Silverman, D. K. (1987). What are little girls made of? *Psychoanalytic Psychology, 4,* 315–334.

Snow, L. (1993). *Walkin' over medicine.* Boulder, CO: Westview Press.

Spanier, G. B. (1976). Measuring dyadic adjustment: New scales for assessing the quality of marriage and similar dyads. *Journal of Marriage and the Family, 38,* 15–28.

Spielberger, C. D., Gorsuch, R. L., & Lusken, R. E. (1970). *STAI—Manual for the State–Trait Anxiety Inventory.* Palo Alto, CA: Consulting Psychologists Press.

Stack, C. (1974). *All our kin: Strategies for survival in a Black community.* New York: Harper & Row.

Stander, V., Piercy, F. P., MacKinnon, D., & Helmeke, T. (1994). Spirituality, religion, and family therapy: Competing or complimentary worlds? *The American Journal of Family Therapy, 22,* 27–41.

Steckel, A. (1987). Psychosocial development of children of lesbian parents. In F. W. Bozett (Ed.), *Gay and lesbian parents* (pp. 75–85). New York: Praeger.

Stein, H. F., & Pontious, J. M. (1985). Family and beyond: The larger context of noncompliance. *Family Systems Medicine, 3,* 179–189.

Steinberg, L. (1987). Recent research on the family at adolescence: The extent and nature of sex differences. *Journal of Youth and Adolescence, 16,* 191–197.

Strauss, N., Gelles, R., & Steinmetz, S. (1980). *Behind closed doors: Violence in the American family.* Garden City, NY: Anchor/Doubleday.

Sue, S., Sue, D. W., Sue, L., & Takeuchi, D. T. (1995). Psychopathology among Asian Americans. *Cultural Diversity and Mental Health, 1,* 39–52.

Surrey, J. L. (1991). "The self in relation": A theory of women's development. In J. V. Jordan, A. G. Kaplan, J. B. Miller, I. P. Stiver, & J. L. Surrey (Eds.), *Women's growth in connection: Writings from the Stone Center* (pp. 51–66). New York: Guilford.

Szapocznik, J., Kurtines, W. M., Foote, F. H., Perez-Vidal, A., & Hervis, O. (1983). Conjoint versus one-person family therapy: Some evidence for the effectiveness of conducting family therapy through one person. *Journal of Consulting and Clinical Psychology, 51,* 889–899.

Szapocznik, J., Kurtines, W. M., Foote, F. H., Perez-Vidal, A., & Hervis, O. (1986). Conjoint versus one-person family therapy: Further evidence for the effectiveness of conducting family therapy through one person with drug abusing adolescents. *Journal of Consulting and Clinical Psychology, 54,* 395–397.

Taffel, R., & Masters, R. (1989). An evolutionary approach to revolutionary change: The impact of gender arrangements on family therapy. In M. McGoldrick, C. M. Anderson, & F. Walsh (Eds.), *Women in families: A framework for family therapy* (pp. 117–134). New York: Norton.

Takaki, R. (1989). *Strangers from a different shore.* New York: Penguin Books.

Taylor, C., & Fontes, L. A. (1995). Seventh Day Adventists and sexual child abuse. In L. A. Fontes (Ed.), *Sexual Abuse in nine North American cultures* (pp. 176–199). Thousand Oaks, CA: Sage.

Toman, W. (1976). *Family constellations* (rev. ed.). New York: Springer.

Tyler, A. (1982). *Dinner at the homesick restaurant.* New York: Ivy Books.

U.S. Bureau of the Census. (1983). *1980 census of the population: Characteristics of the population* (SER. PC80-1-V1). Washington, DC: U.S. Government Printing Office.

U.S. Bureau of the Census. (1991). *Family disruption and economic hardship: Survey of income and program participation* (Current Population Reports, Series p-70, No. 20). Washington, DC: U.S. Government Printing Office.

U.S. Bureau of the Census. (1993). *We, the first Americans.* Washington, DC: U.S. Department of Commerce, Economics and Statistics Administration.

Valliant, G. E. (1977). *Adaptation to life.* Boston: Little, Brown.

Vasquez, M. J. T. (1994). Latinas. In L. Comas-Diaz & B. Greene (Eds.), *Women of color: Integrating ethnic and gender identities in psychotherapy* (pp. 114–138). New York: Guilford.

Vega, W. A., Kolody, B., & Valle, J. (1996). The relationship of marital status, confidante support, and depression among Mexican immigrant women. *Journal of Marriage and the Family, 48,* 595–605.

Walsh, F., & Scheinkman, M. (1989). (Fe)Male: The hidden gender dimension in models of family therapy. In M. McGoldrick, C. Anderson, & F. Walsh (Eds.), *Women in families: A framework for family therapy* (pp. 16–41). New York: W. W. Norton.

Watzlawick, P., Weakland, J., & Fisch, R. (1974). *Change: Principles of problem formation and problem resolution.* New York: W. W. Norton.

Wells, V. K., Scott, R. G., Schmeller, L. J., Hillmann, J. A., & Searight, H. R. (1990). The family of origin framework: A model for clinical training. *Journal for Contemporary Psychotherapy, 20*, 20–23.

Welter, B. (1983). The cult of true womanhood: 1820–1860. In M. Gordon (Ed.), *The American family in social–historical perspective* (3rd ed., pp. 372–392). New York: St. Martin's Press.

Wendorf, D. J., & Wendorf, R. J. (1985). A systemic view of family therapy ethics. *Family Process, 24,* 443–453.

Whitaker, C., & Bumberry, W. (1987). *Dancing with the family.* New York: W. W. Norton.

Winawer-Steiner, H., & Wetzel, N. A. (1982). German families. In M. McGoldrick, J. K. Pearce, & J. Giordano (Eds.), *Ethnicity and family therapy* (pp. 247–268). New York: Guilford Press.

Winer, L. R. (1971). The qualified pronoun count as a measure of change in family psychotherapy. *Family Process, 10,* 243–247.

Yalom, I. D. (1985). *The theory and practice of group psychotherapy* (3rd ed.). New York: Basic Books.

Zborowski, M. (1969). *People in pain.* San Francisco: Jossey Bass.

Zola, I. K. (1966). Culture and symptoms: An analysis of patients presenting complaints. *American Sociological Review, 5,* 141–155.

Index